# THE MUSIC OF
# SIBELIUS

Da Capo Press Music Reprint Series

GENERAL EDITOR
ROLAND JACKSON
UNIVERSITY OF SOUTHERN CALIFORNIA

# THE MUSIC OF SIBELIUS

Edited by
Gerald Abraham

DA CAPO PRESS • NEW YORK • 1975

Library of Congress Cataloging in Publicaton Data

Abraham, Gerald Ernest Heal, 1904-      comp.
    The music of Sibelius.

        (Da Capo Press music reprint series)
        Reprint of the 1st ed. published in New York by
    W. W. Norton, 1947.
        bibliography: p.
        CONTENTS: Hill, R. Sibelius the man.—Abraham, G.
    The Symphonies.—Wood, R. W. The miscellaneous
    orchestral and theatre music. [etc.]
        1. Sibelius, Jean, 1865-1957. I. Title.
    ML410.S54A5    1975            780'.92'4            74-23413
    ISBN 0-306-70716-0

*156780*

Published by Da Capo Press, Inc.
A Subsidiary of Plenum Publishing Corporation
227 West 17th Street, New York, N.Y. 10011

Manufactured in the United States of America

*The* Music *of* Sibelius

# *The* Music
## *of*
## Sibelius

Edited by GERALD ABRAHAM

W · W · NORTON & COMPANY · INC · *New York*

*First Edition*

*Published in England, un-
der the title "Sibelius" in
Music of the Masters series*

PRINTED IN THE UNITED STATES OF AMERICA
FOR THE PUBLISHERS BY RICHARD L. JONES

# Contents

*The* Music *of* Sibelius

# 1

## *Sibelius the Man*

### By

### Ralph Hill

To RE-CREATE THE PERSONALITY of a great man of a past age from his letters and diaries and from the written testimony of his contemporaries is not an easy task; it requires considerable imagination and deep psychological perception. But even these qualities will not help you to re-create the personality of a great man of the present, whom you have never met and whose letters and diaries, if they exist, remain unpublished. And materials for a character-sketch of Sibelius are unusually scanty. The books by Gray, Ekman, de Törne, and Rosa Newmarch (not forgetting the preface to her book by Sir Granville Bantock), all agree upon the fascinating personality of their hero, but fail in varying degrees to communicate their impressions to their readers. Cecil Gray is perhaps the most enlightening, despite his disclaimer that his acquaintanceship with Sibelius is of any but the slightest and most superficial order. On the other hand Rosa Newmarch is singularly unenlightening, considering she had been an intimate friend of Sibelius. She devotes seventy-nine pages to a description of their ' friendship ', but reveals little of any consequence about the man that we do not already know. (To be fair to these writers, however, one imagines that Sibelius's natural reticence and timidity are extremely difficult to overcome, particularly as he believes that his intimate thoughts and ideals should be revealed only in his compositions.)

Like Delius's, Sibelius's creative powers have to be stimulated by the right environment. Freedom and solitude have always been vital necessities in his life as an artist. In a letter to Rosa Newmarch he once said : ' I have come here, to Paris, for a while. Here indeed is solitude! Give me the loneliness either of the Finnish forests or of a great city.' The setting of his country house near Helsinki, sheltered by birches and firs and surrounded by meadows with the glittering surface of a lake clearly discernible in the distance, provides that atmosphere of peace and rest so necessary for a man of

Sibelius's temperament. This love of natural things, of beautiful and awe-inspiring scenery, is the key to Sibelius's make-up as a composer. He is supersensitive to what one might call the natural harmonies and rhythms of nature : curious sounds heard in forests at twilight, the atmosphere of a lonely lake or wind-swept heath, the desolation and majesty of a mountain side. All this kind of thing is profoundly moving to Sibelius and stimulates musical ideas, shapes, and colours. When Rosa Newmarch paid her first visit to Sibelius in Finland— it was in 1910—Sibelius took her to see the great rapids of Imatra, which are the outlet of the waters of Lake Saïma. ' Sibelius,' she says, ' had at that time a passion for trying to catch the pedal notes of natural forces. The pedal note of Imatra no man has gauged, but Sibelius often seemed satisfied with the results of his rapt listening, when he caught the basic sounds of the forests, or of the wind whistling over lakes and moorlands. To share Nature with him is a wonderful but silent experience.'

A ray of sunshine reflected in the water, the falling of a leaf, a shower of rain, are enough to set his musical mind working : one of his first compositions, a piece for violin and cello written at the age of ten, was entitled *Drops of Water*. A curious story is told by one of Sibelius's friends. One summer evening they were out walking together when they came to a shore where some flax and hemp were drying. The hemp gave off a peculiar, offensive smell. Sibelius stopped, looked at the ground and frowned as if puzzled. For a while he was silent. Then his face relaxed and he began to hum and made off homewards. When he arrived at his house he immediately went into the music room, sat down at the piano and began to improvise. ' And soon,' his friend says, ' the sensations evoked by the peculiar smell of the hemp took on a musical form in a grotesque capriccio.' The point of all this is that Sibelius's music is not necessarily an interpretation of such experiences; the experiences merely provoked certain musical ideas which were then developed at length on purely musical lines, though on occasions, of course, Sibelius has set out to write programme music, music intended to evoke a definite mood or to create an atmosphere of fantasy.

Finland is rich in superstitions and legends which have appealed vividly to Sibelius's imagination. He has been a dreamer all his life, a dreamer whose moods would instantly change from melancholy to high spirits, and from high spirits to melancholy. As a boy he loved to wander in the forest and search for fairies and goblins in the gloomiest recesses. A lovely sunset would appeal to his imagination in terms of a fairy world and he would sit and gaze in silent wonder at the changing colours. The fascination of this world of fantasy has remained with Sibelius all through his life and has continually inspired him with musical ideas.

Everyone who has come into contact with Sibelius testifies to the great humanity of the man and the sense of power and strength that he seems to radiate through his steel-blue eyes. Sir Arnold Bax, in his autobiography, compares his impressions of Sibelius when he met him in 1909 and in 1936. Bax says that they might be of two totally different men. 'The massive, bald-headed titan of the latter year, suggesting an embodiment of one of the primeval forces that pervade the *Kalevala*, can at whim transform himself into a purveyor of farcical fun and Rabelaisian joviality. But the earlier Sibelius gave one the notion that he had never laughed in his life, and never could. That strong, taut frame, those cold steel-blue eyes, and hard-lipped mouth, were those of a Viking raider, insensible to scruple, tenderness, or humour of any sort. An arresting, formidable-looking fellow, born of dark rock and northern forest, yet somehow only half the size of the capricious old Colossus of to-day.'

A revealing story is told by de Törne. 'One day,' he says, ' I mentioned the impression which always takes hold of me when returning to Finland across the Baltic, the first forebodings of our country being given us by low, reddish granite rocks emerging from the pale blue sea, solitary islands of a hard, archaic beauty, inhabited by hundreds of white seagulls. And I concluded by saying that this landscape many centuries ago was the cradle of the Vikings. " Yes," Sibelius answered eagerly, and his eyes flashed, " and when we see those granite rocks we know why we are able to treat the orchestra as we do! " '

Sibelius is a true epicurean. He dresses fastidiously; he smokes the best and largest Havana cigars, and he delights in good food and wine. I have heard several stories of his Socratic capacity for good wine and stimulating talk over the dinner table. Henry Askeli, an American, who stayed with Sibelius at his house, describes Sibelius as the perfect host.[1] He can ' eat, drink with his visitor with zest, propose toasts, talk interestingly, relate colourful anecdotes, and laugh without restraint; yet the bourgeois guest soon discovers that the host is very different in his mental make-up. There is something puzzling, far away, hard to understand, about him. It is difficult to form the right kind of an intellectual contact with him, and the

[1] ' Sketch of Sibelius the Man ' in the *Musical Quarterly* (New York, January 1940).

typical bourgeois has to confess to himself that he and Sibelius live in totally different worlds. When evening changes into night, when the visitors have gone and the household has retired, the master often does not even think of going to bed. The silent hours of the night are full of most intensive life to him, and he refuses to waste them. The expression on his face, gay in front of daytime visitors, is now solemn. Those strange, upright wrinkles on his brow are now much deeper. He is looking somewhere far away, and it seems that he has completely forgotten his surroundings. It is impossible to say what he is thinking about, but we may surmise that he is roaming in the limitless world of abstraction. This silent loneliness is to him an opportunity to hear the glorious music of the spheres.'

Most great composers are too prejudiced to make good critics and offer balanced judgment of their contemporaries, though when judging music towards which they are sympathetically disposed their comments are often of great interest and importance. Anyway, the great composers' reactions, whether sympathetic or not, to the music of the past and present are always interesting and often instructive. Sibelius is a typical example. The composer who means more to him than any other is Beethoven : ' I am affected as powerfully by the human side of him as by his music. He is a revelation to me. He is a Titan. Everything was against him yet he triumphed.' The classical school of composers with Mozart at its head, is greatly admired by Sibelius, and he considers that the greatest geniuses of the orchestra are Mozart and Mendelssohn. The music of Wagner is too rich, exotic, and heavily perfumed, even rude, brutal, and vulgar; and Puccini, likewise, is ' too perfumed '. On the other hand, curiously enough, he admires Verdi. He told Walter Legge[1] that Verdi ' has put the life and vivid colour and vitality of Italian street scenes on the stage with music that matches and even intensifies them '. It is also curious, in view of Sibelius's reaction to Wagner and Puccini, that he should be attracted by the luxuriance and over-ripeness of Ernest Bloch.

It is interesting to note that Sibelius agrees with most musicians that the early works of Stravinsky are his best, and that his later continual alterations in style have become irritating : ' Three styles were enough for Beethoven, but I forget whether the last Stravinsky work I looked at was in his tenth or eleventh.' The music of Schönberg apparently means little or nothing to him : an interesting theorist, a philosopher perhaps, but not a great composer. He told

[1] ' Conversations with Sibelius ' in *Musical Times* (London, March 1935).

Walter Legge that in his opinion it was pretentious snobbery for audiences to applaud the later Schönberg: 'There are not twenty musicians in the world who could follow the structure and inner logic of any recent Schönberg work or even get a rough idea of the composer's meaning at one hearing in a concert hall. I flatter myself that I have a sensitive ear, far more sensitive than that of the average concert-goer. And yet when I hear for the first time the more complicated Schönberg works I am completely lost. I have to study the score closely to see what he is driving at. How can the casual concert-goers or the affectationists make head or tail of such music? Alban Berg is Schönberg's best work.'

Among British composers Sibelius entertains a high opinion of Elgar and Bax. He considers that Elgar possessed great genius and more natural musical gifts than even Strauss, whose earlier music he admires more than any other composer of his own time. Elgar 'wrote pages of magnificent music and then, without warning, lapsed into a few bars of vulgarity, only to recover himself as if he had never written a bar below his best'. After reading through the score of Bax's Fifth Symphony, which is dedicated to him, he expressed the opinion that 'Bax is one of the great men of our time; he has a fine musical mind, an original personal style, a splendid independence, and, thank God, he can write a melody, and is not ashamed to do so'.

But there is one composer whose music he will not discuss: himself. 'You know how the wing of a butterfly crumbles at a touch?' he says. 'So it is with my compositions; the very mention of them is fatal.'

# 2

## The Symphonies

### By

### Gerald Abraham

WHETHER OR NOT we are prepared to agree with Mr. Cecil Gray's downright assertion that Sibelius is ' the greatest master of the symphony since the death of Beethoven ', the musical publics of at least Britain, America and Scandinavia have for the last decade or so appeared to accept him as the greatest living symphonist. By general consent he is a symphonist first and foremost; whatever he may have done in other fields, his reputation rests at present on his symphonies and will stand or fall with them in the future. If we wish to understand Sibelius, we must begin by studying his symphonies.[1]

Not that they cover his whole career. When Sibelius wrote his First Symphony he was in his early thirties with some thirty-eight previous opus numbers to his credit. His unmistakable personal style had emerged seven years before in *En Saga*; indeed, it is quite arguable that *En Saga*, *The Swan of Tuonela*, and *Lemminkäinen's Homecoming*, are more perfectly characteristic of Sibelius than the First Symphony itself. Nevertheless, the Symphony provides an admirable starting point for a study of his work in general. It is scored for a normal full orchestra, including harp, bass drum, cymbals and triangle.

The first movement is decidedly the most interesting, comparatively orthodox though it is from the formal point of view. The slow introduction—a twenty-eight bar melody for clarinet, accompanied for sixteen bars by a soft drum-roll, then completely unaccompanied—is itself worthy of close attention. For one thing, it illustrates immediately two of Sibelius's most striking traits : his genius for writing very long-breathed melodies, *unendlich* in the Wagnerian sense (i.e., quite free from any suggestion of stanzaic pattern)—*The Swan of Tuonela* is another instance that occurs to one immediately;

---

[1] The main substance of this chapter appeared originally in *Musical Opinion* (October 1937–October 1938).

and his love of long pedal points. Indeed, everything is calculated for the long view in Sibelius; the reiterated G-B of the second violins for thirteen bars at the opening of the allegro is again typical of his static harmony, though this instance is mild in comparison with the eighty-six bars of nothing but dominant seventh and tonic triad that underlie the beautiful end of *En Saga*, or even the Beethovenian forty bars of tonic fanfare (interrupted by only four bars of subdominant) that conclude *Lemminkäinen's Homecoming*.

But this introduction to the First Symphony is instructive from another point of view. Although Mr. Gray asserts[1] that ' it plays no part in the subsequent developments of the movement proper ', bars 17–19 of it are a note-for-note statement of the main part of the second subject (see Ex. 5 at end of book). And as bars 17–19 are an elaboration of bars 6–7, themselves a consequence of bars 2–3,[2] we may say that the second subject of the allegro is implicit in the very opening bars of the introduction. Nor is the germinal importance of the introduction limited to this point. At bars 11–13, the clarinet dwells successively on the notes E, F sharp, G, F sharp, and ends its phrase with two sustained B naturals (bars 15–16). It may be merely coincidence, but this outline—E, F sharp, G, F sharp, B—is also prominent in both the first subject of the allegro (Ex. 1, bars 5–7) and its first subsidiary theme (Ex. 3). Going on to examine the thematic material of the allegro as a whole, we shall discover similar relationships which—whether deliberate or unconscious—give even this most obvious and conventional of Sibelius's first movements remarkable organic unity.

As Mr. Gray points out, the first subject proper is strikingly akin to that in the first movement of Borodin's Symphony in E flat. I give both themes for comparison (see Exs. 1 and 2). Admittedly, the relationship is merely one of melodic outline, not of rhythm, inflection, or general feeling. But, more curious still, there is a similar relationship between the latter part of the Borodin theme and Sibelius's *second* main subject (Ex. 5). Moreover, there are other Borodinesque traits in this first Sibelius Symphony : the throwing of the orchestral weight on to the second crotchet (bar 10 of Ex. 1), while only tuba and a drum mark the down-beat (cf. the scherzo of Borodin's Second Symphony), the overlapping descent of a figure through the orchestra coming off the climax just before the appearance of the second subject, the character of the scherzo with its quick

---

[1] *Sibelius: the Symphonies* (' Musical Pilgrim ' series). Oxford University Press, 1935.
[2] These points can easily be verified from the miniature score.

repeated notes, the brassy scoring of the whole symphony. And, as we shall see when we come to investigate the Second Symphony, Sibelius was even influenced by the peculiar method of symphonic thought in the first movement of Borodin's E flat Symphony.

Common to both Borodin and Sibelius, too, is the device heard at bar 5 of Ex. 1 : the modification of a motive by the addition of a prefix, which then itself becomes important.[1] (Naturally, in none of these cases, is there any question of Sibelius having echoed Borodin; he has made all these devices and idiosyncracies absolutely his own; but there seems to me a good deal of evidence that he borrowed them from Borodin in the first place.) On the other hand, two features of Ex. 1 are entirely peculiar to Sibelius and very common in his melodic lines : the attack on a long sustained note (sometimes a note several times repeated), which is then broken off, as it were, in some striking, melodic epigram (cf. the third main theme of *En Saga*), and the insertion of an unexpected triplet (cf. *The Swan of Tuonela, passim*).

Ex. 1 is followed, after five transitional bars, by two subsidiary themes (Exs. 3 and 4), the first being given to the wind, the second to the strings. Here again several points are noteworthy : the rhythmic identity of these themes (particularly the striking little rhythmic kick in the second bar of Ex. 3 and the third of Ex. 4, already heard twice in the five transitional bars, and constantly recurring throughout Sibelius's music, e.g., in the main melody of the andante of this symphony), the ' slow trill ' effect of Ex. 4 (cf. *The Swan* again), and the almost-identity of the last bar of Ex. 4 with bar 10 of Ex. 1.

The remarkable harmonic simplicity that prevails practically throughout the first group of themes, continues for some time in the second group, the theme for flutes in thirds, Ex. 5, being accompanied for some time by a simple alternation every half-bar of an F sharp major triad, and a first inversion of a C sharp minor chord. The effect of these thirds—so unlike the sensuous, Italianate thirds of Liszt and Richard Strauss, partly because of the tonal peculiarity of the theme, partly because it is not cantabile—is yet another of Sibelius's pet devices. One again notes the unexpected triplet, here in the melodic form Sibelius usually gives it : a contraction of the motive of the second bar. After a short pizzicato treatment of this theme, a foretaste of a still more striking all-pizzicato passage in the development section, a pendant, Ex. 6, embodying one or two already-

---

[1] For examples of this procedure in Borodin, I refer readers to the chapter on *Prince Igor* in my *Studies in Russian Music* (William Reeves, 1935).

noticed peculiarities of Sibelius's melodic writing, is played by the wood-wind. The re-appearance in the bassoons of the first motive of Ex. 5, as a counterpoint to Ex. 6, establishes a relationship between the two second-group themes similar to that connecting the three which constitute the first group.

The exposition concludes with a passage peculiarly characteristic of Sibelius's use of ostinato effects, though in later works he seldom, if ever, marks such a passage Poco a poco più stretto e crescendo as he does here. Arising naturally out of the crotchet movement of Ex. 5, and the three-crotchet motive of Ex. 6, Sibelius introduces an incessant figure of regular staccato crotchets on the wood-wind in two parts, and continues it for twenty bars, with a stretto effect towards the end. This, like Ex. 5, is accompanied merely by a pair of B minor chords, a tonic 6-4, and a dominant seventh. The striking effect is psychological rather than merely physical.

The working-out section, comparatively short, falls into three parts :

(a) Brass chords, against which the strings play descending chromatic scales; the opening motive of Ex. 5 also appears on the strings.

(b) The motive from Ex. 5 emerges pizzicato; Ex. 6 and, once, Ex. 1 re-appear; but Ex. 5, now entire, predominates.

(c) A wood-wind motive derived from the first three notes of Ex. 1, but breaking off into chromatic scales in thirds, evokes ascending chromatic scales on the lower strings (Ex. 7).

Two points here are specially noteworthy : first, that (a) appears to be a mere inorganic interpolation *until* we hear (c) which balances it structurally; second, that (c) is not only the end of the development, but may also be regarded as the beginning of the recapitulation —distorted.

This telescoping process is then carried still further. As Ex. 7 goes on, Ex. 4 is presently played against it, *largamente e energico*, by all the upper strings. And when Ex. 7 finally dies out, leaving Ex. 4, this latter theme develops an almost gushingly lyrical little pendant (Ex. 8). The tutti return of Ex. 1 again at the end of the first theme-group, as in the exposition, powerful and undistorted, is overwhelming in its effect : we have heard only one brief fragment of it in its true form since the parallel passage in the exposition. The rest of the recapitulation is normal, except for one important point : the main second theme *as a whole* is omitted. The motive that counterpoints with Ex. 6 is present, but that is all. The characteristic curt end of the movement is also noteworthy.

This somewhat detailed analysis—and one less detailed would be useless—shows, I think, how closely knit, how beautifully organic, is even this apparently most sectional and square-cut of Sibelius's first movements, how unconventional beneath the appearance of convention. The difference between this and Sibelius's more mature symphonic movements is that here the ' members ' are still separate, the joins obvious; the later ones are not more organic but higher types of organism. (And, of course, less lyrical, less romantic in character.)

The remaining three movements of the First Symphony repay study much less. One notices interesting points : the reply of the clarinets in sixths to the string melody of the slow movement (anticipating, in spirit rather than in letter, the clarinet reply to the famous oboe melody of the trio of the Second Symphony), the very curious wood-wind fugato in the same movement (a movement that one too often hears sentimentalised), the use of part of the first movement introduction to introduce the finale, the pizzicato chords at the end of the finale, and the recurrence of various already noted idiosyncrasies of Sibelius's writing. But, generally speaking, these three movements are not only on a lower musical level than the first, but much less characteristic of Sibelius.

Sibelius's Second Symphony shows none of the superficial resemblances to Borodin that appear in the First—except that the scherzo has, perhaps, something in common with those of Borodin's symphonies. On the other hand, Sibelius's innovations in the inner organism of his first movement—described by Mr. Gray as ' a veritable revolution . . . the introduction of an entirely new principle into symphonic form '—are fully anticipated in Borodin's First Symphony. Mr. Gray says :

> Instead of presenting definite, clear-cut melodic personalities in the exposition, taking them to pieces, dissecting and analysing them in a development section, and putting them together again in a recapitulation, Sibelius inverts the process, introducing thematic fragments in the exposition, building them up into an organic whole in the development section, then dissolving and dispersing the material back into its primary constituents in a brief recapitulation.

But Borodin had done this sort of thing more than thirty years earlier. (Incidentally, Sibelius himself had done something very similar in *Lemminkäinen's Homecoming*, written some years before the Second Symphony.)

This is not the place to analyse the first movement of the Borodin symphony.[1] But, roughly speaking, this is Borodin's method. A

[1] I must refer the reader who is interested in the matter to the chapter ' Borodin as a Symphonist ' in my *Studies in Russian Music.*

slow introduction does, in contrast with Sibelius's procedure, present 'a definite, clear-cut melodic personality' (Ex. 2). But, having stated it once, he leaves it at that. The ensuing allegro, which we are accustomed to look upon as the 'first movement proper', begins with mere thematic fragments; not until bar 28 do we get as much as three bars of the theme in a connected form. The second subject, too, consists only of two melodic scraps presented separately, then related to each other. In a quasi-development section, repeated again later, we are confronted with a sort of mosaic structure in which the fragments of both first and second subjects are ingeniously dovetailed; but it is only in the andantino coda that Borodin lets us into his secret: that *all* these thematic fragments are really parts of a single idea, here stated for the first time. Sibelius does not follow this procedure exactly. He has no slow introduction and no final coda synthesis; the general architecture of his first movement is quite different. But the essentials are the same: the preservation of the superficial appearance of orthodox sonata-form and the substitution for the old sonata principle (the statement of two main themes and keys, or group of themes and keys, and the working out of a sort of drama in which they are the protagonists) of this new principle of synthesis.

Incidentally, in discussing the general architecture of the movement I feel obliged to disagree entirely with Mr. Gray's analysis. He says that 'in the First Symphony the initial movement is built up on definite first and second subjects; here there are none in the accepted conventional sense of the words.' If it be granted that a 'subject' may be a whole group of themes, as in the First Symphony, the subjects of the Second are quite as conventional. Mr. Gray regards the whole of the first-subject group as an 'introduction' and then speaks of the perfectly obvious second subject in F sharp minor (Ex. 12) as that which 'would in ordinary parlance, no doubt, be called the "first subject".'

The opening chordal figure itself has some thematic importance,[1] or (at least) importance as a binding agent, for it is used not only at once to accompany the first main theme (Ex. 9), but later as the accompaniment to the second subject on its first appearance (see Ex. 12). At the end of each of these wood-wind phrases, the horns echo the motive $x$, but with the quavers now broadened out into a quadruplet group of crotchets, a foretaste of the alla breve time that

---

[1] A rising three-note figure also plays an important part in the thematic material of the slow movement and of the finale, though this, of course, may be only coincidence.

prevails throughout the remainer of the first-subject group. This group consists of no fewer than three more themes, presented with an apparent disconnectedness that is obviously deliberate. They are a theme for bassoons accompanied only by a drum-roll (Ex. 10), a melody for first and second violins unison and quite unaccompanied (Ex. 11), and a third theme for strings which I need not quote. A sixteen-bar codetta makes a half-hearted pretence at tying these disparate elements together, and then an eight-bar pizzicato passage (again in 6-4 time, and growing out of the first three notes of the wood-wind theme, Ex. 9) leads to the main theme of the second group (Ex. 12). The long sustained first note, the quasi-trill and the curt end are all thoroughly characteristic of Sibelius's melodic style. When quoted only melodically, the theme, of course, appears to be in D major; only the context shows that the C sharp is the dominant of F sharp minor. The remaining elements of the second subject, all subsidiary, are three : an incessant quaver figure for strings, almost entirely on three notes, F sharp, E, D sharp; the chordal figure of the opening of the movement; a figure of dropping fifths (D sharp, E, A, D, G, C natural, F natural, B flat, E natural) played by all the wood-wind in octaves, fortissimo.

So much for Sibelius's exposition, which is perfectly orthodox. But from the very beginning the development is marked by the ' synthetic ' principle. Ex. 12 on the oboe is immediately answered by a bassoon theme derived from the ' horn echo ' of Ex. 9; this is repeated with the falling-fifths theme morticed into its opening; and the whole is further welded together by the already mentioned quaver ostinato figure as accompaniment (now in thirds).

The development may be considered as tripartite :

(*a*) Based on the complex of themes just described, but with the dropping fifths becoming more and more important (46 bars).

(*b*) Beginning tranquillo (with one reference to Ex. 12 and then with Ex. 9 played simultaneously with its mirror-inversion) but gradually quickening in pace and becoming fuller in scoring. This latter part is based on a theme with several melodic features in common with Ex. 11, first unobtrusively woven in, then gradually wrought to a climax with much imitation and stretto (46 bars).

(*c*) Poco largamente. Based on the same material as (*a*) except the dropping fifths, but much more fully scored and ending with a short but tremendous crescendo (20 bars).

Then comes the peak of the whole movement : a magnificent synthesis of the seemingly disparate elements of the secondary first-subject themes, a synthesis of which I quote only a part, as Ex. 13, and that only in skeleton. But this synthesis is not, as Mr. Gray says, part of the development, but rather the beginning of the recapitulation—as the return to the tonic key shows. (Or we might perhaps regard this as a telescoping of the end of the development with the beginning of the recapitulation, as in the corresponding passage in the First Symphony.) All that happens is that the first-subject material is recapitulated in a different order and partly in the new forms evolved in the course of the development: the variant of the ' horn echo ' of Ex. 9 already heard at the beginning of the development, the theme from the middle section of the development ' with features in common with Ex. 11 ', Exs. 10 and 11 on the brass, Ex. 9, and then Ex. 9 counterpointed with the third theme which I have not quoted. It will be observed that just as in the First Symphony, the first theme (Ex. 9) recurs first in a dis-guised form, and in its original shape only at a later point in the reprise.

The rest of the recapitulation is perfectly normal, except that the second subject returns in B minor, leaving the tonic key to be restored by the opening chordal figure, which returns with Ex. 12 as in the exposition and actually has the last word.

As in the First Symphony, the three remaining movements are structurally much less interesting than the first. Naturally, they are full of things that no one but Sibelius could have written: the seemingly endless tramp of pizzicato bass quavers at the beginning of the andante; the lovely oboe melody of the lento trio in the third movement, with its nine repeated B flats; the overwhelming effect in the finale of an ostinato figure—essentially a mere five-finger exercise affair—which heightens the power of the inexorably marching second subject to an almost intolerable degree. On the other hand, this second subject itself is a sort of third cousin of the motto-theme of Tchaikovsky's Fifth Symphony: the main part of the scherzo is Borodinesque, and one section of the slow movement shows the influence—unusual in Sibelius—of Wagner (*Tristan*). The trio is pure Sibelius, however, and somewhat akin in feeling to the ' Pastorale ' in his music to *Pelléas et Mélisande*, written four years later.

The one really striking structural feature of the latter part of the symphony is the manner of the fusion of the scherzo with the finale. After the repeat of the scherzo, the trio also returns. But new elements are gradually woven in and gradually become more clearly defined; and as the music grows naturally and organically into the finale, we discover that these new elements are actually the material of the opening of the finale.

Karl Ekman, in his biography of Sibelius, tells us that Sibelius considers that the 'essence of symphony' lies in 'its severity and style and the profound logic that creates an inner connection between all the motives.' We have already seen something of this in the relationship between the themes of the first-subject group in the First Symphony and (a little differently) in the development and 'synthetic' opening of the recapitulation in the first movement of the Second. In the Third Symphony, Sibelius makes these inner connections much subtler than in the two earlier works. But, as I have already said, it is not that the Third and its successors are more organic works : they are *higher* types of organism.

All students of Sibelius agree that the Third Symphony is more classic in feeling than its predecessors. The scoring is dominated by the strings; there is no more of the brassy, quasi-Russian manner of handling the orchestra. The whole work consists of only three movements; and this time the chief interest lies not in the first, which is the most orthodox of all Sibelius's first movements, but in the last, which carries the fusion of scherzo with finale (already seen in a rudimentary state in the Second Symphony) to a remarkable degree of organic unity. It is true both Tovey[1] and Gray agree that the slow movement (andantino con moto, quasi allegretto) 'combines the functions of slow movement and scherzo'. It does to some extent, but not more so than the allegretto of Beethoven's Seventh Symphony. But of the obviously bipartite third movement, the first part is definitely scherzo-like in character, while it is only in the second part that a big finale tune, comparable with that in the Second Symphony, emerges.

I have just said that the allegretto moderato is 'the most orthodox of all Sibelius's first movements.' In clearness and simplicity of outline, indeed, it is comparable with a Haydn or Mozart first movement. The one point in common with the first movement of the Second Symphony is the fusion, very simply effected by overlapping, of the end of the development with the beginning of the reprise. Nevertheless, the organic unity of the movement is far in advance of anything in the Viennese classical masters; and even the general architecture is held together in a way that had classical precedents but had never before, I think, been so fully developed. The second main theme is anticipated before the end of the first-subject section,

---

[1] *Essays in Musical Analysis*, Vol. II (Oxford University Press, 1935).

and most of the latter part of the second-subject section is evolved from first-subject material. (That sounds as if it might lead to confusion : actually, everything is perfectly clear.)

The ' inner connection between all the motives ' is remarkable. Take, for instance, the child (Ex. 14) born of the marriage of the first main theme (Ex. 15) with the quite unrelated subsidiary material (Ex. 16). And, as Tovey points out, the continuation in the development section of the second subject gradually tends to resemble the opening of Ex. 15, but with sustained instead of repeated notes. From the motive *y* in Ex. 16 also grows a tremendous quasi-ostinato semi-quaver figure (said, according to Tovey, ' to represent the composer's impression of fog-banks drifting along the English coast ') which dominates not only the greater part of the second subject but the whole of the development. It is not exactly thematic, but it exercises a binding function similar to that of the chordal-accompaniment figure in the Second Symphony, and produces a psychological effect akin to that of Sibelius's other long ostinato passages.[1]

One other remarkable point in this first movement : of the thirty-seven bar first-subject section, eleven bars are in unison and in a C major unblemished by a single accidental, and twenty-two are harmonised simply by an actual or implied C major triad. Two bars based on the A minor triad and two bars of mild chromatic chords are therefore the sole deviations from the tonic chord throughout the first subject. Similarly, the main part of the second subject—which appears to be in D major and is shown to be really in B minor only as it ends—is harmonised almost throughout with the tonic-suggesting interval D–F sharp, the only deviation being an occasional E treated as an appogiatura to D. These are particularly striking examples of that static Sibelian harmony to which I have drawn attention earlier.

The pleasant andantino, quasi allegretto, one of the weakest movements in the whole of Sibelius's symphonies, has but few features of interest. Yet the constant interplay of 6-4 and 3-2 is charming; and the persistent melodies in thirds, the wood-wind quaver passages (also in thirds) and the prolonged *pizzicato* passages for the whole force of strings are all characteristic of Sibelius.

By far the most interesting part of the symphony is the third. Broadly speaking, it consists (as I have said) of a 6-8 scherzo, which

[1] I am tempted to suggest that Sibelius may have taken a hint for these ostinato passages from Bruckner.

merges almost imperceptibly into an almost march-like finale. Analysis of the first part is extraordinarily difficult—indeed, almost impossible. Scraps of motives and of figuration are tossed about in a way that suggests Debussy's pointillistic technique on the one hand and the sketchy outlines of Beethoven's last quartets on the other. Yet careful study does reveal an underlying formal design; and although this mere skeleton is much less important than the organic tissue of inwardly connected themes that covers it, the tissue cannot be properly understood until we understand the skeleton.

(*a*) Allegro (ma non tanto), 50 bars.—Various scraps of wood-wind melody, apparently unrelated but soon shown in Sibelius's familiar way to be related not only to each other but to the chief theme of the second movement. Tripping staccato quaver-figures on the first violins, divided and muted. All these thematic beads are strung together by a viola figure, a sustained C ending in a slow trill.

(*b*) Meno allegro, 19 bars.—Strings, twice reinforced by the horns, weave a background to more melodic fragments from a new, wavy figure (Ex. 17) worked in close imitation.

(*c*) Più allegro, 16 bars.—New staccato quaver figure. After seven bars, the wood-wind introduces two motives in duple time, a falling major third and a rising diminished fifth, the first hints of the true finale theme. At the same time, a pedal C appears in the bass.

(*a*) Allegro (non tanto), 26 bars.—The pedal C continues for eighteen bars, largely replacing the viola figure as ' string ' to the thematic beads. The falling third and rising fifth reappear at the end.

(*b*) Più moderato (but gradually quickening), 72 bars.—Ex. 17 serves at first as accompaniment to a longer stretch (eleven bars) of the finale theme on horns and violas; then develops as before—in its own right, as it were—and quickens to a rush of continuous quavers. Into this is woven a motive (Ex. 18) extracted from one of the melodic scraps of (*a*), and the rush of continuous quavers leads naturally to the return of

(*c*) (62 bars), marked by the reappearance of the ' new staccato quaver figure '. Ex. 18 is also very prominent, and is now welded on to Ex. 17. The music grows quieter, and, towards the end, part of the finale theme reasserts itself on divided violas marcato (Ex. 19), and finally triumphs over the last flying fragments of the scherzo.

The rest of the movement may be considered as finale proper. The time signature changes to 4-4, and the finale theme marches on to the end in a comparatively simple strophic form, cunningly varied so as to build up (with comparatively slight means) a cumulative effect of great power. A striking feature of this last part of the movement is the unobtrusive introduction and increasing importance of the motive *x* from Ex. 16 (first movement). As always when Sibelius makes thematic cross-references from one movement to another, it is done so unobtrusively that one is half in doubt whether the reference is intentional or only a subconscious recollection. But, deliberate or not, these subtle links strengthen the organic unity of the symphonies enormously—and far more satisfactorily than the crude use of motto-themes (à la Tchaïkovsky) or cyclic themes (à la Franck).

Similarly, although the first, scherzo-like portion of the third movement *can* be divided into recognisable sections, as I have shown above (indeed, *must* be for the purposes of analysis), the essence of the movement is its continuous organic growth. One can speak of its ' sections ' only as one can of the limbs of an animal.

Sibelius's Fourth Symphony is generally recognised as the finest of the whole series : the work in which the composer is most completely himself, and in which his symphonic methods are most uncompromisingly employed. (Its only serious rival in this respect is the Seventh.) Sibelius has here carried compression so far that even many of those who feel the greatness of the music are apparently puzzled by its form and unable to grasp the inner logic which they are conscious is present. Actually, the formal outline of the work is remarkably clear, especially to those who have studied Sibelius's structural methods in his earlier symphonies; and study of the score soon reveals the inner logic.

The first movement, though adagio in tempo and therefore occupying only thirteen pages of the score, is architecturally a model of text-book sonata form—with one modification. We have already seen how, in his first two symphonies, Sibelius telescopes the end of the development with the beginning of the recapitulation; here in the Fourth he takes a small step further by eliminating the recapitulation of the first subject altogether. One feels that the development, being in the same grey, brooding mood, has taken the place of a reprise of the first subject.

The six opening bars may be regarded as an introduction. The motive *x* in Ex. 20 is of the greatest importance later, but here it only generates a sort of alternating pedal or two-note ground bass, F sharp–E. This alternating pedal continues practically throughout the first subject, which need not be quoted. It is a grey, melancholy theme in A minor played by the muted strings, moving largely in even quavers. Finally, the F sharp in the bass triumphs; the alternating bass becomes F sharp–C sharp, and after a mere four-bar transition the second subject (Ex. 21) bursts out in F sharp major. (It will be noticed that the first four notes are the motive *x* from Ex. 20.) The remarkable point is that this second subject (including a soft horn fanfare figure, the echoes of which die away under the shadow, as it were, of Ex. 21) is only nine bars long. There is one transitional bar and then a thirteen-bar codetta (F sharp major), based on the first subject on the strings and Ex. 20 *x* on solo clarinet and solo oboe, brings the exposition to a close.

The development falls into two main parts : (*a*) after four introductory bars evolved from the first subject, a solo 'cello (unaccompanied) propounds a curious syncopated melody combining elements from the first subject and from Ex. 21. This is taken up by the higher strings, still mainly unison, lasts for fourteen bars and then merges imperceptibly into (*b*) sixteen bars of murmuring muted string background Ex. 22 derived from Ex. 20 *x*, against which the wood-wind gives out a three-note motive which Cecil Gray suggests may also be derived from Ex. 20 *x*. (It is marked by an augmented fourth, an interval noticeable in the material of each movement of the symphony.) Ex. 22, with a new figure on solo wind, is worked up to a climax which culminates in Ex. 21, now in A major.

Thus the reprise begins, as already mentioned, with the second subject; but the rest of it is note for note the same as the exposition, even as regards the scoring, except that the codetta is extended by five concluding bars based on Ex. 20 *x*, and that the key is now A major instead of F sharp major. Nothing could be more concise than this movement. In place of the subject-group of the earlier symphonies, we have single short themes; transitional passages are reduced to the absolute minimum; and the recapitulation is drastically shortened.

The scherzo has two striking features. It is interrupted near the beginning by a strange passage in 2-4 time for strings in octaves (Ex. 23). As will be noticed this contains a reference—perhaps only accidental—to Ex. 20 *x*, and continues solely in this rhythm for forty-four bars : it proves later to be a rhythmic distortion of the trio. The other notable feature of the scherzo is that, after the trio (doppio più lento), the scherzo returns in A major as if for the normal repeat, though in the wrong key. But when only four bars of it have been heard, it fizzles out with startling abruptness, just hinting at the real tonic key (F major), and the movement is over. Sibelius has here evidently taken a hint from the end of the scherzo of Beethoven's Seventh Symphony.

Ex. 20 *x* is again noticeable in the flute motive (Ex. 24) which opens the slow movement and, either in this form or in rhythmic augmentation, forms one of its two main elements. This movement, in C sharp minor,[1] is the most loosely constructed of the four. It consists solely of alternations of two elements : Ex. 24 and a motive rising in two perfect fifths. Each is stated first in a rudimentary form; each develops with every repetition. Here and there occur fleeting hints, mere insubstantial shadows, of the preceding movements; and, as Mr. Gray has pointed out, the fourteenth bar from the end happens to coincide with the opening of the finale. But whether these relationships are intentional or accidental, no one but the composer can tell us.

Nothing could be in stronger contrast with this short, rather rhapsodic, movement than the finale : long and comparatively symmetrical, though diffuse in structure. Indeed, this last movement, occupying thirty-one of the sixty-eight pages of the score, hardly seems to belong to the other three. It opens with fifteen introductory bars—a sort of false start, for they lead to nothing. The opening figure is then repeated in a modified form and at once throws out a whole group of motives, which serve as the main part of the first-subject material. Two of these motives are notable : one, given first to the clarinets and outlined by bells (the score, as Mr. Gray points out, indicates ' Glocken ', not ' Glockenspiel '), seems to have originated in the soft horn fanfares of the second subject of the first movement; the other, occurring in a more extended violin theme, is an inversion of Ex. 20 *x*. A declamatory passage for solo 'cello (affettuoso), repeated by a solo violin, and a curious thirty-two bar passage for strings, pianissimo (against which the wind plays an apparently quite unimportant motive, consisting only of a rising third), may also be classed as subsidiary first-subject material.

The second-subject group consists of two elements : (*a*) a somewhat choral-like theme, first played by the wood-wind; (*b*) a syncopated string-figure. The greater part of this section is supported by a monotonous two-chord accompaniment, reminiscent of a passage to which I drew attention in the first movement of the First Symphony.

The development, if one can call it such, consists mainly of a nineteen-bar passage of rushing C major scales for strings, unison (one of the most remarkable of all Sibelius's ostinato effects), against which the trumpets play one of the first-subject motives, the bells another. The recapitulation follows, with the second subject coming *before* the first group of themes; and there is a lengthy coda based mainly on the syncopated theme of the second subject and on the

[1] The key system of the Symphony as a whole is interesting. The keynote of the second movement is a major third below that of the first, that of the third a major third above it.

' apparently quite unimportant ' rising third motive mentioned above as part of the subsidiary first-subject material.

I have described this finale in terms of sonata form partly because it seems probable that Sibelius conceived it so and partly because it seems to me that this is the easiest way of making clear the topography of the whole wood instead of confusing the reader with the tree-by-tree method of pseudo-analysis—' now a fresh theme appears; after this comes another episode ', and so on—a proceeding which tells the explorer what he can very easily find out for himself but leaves him completely unenlightened on the very point on which he needs enlightenment: the ground plan of the composition. On the other hand, it is a pity to put such a freely constructed movement as this finale into a text-book strait-jacket and label it with a text-book label. With equal justice one might say that it is in what modern German theorists call *Bogenform*, with a brief introduction and protracted coda, the apex of the arch (*Bogen*) being the nineteen-bar scale passage, thus: Introductory bars; A, first-subject group; B, second subject; C, brief development; B, second subject; A, first subject; Coda.

The Fifth is perhaps the most approachable of all Sibelius's later symphonies. Yet despite apparent obviousness, despite its rich, melodious diatonicism, it is by no means a concession to a puzzled public, least of all a backward step in symphonic method. Structurally, its opening movement is, at first glance, the most puzzling of all Sibelius's first movements.

Actually it is a perfectly logical synthesis of various methods previously employed. We have already noticed in Nos. 1, 2 and 4 how Sibelius curtails his recapitulations, telescoping them with the developments; in Nos. 2 and 3 we have seen him, with increasing subtlety, organically fusing scherzo with finale; and in No. 4 we have had an instance of a concentrated first movement in slow tempo. Now, in the opening movement of No. 5 we find all these devices employed together, and the result is a piece of musical architecture completely unlike that of any other symphonic movement ever written. So completely, in fact, that no one seems to be quite sure whether it should be regarded as one movement or two. Actually, however, the simultaneous change of tempo-marking and time-signature is not quite as important as it appears to be; it does mark the transition from first-movement-pure-and-simple to first-move-ment-cum-scherzo; but as the dotted minim of the new tempo (allegro molto) in 3-4 time is exactly equal to the dotted crotchet of the opening (molto moderato) in 12-8 time, the difference is purely one of notation. One bar is now written as four, that is all.

The Tempo molto moderato opens with a normal two-group exposition : first group in E flat, second group in G. The horn theme, Ex. 25, with which the work opens, begets a wood-wind pendant of considerable importance but which need not be quoted, and this in turn engenders one of Sibelius's characteristic wood-wind-in-thirds ideas. The three themes of the second group, however, all demand quotation (*cf.* Ex. 26). So far all is plain sailing; but now comes a section which may be regarded as the equivalent of the late eighteenth century repeat of the exposition, though naturally the repetition is here very free and both groups are now in E flat or closely related keys. (The object is obviously to establish both the themes and the tonic key with the unusual emphasis necessary if the equilibrium of this big unorthodox movement is not to be upset altogether.)

The development begins with a fugal treatment of an insignificant scrap of theme linking two groups of ideas in the original exposition but omitted from the repeat. As Sir Donald Tovey puts it,[1] it ' is worked up into a wonderful, mysterious kind of fugue which quickens (by diminution) into a cloudy chromatic trembling, through which its original figure moans in the clarinet and bassoon.' After a largamente development of Ex. 26 (a) the key changes to B major, Ex. 25 rings out on the trumpets (with the already mentioned pendant on the wood-wind), and with the change of time-signature from 12-8 to 3-4, the rest of the development assumes a definitely scherzo-like character.

The scherzo proper is almost entirely evolved from Ex. 25, much of it being woven round an ostinato figure consisting of the first four notes of this theme. The theme of what corresponds to the trio, first stated by the solo trumpet (Ex. 27), is also related to it. Presently flying fragments, first of Ex. 26 (a) (see Ex. 28), then of Ex. 25 (see Ex. 29), appear. Gradually Ex. 27 dies, throwing out a new sprout (which survives and becomes important) at the very moment of death, and imperceptibly we enter on a final section which is neither a repeat of the scherzo nor a recapitulation of the opening molto moderato, but does duty for both; it is thoroughly scherzo-like, becoming even quicker towards the end, but is based on transformations of the material of the molto moderato exposition. The first four notes of Ex. 25 are sounded by the trumpets; Ex. 26 (b)

[1] *Essays in Musical Analysis*, Vol. II.

returns on the horns and is worked up to a clinching climax; and Ex.
26 (c) becomes a giddy, incessant presto dance in even crotchets, a
dance continued for more than fifty bars. The melodic figuration of
the last sixteen bars of the movement is entirely derived from the
first four notes of Ex. 25, while the underlying harmony consists of
the same four notes compressed into a single chord.

The plan and proportions of the whole great movement can be
grasped easily from the following rough outline:

*Tempo molto moderato*
Exposition (35 bars = 140 bars of allegro molto)
Repeat of exposition (35 bars = 140)
Development (43 bars = 172)

*Allegro molto*
Scherzo (second part of development) (104 bars)
Trio (80 bars)
Section corresponding to scherzo-repeat and recapitulation
(289 bars)

The exact number of bars in each section is admittedly open to
challenge; it is not always possible to define precisely where one
section merges into another, but, as will be seen, the architectural
balance of the whole is remarkable: exposition, 280 bars; development, 276 bars (+ 80); recapitulation, 289 bars.

After this very complicated movement, Sibelius gives an unusually
simple one—a set of almost naïve variations, not on a ' theme ' in the
ordinary sense but on a basic rhythm:

The tempo marking, andante mosso, quasi allegretto, is almost the
same as that of the middle movement of the Third Symphony
(andante con moto, quasi allegretto); indeed, the two movements have
a good deal in common, possibly including a common ancestor: the
allegretto of Beethoven's Seventh Symphony. But one feature of
this piece should be noticed: the appearance of the second subject of
the finale as a bass in two of the variations: first nearly, then exactly
as it is heard in the last movement.

The finale is very simple in build, following the outline (though
not the key-plan) of sonata form, but is not without interesting
features. To begin with, the place of the first subject is taken by a
sort of moto perpetuo effect for the strings. The second violins
(divided into four parts) and violas begin it, and gradually the rest
of the orchestra join in; but throughout this section, 104 bars long,

nothing that could be called a theme emerges. Such incessant, non-thematic or barely thematic passages have always been a feature of Sibelius's music and a strangely effective feature. Closely akin to his ostinato figures and rhythms, they produce a similar almost mesmeric effect.

As the moto perpetuo dies away at last, the powerful, swinging second subject enters at once on strings and horns in thirds and *in the same key* (E flat major). After twenty-four bars, a fresh idea enters in counterpoint with this: not merely a theme this time but a lengthy tune, scored for wood-wind in octaves plus the 'cellos in their higher register. The key changes to C, then to C minor, and a quasi-development follows. At least, a section that shares the bustling character of the opening: one can hardly speak of 'development' where there is no theme to develop. A rather slight, fresh idea also appears here.

The recapitulation, shortened and with different scoring and dynamics, is otherwise normal except that the key is now G flat throughout. The music returns to the tonic key only in the middle of the coda: a splendid, broad peroration based first on the melodic counter-theme of the second subject (played by all the strings, except double-basses, in octaves), then by the second subject proper (on the brass). The quasi-stretto effect and the brass writing towards the end remind one of the end of the Third Symphony, and at the same time anticipate climactic points in the Seventh.

The Sixth Symphony, though the Cinderella of the seven, falling (as Cecil Gray has put it) 'between the stools of the appreciation of the many and the appreciation of the few', is both very fine and particularly interesting. The first movement is one of Sibelius's most highly organic compositions, and the work as a whole contains some striking foreshadowings of points in the Seventh Symphony: effects of rather cold diatonic polyphony for strings only; the simultaneous sounding of opposing harmonies in contrasted instrumental groups (e.g. the chord C sharp-E-B-G on the strings against a C major triad on the brass at the end of the first subject of the first movement of No. 6; the D sharp-B of the strings impinging on the F major triad of the horns and bassoons at bar 6 of No. 7); rather deliberate, rising diatonic scales ending on unexpected notes (e.g., the opening of No. 7 and the passage a few bars before the end of the first movement of No. 6); above all, a pronounced strengthening of the tendency, noticeable in much of Sibelius's earlier work (e.g., the finale of No. 3 and the first subject of the finale of No. 5) for the essence of the music to be embodied less in definite themes than in the harmonic-contrapuntal-instrumental texture as a whole. The themes seem to be thrown up, as it were, out of the complex musical stream, instead of the stream of thought being evolved from the themes. Here we have one of Sibelius's very few points of resemblance to Wagner, in particular to *Tristan*. This sort of musical thinking really defies analysis. One can only talk about 'themes' and 'motives', yet the real sense of the music does not lie in the themes as such. At the same time, it is mainly through the recurrence of themes that one recognises the formal outline of a piece of music, and it should be the analyst's fundamental object to make the ouline clear. (Here, again, 'form' in the case of the later Sibelius means something essentially different from Mozartean form, something almost as different as the form of a tree or a human anatomy from the form of a cathedral.)

The opening of the first movement of the Sixth Symphony is characteristic of this non-thematic style. For nearly thirty bars we hear nothing but quietly moving diatonic counterpoint in four or five parts for divided violins and violas only. None of these contrapuntal lines is a melody in the conventional sense of the word, no segment of them is thematic. At the most, one can find only tiny two- or three-note motives, which may or may not be really related to the more definite themes of the work. The little four-note descending scale figure near the end of the finale *may* have been connected in the composer's mind with some of these wisps of counterpoint, but the similarity is just as likely to be accidental.

But out of this vague, almost amorphous piece of polyphonic texture presently grows a more definite theme, divided between oboes and flutes (Ex. 30), which may be regarded as the real first subject. Its tonal peculiarity will be noticed at once : it is in the Dorian mode (white-note scale of D). Although the symphony is usually spoken of as 'in D minor', it is not so described on the score; the first movement has no key signature (except for a few bars), and the finale takes the one-flat signature only towards the end. Both movements end with D minor triads, but if the key of the symphony is D minor, it is a D minor with a flattened leading note.

The material of the second subject is more interesting than that of the first. As Mr. Gray has shown in his 'Musical Pilgrim' booklet on the symphonies, it begins with a striking instance of that method of re-shaping a theme motive by motive which Sibelius seems to have learned from Borodin. The process reminds one of the child's game of altering a word letter by letter, so that 'cat' becomes 'dog' through the intermediate stages of 'cot' and 'cog'. Here the original 'word' is one of Sibelius's typical wood-wind-in-thirds themes (Ex. 31). (The supporting harmony is a C major triad, the tonality indeterminate.) The subsequent derivatives need not be quoted. After two other second-group themes of minor importance the development begins.

Like the corresponding section of the Third Symphony, the development is pervaded from beginning to end by an incessant spiccato string figure (Ex. 32) derived from a motive of the first subject, against which background other thematic fragments (including the oboe motive of Ex. 30) are thrown. As in the Third Symphony, too, the beginning of the reprise is most skilfully dovetailed into the end of the development—Ex. 30 returns on the 'cellos so naturally and spontaneously that we hardly notice its reappearance —but the recapitulation is not actually foreshortened in accordance with Sibelius's more usual practice.

Nevertheless, the reprise is full of interest. Whereas the exposition is hesitant, indeterminate, a collection of seemingly rather heterogeneous elements, the recapitulation is a confident, clear-cut, perfectly welded whole. This is due partly to different scoring and treatment of the material, partly to the replacement of Ex. 31 (and the section derived from it) by a brilliantly scored passage the beginning of which is shown as Ex. 33, which might possibly be considered a further derivative of it (compare Ex. 33 $x$ with Ex. 31 $x$).

The two minor second-group themes are recapitulated in reverse order, and finally synthesised (letter K of the miniature score), after which a quiet, curiously enigmatic coda brings the movement to a close.

The second movement—allegro moderato—is, as usual, the weakest of the whole symphony. And, as rarely happens in Sibelius, one is reminded of other composers : of the mood of the allegretto of Brahms's Third Symphony, of some of Tchaïkovsky's half-playful, half-indolent melodies, and—even Mr. Gray recognises this, though he admits Wagnerian influence nowhere else in Sibelius—of Wagner's *Waldweben.* Exactly as in the scherzo of the Fourth Symphony a repeat of the first section is begun, as if the movement were to be in regular ternary form, and then immediately broken off in the manner of the end of the scherzo of Beethoven's Seventh.

If the scherzo has no points of special interest, the finale amply compensates. The form is peculiar. First we have a series of square-cut four-bar phrases, played antiphonally by answering orchestral choirs : violins, wood-wind and horns; lower strings only; violins, wood-wind and horns; lower strings; wood-wind only; lower strings; wood-wind; strings, and so on. Only two of these phrases need be quoted (see Ex. 34). Then comes a section, 97 bars long, evolved from the motive shown in Ex. 35, which in turn is derived from Ex. 34 (a); its rhythm is that of *x* in that theme, its melodic outline is modified from that of *y*. The form of this middle section is particularly interesting; it is that which modern German theorists, borrowing from medieval German poetry a term revived by Wagner in *Die Meistersinger,* call the *Bar*[1] : two stanzas (*Stollen*) exactly balancing each other, and an ' after-song ' (*Abgesang*)—like the *Stollen* ' as the child to the parent ', yet different—rounding off the whole. In this instance the *Stollen* are respectively 29 and 30 bars long, the *Abgesang* 39.

Then we return to the opening (modified) for 25 bars. After a further 38 bars of allegro assai also based on a variant of Ex. 34 (a), comes a doppio più lento coda of singular beauty which, according to Mr. Gray, ' appears to be an entirely fresh line of thought, bearing no relation to anything that has gone before '. Actually, however, this coda-material (Ex. 36) is founded on Ex. 34 (b), here used as a bass while the melody is a free mirror-inversion of it.

The Seventh Symphony is the most adventurous of all Sibelius's formal experiments. Throughout the last hundred years or so, various composers have experimented with the idea of the complete-sonata-in-one-movement. Schubert was one of the first with his so-called *Wanderer* Fantasia : compressed first movement, adagio, scherzo and fugal finale all based on the same thematic material and running into each other without a break. This was the pattern followed, with variants, by Schumann in his D minor Symphony and by Liszt in his Piano Concertos. Liszt himself experimented in his Piano Sonata, with a single colossal, free ' first movement ', in which the slow-movement element is represented structurally by the second-subject group of themes. This method has found favour, too, in the eyes of some of Liszt's successors, notably Arnold Bax in his first two Piano Sonatas. Then, again, there is the modern British chamber music ' phantasy ' form produced by the Cobbett Competitions, a compromise between the two types used by Liszt, rather rigidly defined by Fuller-Maitland in the second edition of Grove as ' a

[1] This is the form in which Hans Sachs teaches Walther to cast the *Preislied.*

continuous movement (in which) the development section of the sonata form is . . . replaced by a movement in slow tempo, which may include also a scherzando movement. In any case a logical connection with the thematic material of the first part is maintained. A return to the characteristics of the first part of the movement is made, but not necessarily a definite repetition, and a developed coda is added as finale.' Incidentally, Schönberg's early Quartet in D minor and *Kammersymphonie* are constructed on very similar lines.[1]

Now these structural plans may not be inherently bad as plans, but no one has yet contrived to produce from them a genuinely organic whole. The ' colossal first movement ' type usually proves unwieldy. The ' four-movements-in-one ' obstinately remain four; the joins are almost invariably arbitrary and obvious, instead of natural and organic. Theme-transformation on deliberate, Lisztian-Franckish lines is a rather mechanical way of binding several pieces of music into a unified whole.

The most remarkable aspect of Sibelius's Seventh Symphony is that it is an *organic* symphony in one movement; not merely a long movement in which various sections correspond to slow movement, scherzo and so on, but a single indivisible organism. Even in the transition from the scherzo to the finale of the Second Symphony, Sibelius had shown his superiority to the most skilful of musical carpenters. In the third movement of the Third Symphony and the first of the Fifth, he had in each case grafted two normal movements into a single organic whole. Here in the Seventh he carries the process a stage further, and combines it with the intense compression of the Fourth.

The build of the symphony as a whole can be shown only by plotting out its ' sections ', though its superiority to other one-movement works of the same type lies in the very fact that it is *not* sectional in the conventional sense, that the sections merge gradually, imperceptibly and without any break in the logical tissue of the music. Still, analysis reveals the following ground plan :

A  EXPOSITION. Adagio (92 bars; pages 1–12 of the miniature score).
B  DEVELOPMENT. Un pochettino meno adagio (41 bars; pages 12–20).
    TRANSITION (22 bars), gradually quickening the pace to, and introducing the themes of,
C  SCHERZO. Vivacissimo (53 bars; pages 23–29).
    TRANSITION (13 bars), gradually slowing down to

[1] Mr. Cherniavsky discusses this subject further on pp. 158–9.

D DEVELOPMENT (continued). Adagio (20 bars; pages 30–36).
TRANSITION (16 bars), quickening to
E ALLEGRO MOLTO MODERATO (151 bars; pages 40–59).
F SECOND SCHERZO. Presto (40 bars; pages 59–64).
TRANSITION (27 bars), slowing down to
G RECAPITULATION. Adagio (50 bars; pages 68–76).

Naturally the exact length given here for each section is open to challenge; it is seldom possible to determine just where each begins and ends. Similarly, the terms 'exposition', 'development', 'scherzo', are offered only tentatively. In a sense, practically the whole symphony is one vast development.

Let us now see how the living thematic tissue covers this structural skeleton. We can no longer speak of 'first' and 'second' subjects or groups in the conventional sense; but the first germ of thematic importance occurs at bar 6, the sustained B of the violins dropping to A on the last quaver of the bar. This at once generates Ex. 37 (*b* being obviously derived from *a*) on the flutes. And the echo of Ex. 37 (b) on the clarinets overlaps the beginning of another important, though apparently insignificant, theme (Ex. 38) on the first violins, which is immediately counterpointed with the rising scale with which the symphony opens.

But the main feature of what I have called the A section is a sustained stretch of pure diatonic polyphony evolved from the first four notes of Exs. 37 (a) and 37 (b), begun by divided violas and 'cellos, while the rest of the orchestra joins in gradually. At its peak, reached in a C major triad, a solo trombone intones Ex. 39, one of the most impressive themes in the work. It will be noticed that this, too, appears to be derived from Ex. 37 (b). The rest of the A section, and of B too (into which it passes imperceptibly), is based almost entirely on themes already heard. The new material introduced is hardly important enough to need quotation.

Towards the end of the ensuing transition passage we hear the two main themes of the first scherzo (C) (Ex. 40); Ex. 40 (a) is evidently derived from Ex. 38; Ex. 40 (b) partly from the first three notes of Ex. 39, and partly (last four notes) from Ex. 38.[1] At the end of this section the bustling crotchets settle down into a chromatic murmur (adagio, quavers) in C minor, against which the first trombone again plays Ex. 39, marcato (section D). A reverse process of quickening up the quavers underlies the transition to the allegro molto moderato (E).

[1] Mr. Gray remarks that Ex. 40 (b) ' does not appear to be derived from, or related to, any of the foregoing material '.

This section is rhythmically, structurally and thematically more clear-cut than most of the remainder of the symphony. Though not in the least ' romantic ', the music reminds one of the early Sibelius of *En Saga* and *Lemminkäinen's Homecoming*. The themes (Ex. 41) appear to be new; yet Ex. 41 (a) has points in common with Ex. 39, and Ex. 41 (b) with the polyphonic string passage, while Ex. 41 (c) is shown by a connecting theme, Ex. 42, to be related to the latter part of Ex. 41 (a). In fact, Ex. 42 is the link connecting all three of the Ex. 41 themes; its last five notes seem to be derived from bar 2 of Ex. 41 (b). This allegro is particularly clear in outline :

INTRODUCTION 27 bars (Exs. 41 (a) and (b) ).

X  30 bars, C major (Exs. 41 (a), 42 and 41 (c) ), and seven-bar codetta on the motive *x* in Ex. 38 and a reference to Ex. 40 (b).

Y  53 bars, various keys (Exs. 41 (a), 41 (c) and other thematic fragments).

X  25 bars, E flat (Exs. 41 (a), 42 and 41 (c) ), and nine-bar codetta as before.

The second scherzo (section F) springs immediately from the preceding codetta. The germ is a motive, Ex. 43, probably derived from Ex. 40 (a). And again, as at the end of the first scherzo, the quick crotchets are converted into an ostinato accompaniment—this time very different, however.

All this is wrought to a tremendous climax : the final recapitulation has begun. There are suggestions of the polyphonic passage; there is a short passage for flute and bassoon, entirely developed from Ex. 37 (b); and the symphony ends with a powerful statement of the motive *x* in Ex. 38, D-C B-C, constituting (as Mr. Gray puts it) ' a kind of triumphal Q.E.D. to the whole proposition put forward at the outset.'

So much talk about structure and thematic derivations may disappoint the reader who has been overwhelmed by the emotional force of the Seventh Symphony. But if he has been overwhelmed, that is enough. He will not profit by matching his emotional impressions with a critic's; on the other hand he may profit by hearing not only how Sibelius feels musically but how he *thinks* musically.

# 3

# The Miscellaneous Orchestral and Theatre Music

By

Ralph W. Wood

WHEN WE VIEW SIBELIUS as a whole, comprehensively but not cursorily, surveying all his work as a composer and all that we know of his life outside that work, two things seem clear (if that word may be used when both the things are, in fact, rather matters of mystery). He is a natural composer, a person whose mind appears to have worked always in terms of music, who has always been turning spontaneously into music his thoughts and feelings of every description. Secondly, an artificial enigma added to the natural one, he has generally left unspoken and unwritten, withheld from his fellow-mortals except in the implications of his works themselves, his opinions about the nature of music and the functions of composers and the problems of musical creation. A sentence here and there in his letters, patches of conversation with friends and colleagues, obiter dicta to pupils, such as Mr. Hill has quoted : enough of those, in fact, to make it uncertain whether his reticence has been deliberate. But reticent he has been; unformulated his outlook has remained— perhaps even to himself.

One may decide that, on the whole, this is as it should be. No additional value could possibly be given to either his best works or his worst ones by any verbal elucidation of his theories and motives, or by any hypothetical light that might be thrown by philosophy or science on the phenomenon of a ' natural composer '. But what is more or less important is that one should realise that such hints as biographers and anecdotists do give us of Sibelius's outlook on music in general, on his problems as a composer, and on the relation of those things to the rest of his life and to anybody else's life, amount to nothing better than superficial surmises. Such surmises are offered to us, of Sibelius as of many another creative giant, rather too frequently and facilely.

Behind the symphonies, behind the songs, behind the piano pieces, behind the thin trickle of chamber-music and the steady gush of choral works, behind the amazing cross-section of his entire composing career, there is a human mind, a human frame, human characteristics and foibles and interests, human opinions about music, all the concentrated disparities that make up a man, this man represented for us by the words ' Jean Sibelius '. Behind the music that is what the word ' Sibelius ' means to a musician stands, sits, lies, sleeps, eats, drinks, smokes, talks, reads, travels, thinks, dreams its flesh-and-blood creator; but in relation to the music it is simplest to accept the man as an impenetrable mystery.

Nevertheless there is one point at which man and music both, together, force themselves, behind a large, insistent question-mark, upon the puzzled attention of all zestful musicians. Since his sixtieth year no new work from Sibelius's pen has been published or performed.[1] When Beethoven died at only three years short of sixty his creative life seemed anything but in decline. With the stupendous post-sixty achievements of Verdi (one of Sibelius's favourite composers, as Mr. Hill has already pointed out) we are all of us familiar. The quality of Richard Strauss, it is true, has been deteriorating for many years—since he was about forty; but we increasingly realise that it was a quality, even at its best, very far from first-rate. Not Fauré nor Haydn nor Handel nor Bach nor Domenico Scarlatti was a spent force at sixty, and neither is Stravinsky. There are, of course, a few contrary examples. The truth is that not very many very great composers have passed the age of sixty; and the silence—after that age—of one of them in spite of his continuing to live seems the more lamentable.

That Sibelius has actually written no music since about 1929 is scarcely credible. Among the other characteristics of the ' natural composer ' he was born with that of fertility. From boyhood, he composed unceasingly and profusely. To believe that all that creative activity, till then the overwhelmingly dominant factor in his life, year by year, month by month, day by day, could come to an abrupt end is next to impossible. Even Rossini, during his forty years of self-imposed retirement, could not refrain from composing a number of trifles (and very admirable trifles, too); but that is a very different case. With Sibelius it is open to us to imagine that reasons of health and of increasing self-criticism, either or both, have had something to do with his long silence. Whatever the reasons, speculation about

---

[1] With immaterial exceptions, such as the Two Psalms for mixed chorus (1925-7) and the two small sets of salon pieces for violin and piano, Opp. 115 and 116 (1929).

them forces us to include, for once, the man as well as his music in our inquiring scrutiny.

We have, in fact, been told that an Eighth Symphony has long been completed and only awaits Sibelius's death for its première. There is really no room for doubt that much other music has struggled past, whatever his accumulations of infirmity or of critical severity since 1929. For no-longer-young music-lovers who happen to recognise Sibelius's stature it becomes a tantalising race between his death and theirs.

Sibelius's most recent orchestral work to be given a hearing was the music to *The Tempest,* written for the production of that play in Copenhagen in 1926. But to his music for the stage, an interesting and considerable section of his output, we shall turn later in this chapter. In 1925 *Tapiola* had appeared; in 1924 the Seventh Symphony and two small pieces for string orchestra; in 1923 the Sixth Symphony.

*Tapiola* is called by the composer a tone-poem, and the score is prefaced by a quatrain of which the English version given is as follows:

> Wide-spread they stand, the Northland's dusky forests,
> Ancient, mysterious, brooding savage dreams;
> Within them dwells the Forest's mighty God,
> And wood-sprites in the gloom weave magic secrets.

The origin of the lines is not divulged. Tapio, by the way, is the name of the God of the Forests in Finnish mythology. The work is laid out for 3 flutes (3rd alternating with piccolo), 2 oboes, English horn, 2 clarinets, bass clarinet, 2 bassoons, double bassoon, 4 horns, 3 trumpets, 3 trombones, 3 kettledrums, and strings. It is dedicated to Walter Damrosch, the American conductor and composer, who had commissioned the work for the Symphony Society of New York, which gave it its first performance on December 26th, 1926.

The four prefatory lines quoted above are a complete exposition of the music's intended extra-musical significance. The work is, indeed, a very typical example of music's extraordinary power of suggestion. No one, it is fairly safe to declare, would deny that in these 634 bars of orchestral sound, heard after the quatrain has been read, the quatrain's idea-content is eloquently expressed. Even to some people not particularly musical the ' programmatic ' force of *Tapiola* is likely to be evident. Every word of the quatrain, and a good deal more that one may be able to imagine for oneself about a Northern forest and its deity, is to be found in this piece of music.

But now we must face two further facts, very important ones. The first is that if this composition were to be heard without its title being given, and of course without any mention of the prefatory lines, it is doubtful if the hearer would hit on its intended extra-musical meaning. The second fact is that to a thorough musician the work is entirely enjoyable without the programme being either known or even guessed at. These are facts. They are worth pondering over, because they have a great bearing on musical aesthetics, and indeed aesthetics in general, and because they are rather unfortunately ignored by a great many people. Music has tremendous powers of interpreting a given programme (or of evoking ideas associated with a mere extra-musical title); but it is very difficult to guess the programme, or the title, if one hears the music without being told them. On the other hand, it is easy, quite a natural process, for a musical person to get rich musical enjoyment from a piece of programme music (if it is good *as* music) without knowing or caring anything about its programme at all. Which brings us to the musical content and character of *Tapiola*, the most recent work known to us of an extremely mature and profound and individual musician—of a ' natural composer ' : which means not only one who automatically tends to throw into musical shape his physical and mental reactions to everything in life outside music, but one who does actually ' think *in* music '.

The most important kind of ' thinking in music ', the most important form that it takes, is the achieving of continuity of growth. That is to say, this most important kind of thinking can be felt to exist in a composition when every successive section of it, every successive line, every successive phrase, every successive bar, is only what it is because of what the immediately preceding section, line, phrase, bar, and all their predecessors were. When the music is ' thought ' in that sense, it has a thread of interest from start to finish that demands, and rewards, concentrated attention from the listener. It can only be appreciated fully if given that concentrated attention. One cannot listen to it with half an ear, or in spasms, with interruptions to attend to other things. No bar of it can be savoured fully, and some cannot be at all, unless one has intently listened to all the previous bars (whereas, of course, in a great deal of music it is possible to enjoy various patches without any reference to what has preceded them). This is the most important kind of musical thinking, some would say it is the only real kind, but it is also the most rare. Sibelius, however, is its most thorough-going exponent. And *Tapiola* is one of the best examples of it in existence.

In *Tapiola* every thematic element seems to grow from previous ones. It is, in fact, almost monothematic; practically everything that can be called theme in it is felt to be derived ultimately from the short phrase with which it opens (cf. the first movement of the Fifth Symphony). Moreover its textures are merged into each other with the utmost conceivable smoothness and gradualness. It is, as may be imagined, a work almost impossible to divide into sections; but if you do in some rough way make such divisions you have to observe that, long before one section has finished, the elements of the following one are usually already present, slowly accumulating prominence as the elements of the present one recede. Bars 3–6 of *Tapiola* are shown in Ex. 44. Now, if instead of a mere transition from the colour, intentionally a close relative, of three trumpets to that of three flutes, on the same chord, you imagine a transition from one texture and one type of motion to a totally different texture and motion, a transition achieved in, say, thirty bars instead of in three, but with equally perfect smoothness and imperceptibility, you have what constantly happens in *Tapiola*.

There is, as a matter of fact, one striking exception, at p. 19 of the miniature score. Yet one may note that although the material thus abruptly introduced at letter G (derived, nevertheless, from the opening theme) lasts for 60 bars altogether, the first re-entry of a phrase (heard some time previously) that is to be prominent in the section following those 60 bars occurs (*ppp* on a bassoon) when only 16 of them have gone by, and from that point onwards the ensuing texture and material gradually intrude themselves. This 60-bar passage ends on p. 30 of the miniature score, where the violin and 'cello parts are the final muttering of the material that came in at letter G.

This extraordinarily close continuity is bound to strike anyone who hears *Tapiola* with an ear for anything beyond its programmatic effect but it contains a number of other remarkable technical features that are less apparent. One may as well note at once that Sibelius's music tends to sound simpler than it looks. This is partly because he has so extraordinarily original, and at the same time so extraordinarily sure, a flair for distribution : distribution as regards texture and as regards movement. Whether one is taking the vertical or the horizontal view, what the score offers to the eye in space as a baffling litter of not obviously related fragments, the ear, working in time, receives as an unquestionable, unquestioned unity. Many more or less cultivated listeners do, in fact, at some time or other in their careers find his best music obscure, but only in one aspect—that of form; and there the trouble is not that the music fails to hang together, that for the ear, as for the eye, it is a jumble of unrelated, separate bits, but on the contrary that it hangs together with such remarkable cohesion, its continuity is so unbroken (its continuity above all, remember, not just of technical ingredients but of *thought*) and so without separation, that the ears, and behind them the minds, of musicians over-used to the far lesser continuity of most other comparable composers find the absence of signposts and boundary-marks bewildering and the consequent call for absorbed and long-breathed attention too exacting. It is paradoxical but true that a work by Brahms or Dvořák or Tchaïkovsky is a good deal easier to follow than one by Sibelius not because there is more connectedness in any of the former but because there is less. One does not, in fact, ' follow ' Brahms or Dvořák or Tchaïkovsky as, if one is to make sense of him at all, one has to follow Sibelius. And so the word ' easier ' means not less difficult (for actually it is not merely difficult, but *impossible*, to ' follow ' Brahms or Dvořák or Tchaïkovsky as one can ' follow ' Sibelius) but ' less exacting ', ' making less demand, both as to intensity and as to duration, on one's concentration and interest '. And of course this quality of Sibelius's is most noticeable in his symphonies, where complete absence of programme coincides with his most advanced constructive achievements (i.e. absence of extra-musical ideas leaves musical thought fullest possible play). *Tapiola*, indeed, is not conspicuously easier to follow with the ear than with the eye; both in texture and in movement it is a score comparatively simple to read. In it, for one thing, Sibelius's habit of writing for the orchestra in family blocks (as opposed to the complex inter-family doublings and blendings of a Strauss or an Elgar) is very much in evidence. Nevertheless a twentieth-century Berlioz, writing another *Traité d'instrumentation* would be able to quote copiously and staggeringly from its pages. He would certainly want to bring to our notice the iterations, near the beginning, of the opening motive, by the violas ' divisi in 4 '; eleven of them, at two-bar intervals, the first quite loud, the last (by which time 'cellos, basses, all the violins, bassoons, trombones, and even trumpets, have with successive entries become united in the slowly accumulating background that leads to the next passage)—the last, *ppp*. They are extremely beautiful. And of course he would cite that ' next passage ', beginning at letter C on page 10. The violins, joined after a while by the violas, then by the 'cellos, and then by the basses, continue that pedal background of major seconds, through several modulations, for no fewer than 76 bars, while arresting developments of various kinds on the wood-wind and brass hold us enthralled. The whole of this passage is hypnotic in its power; one feels almost literally spell-bound. Then there are the harmonics—a couple of bars on double-basses in the course of the fluttering, darting section following letter G already mentioned, and later on some twenty or thirty bars of them for all the lower strings (cf. pp. 32–3 of the miniature score). The twentieth-century Berlioz would not overlook the trumpets-flutes transition quoted as Ex. 44, and he would probably be able to base a whole chapter on Sibelius's employment of the timpani, as illustrated in this score alone. He would be fascinated, too, by the uses to which the very lowest register of the flute is put, once more a thing very characteristic of all Sibelius's music but amply demonstrated in this single work (pp. 4, 30, 35, and 55–6). (The low B of the second flute in the final allegro moderato is not on the instrument—as made in England, at any rate—and the note is simply omitted in English per-formances. The *fff* markings of such passages are, of course, quite idealistic.) Without doubt our Berlioz would mention the ' poco a poco senza sordini ' passage for the violins on p. 51. Less sensationally, but perhaps more usefully, he would quote some at least of the many extremely beautiful chordal colours drawn in this work from wood-wind and brass in combination, especially in the lower registers.

It is perhaps in his harmony that Sibelius's methods are most deceptive of all. Apart from the Fourth Symphony, it is not easy to call to mind any work of his—any, at least, with which we are at all familiar—the harmonic idiom and structure of which do not sound in these days thoroughly conservative. Yet the truth is that if we look at these scores, instead of hearing them played, we become aware of numerous procedures that are extremely startling. Not a twentieth but only a twenty-first or twenty-second-century Ebenezer Prout could be expected to disgorge dogmas of harmony and counterpoint in which these procedures were assimilated. In this sense *Tapiola* is one of Sibelius's works in which the disparity between look and sound is widest. On paper its pedal-points, passing-notes, the extremely close intervals in the bottom register, not to speak of such ingredients as a long canonic passage in which both ' voices ', a major third apart, are themselves doubled in major thirds, at times produce sights that could appal the imagination of a person who had never heard the thing played.

Cecil Gray has written of *Tapiola* : ' Even if Sibelius had written nothing else this one work would be sufficient to entitle him to a place among the greatest masters of all time '. It is not an overstatement. To hear this piece of music is an overwhelming experience. To study it (having heard it) is a comprehensive education.

Karl Ekman attributes to the composer, among many other things, the statement : ' Composing has been the guiding line in my life, and it still is so. My work has the same fascination for me as when I was young, a fascination bound up with the difficulty of the task. Let no one imagine that composing is easier for an old composer if he takes his art seriously. The demands one makes on oneself have increased in the course of years. Greater sureness makes one scorn solutions that come too easily, that follow the line of least resistance, in a higher degree than formerly. One is always faced with new problems. The thing that has pleased me most is that I have been able to reject. The greatest labour I have expended, perhaps, was on works that have never been completed.' That statement is extremely well worded. And it is thoroughly intelligible. It makes very good sense, both as a generalisation and in the light of Sibelius's own masterpieces. But it only makes more acute a perplexity to which we now come.

As we have already noted, *Tapiola* was immediately preceded in Sibelius's creative career by his Sixth and Seventh Symphonies, and a very tremendous climax to that career they and *Tapiola* form. Between the composition of the Fifth Symphony, which (with its several revisions) extended through practically the entire duration of the 1914–18 war, and that of the Sixth (1923–24) there lay, however, a stretch that contained no major work at all, for orchestra or for any other medium. The orchestral output during those five years or so was, in fact, as follows : the Humoresques for violin and orchestra, Op. 87b and Op. 89, two marches, Op. 91; *Valse lyrique, Autrefois* and *Valse chevaleresque*, Op. 96; the *Suite mignonne* for two flutes and strings and *Suite champêtre* for string orchestra, Op. 98; and the *Suite caractéristique*, Op. 100.

The *Suite caractéristique*, composed in 1922, consists of three short pieces lasting only some five minutes altogether. They are very commonplace, to all appearance absolute hackwork—by any standard, leave alone Sibelius's. The *Suite champêtre* contains, again, three pieces, their total length only a little more than that of Op. 100 and their content nearly as worthless, though not quite so utterly dull. Despite their slightly greater enterprise, however, they are cheap

45

and irritating. Their titles are *Pièce caractéristique, Mélodie élégiaque,* and *Danse,* and they are all in D minor. The other 1921 product, the *Suite mignonne* for two flutes and strings, is likewise quite meritless and, indeed, offensive. Once more, it comprises three numbers; *Petite scène, Polka* and *Epilogue.*

It is quite impossible to over-emphasise the contrast in almost every respect between these works and such things as *Tapiola* or the Seventh Symphony. Perhaps it would be going too far to say that from internal evidence alone one could not possibly imagine them to have come from Sibelius's pen. (Even, that is, if one did not know that throughout his whole career he had been producing, side by side with music of the very finest calibre, salon pieces of this type, sometimes for orchestra, more often for instrumental soloists, notably pianists.) A musician's most innate characteristics, quite unconscious and involuntary as they are, have a way of bobbing up in his worst works just as much as in his best ones. In fact, perhaps more. For into his best achievements a great composer puts so much conscious, deliberate thought, so much inquiry and searching and problem-solving and self-criticism, that inborn tendencies are rather likelier to be flattened out than when he is in a more ' unbuttoned ' state of mind. In this connection it is interesting to note that Sibelius's symphonies on the whole are both more different from each other and (the last four, at least) more different from the remainder of his output than his symphonic poems are; and, magnificent as the symphonic poems are, few students of the composer would dispute that his most important creations are his symphonies.

The trivial suites, Opp. 98 and 100, whose existence forms a second personal enigma to add to the one already discussed (Sibelius's silence since 1929), do perhaps, then, contain little turns of idiom that would enable a close observer to connect them with Sibelius. The pieces are, of course, all straightforward specimens of pattern-work, as nearly devoid of any ' growth ' within themselves as it is possible for music to be. With Sibelius this is an important point.

Broadly speaking, there are two methods of design in music. By ' design ' one means that which gives the listener a sense of shape, of orderedness, even (when the music is not a setting of words and has no literary or pictorial title) of intelligibility. The two methods can be conveniently labelled ' pattern ' and ' growth '. To *balance* eight bars of material by another eight is to make a pattern. To write a rondo describable in academic form-jargon, as, say, ABACABA is to make a pattern. To write a second bar of a melody that is *compatible* with the first, that falls acceptably on the ear after and in conjunction with the first, is to produce a tiny piece of growth. To write a whole movement in which each section emerges naturally from the one before it—so naturally that to divide the thing into sections at all is neither an easy nor a sensible task—is to achieve growth.

Obviously no music is quite without pattern or quite without growth. No process of musical structure is conceivable without both principles being to some extent involved. Nevertheless, so far as the construction not of separate tunes or phrases, etc., but of whole movements is concerned, most music will be found to rely in the main on just one of those principles, *either* on pattern *or* on growth. It needs to be emphasised that growth implies not merely developmental adaptations of technical ingredients but a genuine continuity of thought and progression of feeling. It is difficult, but not impossible, to achieve growth without using the technical adaptations (so beloved of the academicians) at all; it is easy to fill a whole movement with technical adaptations, but still to fail to achieve continuity or growth. (That, in fact, was a feat performed by Brahms in almost every movement he wrote). Lastly, it need hardly be said that growth, as the predominant factor in the construction of a whole movement, is much less common and more modern than pattern.

Easily the most notable examples to date of the use of the ' growth ' principle are supplied by the symphonic works of Sibelius, and it is significant that precisely those works have often been accused of formlessness—by people whose ideas of form are confined to pattern. As we shall see later, Sibelius has a very wide scope. And (side by side with the amazing capacity for creating form by growth rather than by pattern that is, some will be inclined to think, his greatest contribution to music) he has both a consummate mastery of pattern technique and a gargantuan interest in the literary and pictorial ideas to which it can be applied in the writing of programme music. If it is true that his finest creativeness has been put into the symphonies, nevertheless so far as external evidence goes we could imagine him just as interested in writing symphonic poems and interpreting musically the *Kalevala*, the corpus of Finnish mythology; and certainly his own authentic personal style, the most fundamental aspect of him as a composer, is (as already noticed) rather more uniformly present in the programme works than in the absolute ones. In his maturity he has, as a matter of fact, applied the principle of growth very comprehensively to programme music—as we have seen in *Tapiola*; and in any case it is so peculiarly and strongly the method to which his musical intelligence has always inclined him that it has been in some degree operative in what one instinctively feels to be his most serious compositions right from the start of his career. Its extremest uses in his work are probably (entirely successful) the first movement of the Fifth Symphony and (not quite successful, even in the hands of the best conductor) the Seventh Symphony. Even in those, however, there are certain very effectual elements of ' pattern ' technique : to give only two examples, the beautifully placed and balanced modulations (bars 41 and 158) in the movement from the Fifth Symphony and the appearances of the big trombone motive in the Seventh (cf. the two wood-wind shrieks, bars 139 and 499, in *Tapiola*).

What we have to ask ourselves is (whether or not Sibelius has been as interested in writing symphonic poems as in writing symphonies) what interest he can possibly have taken in writing such things as his Opp. 98 and 100. After all, we have that statement of his already quoted : ' . . . My work has the same fascination for me as when I was young, a fascination bound up with the difficulty of the task. Let no one imagine that composing is easier for an old composer if he takes his art seriously . . . scorn solutions that come too easily, that follow the line of least resistance . . . pleased me most is that I have been able to reject . . . ' Not a word of it has any meaning, in relation to the *Suite caractéristique, Suite champêtre* or *Suite mignonne*. One cannot possibly believe that these were serious works in any sense of the phrase or that he had them at all in mind when making that statement. It remains to wonder why he produced them, what purpose they, or the writing of them, served. Whatever hypothesis we may form, arising out of that wonder, it is quite impossible to reconcile it with the fact that this same man is responsible for the seven symphonies and for the train of other orchestral masterpieces that began with *En Saga* and ended, so far as is known at present, with *Tapiola*—and (may one add?) with the fact that he has been in receipt of a government pension since his early thirties. However carefully one considers the matter, it remains an insoluble conundrum : a complete contrast to the superficially comparable case of Elgar, where in fact the best works and the worst not only have quite clear indications of a common authorship (so, though in a lesser degree, have the Sibelius ones) but are not in any respect such as to make that common authorship difficult to comprehend. To detect in *Falstaff*, *Gerontius* and *Salut d'amour* the same man's

' musical fingerprints ' (as Ernest Newman has called them) is not, ultimately, a matter for surprise : to detect the same fingerprints in *Tapiola* as in the *Suite champêtre* is to find all one's spiritual, philosophical, aesthetic and intellectual canons at fault.

The *Suite mignonne* of 1921 was preceded by the *Valse lyrique, Autrefois* and *Valse chevaleresque*, Op. 96, of 1920. The last-named, which is scored for the usual double wood-wind, 4 horns, 2 trumpets, 3 trombones, 2 kettle-drums, side-drum and strings, seems just like some hitherto undiscovered—and, after all, not terribly worth discovering—specimen of one of the Strauss family's handiwork. Cecil Gray writes that ' Sibelius . . . and not by any means alone among distinguished composers . . . cherishes an ardent affection for the Viennese waltz, and particularly for its greatest master, Johann Strauss the younger '. He goes on to describe the numerous waltzes Sibelius has written as ' a kind of " Hommage à Strauss " ', and then says that he believes one would please Sibelius ' more by saying that they were worthy to be compared with those of the master than by praising any of his other works '. It may be true; we have already recognised that Sibelius is a most inexplicable person. But is he actually so inexplicable as to combine with his colossal musical intelligence, his colossal insight and power and his colossal technical acumen, an unawareness that Johann Strauss's music owes its enduring deliciousness to the essential fact, among others, that it came sincerely, naturally, purely from Strauss's own musical consciousness, using the idiom that was Strauss's own, and was not in any way pastiche? Oddly enough, the *Valse lyrique*, Op. 96, No. 1, is not even remotely Straussian. Published by a London firm in what perhaps it would regard as the bad old days, the back cover of the piano transcription advertises, with perfect congruity, waltzes by Charles Ancliffe and Kenneth J. Alford.

The other part of Op. 96 is *Autrefois (Scène pastorale)*, a modest piece for strings, 2 kettle-drums, 2 horns, 2 bassoons, 2 clarinets and 2 flutes, the clarinets, however, only being used when two wordless voice parts (soprano and contralto) that are also in the score cannot be supplied by actual singers. In its opening section, duly returning at the end, it is as empty as the other works just discussed. But the middle section is quite discrepantly poetic, with unexpected melodic and harmonic lustres, delicate pianissimo kettle-drum entries in Sibelius's best manner, and the ostinato for the violins quoted as Ex. 45 (during a prevalent tonality that leans towards B flat major but in which the dominant, F natural, is always replaced by A or G). At any rate it gives a taste of Sibelius's individuality and fussiness in matters of detail, even if the thing does remain on a cabaret level. It is in this middle section that the voices, or clarinets, make their appearance.

The two marches, Op. 91, from 1918, need not detain us long or exercise our faculties, spiritual, philosophical, aesthetic or intellectual, very much. The *Scout March*, for example, which employs a four-part choir as well as full orchestra, reminds one strongly of the songs being produced nowadays in Soviet Russia for popular and mass singing (e.g. Red Army songs); it is ' go-ey ', straightforward, strong. In these marches, which are really in a very different class from the suites and valses of 1920–22, we can observe not only careful craftsmanship, but even some degree of enthusiasm.

But it is a relief to turn to the six Humoresques for violin and orchestra, which might be said to form a kind of oasis, and a sizeable one, in the otherwise uninteresting, unimportant and even rather deplorable desert expanse of stave-filling done by Sibelius between the final revision of the Fifth Symphony and the completion of the Sixth, but for the fact that actually they date not from the middle but from the very beginning of that six-year period. They are quite evidently serious works, individually not large in scale or range, but full of interest, not at all ' pattern ' stuff, containing a good deal of technical exploration—in some ways obviously, in effect whether or not in intention, studies for that next symphony. They are absolutely characteristic Sibelius in their unexpected methods and in the flavour of their material. It is a pity that none of our leading fiddlers has managed yet to discover them. Their musical interest is equalled by the scope they offer for first-class violin-playing. I have unfortunately been unable to find a score of Op. 89, No. 4, in G minor.

In the experimentalism (so far as Sibelius is concerned) of their harmony the Humoresques are almost unparalleled in his output. The first, in D minor but with a great many B naturals, makes much use of augmented intervals and modulates with exceptional frequency and freedom. The second, allegro assai, a perpetuum mobile in D major, but with great insistence on flattened supertonic and flattened submediant, has Ex. 46 as its subject. And then there is the fifth. This score—it is laid out for 2 flutes, 2 clarinets, 2 bassoons and strings—settles down after a few bars of G minor into a deceptively straightforward E flat major; but very soon we find ourselves in the midst of experiment again, and presently arrive at Ex. 47.

Harmonically the least forward-looking, and as it happens

altogether the least Sibelian too, is the fourth. This 6/8 andantino in G minor has, in fact, rather a flavour of Grieg, given partly by its actual theme and partly by its often semitonally sliding chromatic harmonies. Yet although it does not sound very characteristic Sibelius, an analyst will find it in fact more a preparation for, say, the opening of No. 7 (least characteristic of the symphonies, at any rate in its material) than for anything in the Sixth Symphony. It is very interesting and pleasant music, all the same, and the solo-part is very showy.

Nos. 1 and 5 are both marked 'Commodo'. No. 2 is a brisk 3/4 that adds to its harmonic interest the seductions of much cross-rhythm. (The substitution of ♩. ♩. for ♪. ♩ ♩ is a procedure for which the composer most memorably showed his affection in, of course, the middle movement of the Third Symphony.)

In some ways, at least, the third is the most striking of the Humoresques. The accompaniment is for strings only; six first violins div. a 3, six second violins div. a 3, four violas div., four 'cellos div., two double-basses div.—all 'con sord.' except, of course, the double-basses. Its initial direction reads 'Alla gavotta (♩ = 88)', but it is very far from a conventional specimen of that dance. The violins start by themselves (Ex. 48). The solo violin part is for a virtuoso (though not for an exhibitionistic one), with its double- and treble-stopping passages and its artificial harmonics; and the scoring of the accompaniment is that of a virtuoso orchestrator : apart from the opening effect, used at intervals throughout the piece, there are, for instance, harmonics for all the lower strings.

The Humoresques, one can only finish by repeating, are thoroughly worth-while music, the neglect of which is to be deplored. They demand fine violin-playing, both technical and intellectual; it is to be believed, when we carefully scan the ranks of our leading performers, that they would manage to obtain it. They also demand intelligent, enterprising, unconventional programme-planning; and that, alas, seems to be where they demand too much. Cecil Gray refers disparagingly, à propos of these works, to 'their intrinsic musical interest, which is frequently slight and sometimes even less than that'; but here, for once, is an instance where the composer's own opinion may be accorded more respect than his critic's. Sibelius wrote about the Humoresques, in a letter, a sufficiently flimmery-flummery phrase about 'Life's sorrow and rays of sunshine' but went on : 'I like them very much. They are " large size ".' Gray prefers to the Humoresques the two pieces for violin and orchestra that Sibelius wrote some three years previously—his Op. 77, *Laetare anima mea* and *Devotion* (*Ab imo pectore*)—though it is true that they as well as the Humoresques are covered by his adverse remark quoted above.

Sibelius's operations and projects as a composer at that time, at the beginning of the 1914–18 war, are interesting and—in their profusion and incongruity—typical. He had just got back from a triumphant visit to America, re-landing in Finland on July 10th, 1914. He had in mind the writing of a symphonic poem, *King Fjalar;* approaches had been made to him about doing an opera, to be based on Aho's *Juha*; and he had also before him a request (well garnished with pecuniary allurements) for a ballet, a ballet on *Karhun Tappajaiset* (*The Bear Hunters*)—a *Kalevala* subject. Ekman relates how Sibelius decided against these stage invitations, and quotes a letter in which the composer wrote : ' I cannot become a prolific writer. It would mean killing all my reputation and my art. I have made my name in the world by straightforward means. I must go on in the same way. Perhaps I am too much of a hypochondriac. But to waste on a few *pas* a motive that would be excellently suited to symphonic composition! ' No one doubts Sibelius's sincerity, nor on the whole his great intelligence and wisdom; but such a passage as that, from the pen of the man who was going to compose just what Sibelius composed between 1914 and 1923, is to be called ' rich '! Actually during the first few months of the war he wrote about twenty short pieces, mostly for piano solo, after which he produced the two works for violin and orchestra and a lot of small stuff for violin and piano. The period ended with the appearance of the first version of the Fifth Symphony, upon which he had apparently been in some degree working since at least September 1914.

*Laetare anima mea*, Op. 77a (dedicated to Ossian Fohström) is a quite peculiar offshoot. Is it, perhaps, to be connected with Sibelius's avowed very great admiration for Palestrina? (As we have seen in the case of waltzes, he is not too wise to imitate, apparently in all seriousness, masters whose music he enjoys.) Despite its completely uncharacteristic flavour it is like nearly everything else of Sibelius in that it uses very unconventional technical methods. It is scored for solo violin, 2 flutes, 2 clarinets, 2 horns, 4 kettle-drums, harp and strings. For all its title, and for all its E flat major main cadences, it is a grave, slow-moving piece, largely in the minor; ' moderato assai ($\lrcorner$ = 60)'. The horns are in their low register throughout and the clarinets practically throughout. The sound of two kettle-drums together, at different pitches, is more frequent than that of one kettle-drum only. On the whole it is probably by far the most monotonous piece of music Sibelius has ever written.

*Devotion* (*Ab imo pectore*) is for violin solo, 2 flutes, 1 clarinet, 2 bassoons, 4 horns, 3 trombones and strings. It is an extreme contrast to its companion piece, being virtually one continual modulation, full of sequences, and having a changeful texture with very many rests sprinkled over the staves. All the same, it is not very good Sibelius. Ex. 49, however, could hardly have been written by anyone else, so usual in Sibelius and so unusual otherwise is that kind of flute and bassoon doubling.

It is perhaps appropriate, in passing back from this decade (which out of the most vigorous fertility saw the bringing forth of so little of much importance apart from three stupendous symphonies), to reiterate a point concerning Sibelius, at any rate as an orchestral composer, that is relevant to such minor products as we have just dealt with no less than to such masterpieces as the *Tapiola* of his Olympian maturity or the very considerable ones of his middle period, to which we are coming. In fact, it is perhaps the more striking in connection with the works of no account, where their very insignificance throws it into greater relief.

Practically always, we remind ourselves, then—practically always Sibelius's scores look much more original than they sound. Just like Beethoven's (the only real comparison), his technique, his method of constructing musical texture and musical motion, is, as if automatically, quite different from anyone else's, much more different than one would guess from hearing the results, which often (though, as we have seen, not always) sound strongly characteristic and personal in an almost indefinable way but *not* ' different ' and original in the pioneering, iconoclastic way that such absolute difference of technical method would lead us in theory to expect. The point is that —again, like Beethoven—he uses no new idiom or vocabulary. He uses more or less familiar ingredients : that is why one has no sense of iconoclasm or pioneering when listening to his music (with perhaps the single exception of the Fourth Symphony). Thus it is only in comparison with his usual conservatism that the harmony of the Humoresques can be called, for him, experimental. What makes his methods unique is the way he builds his texture and movement and form, the way he *uses* the ingredients. In that sense he is, indeed, much more experimental than he ever sounds. His scores simply swarm with what the student has to admit are the most striking innovations, always, of course, introduced strictly in furtherance of his immediate end at the moment but a good many of them developing into habits as he notes their success and the general principles that, at any rate for his particular idea of composing in general, they embody. One is reminded of the fact that when Cecil Forsyth was at work on his justly famous book on orchestration he discovered, quite to his surprise, that far more examples of innovating in orchestral technique occurred in the music of Beethoven than in any other one composer's. There the innovations were; but so sweepingly were they assimilated into Beethoven's whole dominating style and personality that as innovations they passed unnoticed. The same is true of much of the detail of Beethoven's musical construction, and likewise of Sibelius's. As for Sibelius's orchestration, it is probable that, just as a contemporary Berlioz could make great play with *Tapiola* as already suggested, another Forsyth of a century hence would make the same discovery about Sibelius's orchestral works as a whole as the Forsyth of 1912 made about Beethoven's. And that discovery would depend much less on passages that instantly jolt the listener into consciousness of their unusual scoring than upon passages in which he is unaware of anything unusual at all (the art that conceals art!), and it would be notwithstanding the fact that Sibelius came after Berlioz, was contemporary with Debussy and Rimsky-Korsakov, and had the prodigious Stravinsky close on his heels. He makes the whole parcel of them seem stereotyped, this lone figure of a composer who has had the deceptive effrontery to name Mozart and Mendelssohn as his idols among orchestrators.

The visit to America from which Sibelius returned just before the outbreak of the 1914 war had been undertaken in response to an invitation by the wealthy connoisseur, Carl Stoeckel, who asked him to accept his personal hospitality, to conduct a Sibelius concert in the 1914 musical festival on his estate (in the series of practically world-famous Norfolk Festivals), and to write a new work for the occasion. *Tapiola* was in 1925 the glorious outcome of one American commission; in 1914 *The Oceanides* had been another.

*The Oceanides*, tone-poem for large orchestra, Op. 73, is dedicated to Mr. and Mrs. Carl Stoeckel, was written in the winter of 1913–4, and was first performed in June 1914. The orchestra it calls for comprises piccolo, 2 flutes, 2 oboes, English horn, 2 clarinets, bass clarinet, 2 bassoons. double bassoon, 4 horns, 3 trumpets, 3 trombones, 4 kettle-drums, ' *Stahlstäbe* ' (celesta?), triangle, 2 harps, and strings. It has been described by several writers as an experiment in impressionist technique, à la Debussy—possibly because of the harp harmonics and glissandos, the muted string tremolos, the doublings in fourths, and so on, with which it abounds. Cecil Gray goes so far as to say that ' the orchestral technique in this work is strikingly different from that encountered in any other of Sibelius, and consists in a kind of "pointillisme"'. That is a considerable exaggeration. As we go back into Sibelius's earlier works we shall encounter a good many foreshadowings of the type of scoring that admittedly reached its zenith, so far as he is concerned, in *The Oceanides*. It is true that the total aural effect of this work is markedly different from that of any other of his works. But the same can be said of most of his tone-poems. Look, too, at the striking dissimilarity of the seven symphonies, both from each other and from most of his other works; this is simply one of the aspects of his gigantic stature as a composer. But the total aural effect of a work is quite another matter from the details of its technical processes; and most of Sibelius's works are as recognisably all in the same line of technical development (likewise, of course, exhibiting the same ' finger-prints') as they are, as self-contained entities, sharply distinguished from each other.

The opening four bars of *The Oceanides* (Ex. 60) are such that, it is safe to say, no other composer would ever be suspected of having written them, and such that, further, anyone reasonably familiar with Sibelius's previous output would instantly attribute them to him. Perhaps the ' impressionist ', ' pointilliste ' description is, after all, misleading just for the usual Sibelian reason, viz., that the effect of the score on the listener's ear is so much more straightforward and coherent and simple than its effect on the student's eye. Still, the technical label does not matter; one must hear the music. It is a very lovely work, unbelievably involved in craftsmanship, comparatively quite clear in its outlines for any listener who is accustomed to Sibelius's methods of dealing with musical ideas. It is based on two small, much-used, haunting themes (Exs. 51 and 52). The scoring of the second (subsequently much varied, but long maintaining its basic principle) is shown in Ex. 52. In the eighth bar of the work is a further passage that is used quite a lot all through, among other things in conjunction with the second of the two themes quoted. Ex. 53 shows the whole of the part allotted to the *Stahlstäbe* and also illustrates a feature of this particular work that really is quite untypical of its composer, namely the frequent doublings, the blendings of diverse timbres. (Is *that* what Gray calls ' pointillisme '? Strictly speaking, it is the very reverse, since an *actual* blend of colours is precisely what the pointilliste painters avoided.)

Just over a year before *The Oceanides* Sibelius composed *The Bard*, Op. 64, a piece of music that, in fact, compares very interestingly with *The Oceanides* in several aspects. Both are described as tone-poems for large orchestra; but *The Bard* dispenses with piccolo, English horn, and double bassoon, and uses only the usual complement of kettle-drums and one harp. (On the other hand, it contains one of the five notes that are all Sibelius in his whole published output has written for the tam-tam; it is *ppp*, accompanying the first of the E flat major chords into which the final cadences all resolve, the piece having been in E flat minor.) *The Bard* is the shortest of Sibelius's tone-poems, and contains nothing of drama or action. Musically, it is a brooding over a handful of minute motive-fragments that develop very little, when at all. The harp's part is dominating (obviously in characterisation of the title) but extremely simple. The structure of the piece, both progressional and textural, is very typical mature Sibelius, and also, as it happens, does go a long way in foreshadowing the allegedly isolated ' impressionism ' of *The Oceanides*. It is, in fact, a very interesting point in the transition to the latter work's extraordinarily complex orchestral technique from the much more solid, block methods (but always full of unexpected features and strange finesses) of Sibelius's early orchestration. The Fourth Symphony, with the opus number immediately preceding that of *The Bard*, had also been full of significant tendencies. For example, no one can fail to observe how, in that Symphony, Sibelius's predilection for stretches of thin, close counterpoints in small-length notes, in which often one voice is syncopated, becomes very prominent. The two bars between letters G and H in *The Bard* (pp. 11–12 of the miniature score) show the development of the same habit; observe how the percussion pattern started on the last half-beat of the first bar, continues throughout three more bars, outlasting the final morendo mutterings of the double-basses and projecting into the beginning of the ensuing texture, in which, against held chords on the horns, with occasional timpani rolls and harp glissandi, a melodic ejaculation started *mp* on flutes and oboes (in octaves) is at length taken up by all the wood-wind and all the strings except double-basses and leads to a big climax. And then on the penultimate page we have one of the most strange-*looking* passages in all Sibelius : a favourite employment of the flute in its lowest register, as something very like an extra trumpet, being carried to an astonishing extreme. The lowness of the *trumpet* register here is the crucial factor.

Sibelius told his pupils, among them Bengt de Törne, and Bengt de Törne in his book *Sibelius : A Close-Up* has told the world, that one of the most essential things in the art of orchestration is to remember that the orchestra is not a piano and has no sustaining pedal. He urged that it was necessary constantly to bear that in mind and to incorporate sostenuto-giving devices in one's scores. All his work contains examples of the application of that principle, but none more careful and elaborate than we can find in *The Bard*. It is always a question not only of providing sostenuto points, of course, but of relinquishing them in the least conspicuous manner possible (cf. p. 2, bars 1–3; bars 3–7 after letter A; bars 1–5 after letter B). Much use is made in *The Bard* of the type of device shown in Ex. 54 (cf. Ex. 48 from the third Humoresque). There is a very great deal of divisi work for muted strings; the 'cellos are often in four parts. *The Bard* is a quiet and unostentatious work, but a beautiful one, written with almost incredible elaboration and care. The composer was forty-eight and may be considered to have reached the apex of his purely technical powers, prior to the remarkable advance into quite unprecedented continuity and ' growth ' (accompanied, and, indeed, largely accomplished, by the system of bit-by-bit thematic transformations)[1] embodied in the Fifth Symphony, its successors and *Tapiola*.

The close neighbour of *The Bard* in Sibelius's list of compositions is, as has been mentioned, that obviously climacteric masterpiece, the Fourth Symphony, but between the two, though bearing later opus numbers, came the second set of *Scènes historiques* (though it is not clear whether, or how far, these were a revision of much earlier work), a couple of part-songs, some of Sibelius's most interesting piano music (the three Sonatinas and two Rondinos) and the first of two Serenades for violin and orchestra. (The other Serenade dates from just after *The Bard*.)

In the two Serenades the soloist is accompanied by an orchestra of moderate dimensions. They are both considerable works, whether viewed as essays in composition or as vehicles for the display of virtuosity or near-virtuosity by violinists. Otherwise they are quite dissimilar to each other.

The first is in D, andante assai. The opening eight bars are worth quoting (see Ex. 55) both because they exhibit well the personal flavour

[1] See p. 330.

of Sibelius, so very strong although so simple and so clear of violent idiosyncracies, and because they contain all the thematic bases of the piece, which broods over them, rather than develops them progressively, somewhat in the mánner, technically speaking, of *The Bard*. The G sharp is worth noting, for the sharpened fourth is one of Sibelius's favourite modal-tendencies. Gray refers, *à propos* of the Sixth Symphony, to ' this modal atmosphere, unusual in the music of Sibelius '. But Sibelius's music, though practically never without a strong sense of tonality, does quite often give basic employment to notes not to be found in the diatonic major or minor scales of the key of the moment; in other words it is often what an English theorist of the past few decades would call ' modal ', though it is doubtful whether Sibelius himself thought of it in that way. It is an odd fact about this piece that a great proportion of the accompaniment is pitched so low that one would have guessed the solo instrument to be a 'cello or bassoon rather than a violin.

The Serenade, Op. 69, No. 2, is in G minor, lento assai. Unlike its companion it has two quite distinct, indeed extremely contrasted, subjects. Its form is a matter of simple pattern—ABABA—and each return from B to A is accomplished by the artless process of rather more than a bar's silence, marked with a ⌒ . Before the break subject B comes to a stop; after the break subject A restarts. There are no transition notes whatever. This is quite staggeringly unlike Sibelius's usual practice. It is quite a pleasant work, however, though the bright ending is perhaps not quite satisfactory.

The decade that culminated in the appearance of the Fourth Symphony was, so far as orchestral music is concerned, very fertile. It produced three symphonies, three other big orchestral canvases, three ' dance-intermezzos ', three works for strings and one for small orchestra, the Violin Concerto, and incidental music to six plays. Sibelius also composed during this period 29 songs, 13 piano pieces, *The Captive Queen* (ballad for chorus and orchestra) and the superb String Quartet *Voces intimae*.

The date of the Fourth Symphony, 1911, was the year also of a *Valse romantique* for small orchestra, a Canzonetta and the *Rakastava* suite for strings, as well as the incidental music to *The Language of the Birds*. Gray gives 1893 as the date of *Rakastava*, but this must refer to the male-voice chorus from which the material of the suite was taken; in any case the chorus was more probably not written till 1895.

We often loosely refer to *Rakastava* (*The Lover*) as a suite for string orchestra, but actually the score contains parts for a kettle-drum in the first and last numbers and a triangle in the middle one. The titles and keys of the three are : (1) *Rakastava—The Lover* (D minor), (2) *The way of the lover* (B flat major), (3) *Good evening, my love! Farewell!* (F major—D minor).

The opening of No. 1 (Ex. 56) admirably illustrates both Sibelius's subtle harmonic style in this work, quiet with poignant flashes, and the metrical subtleties characteristic of his maturity. (Cf. the strange metrical complexity of the brass pronouncement in the first movement of the Fourth Symphony : last bar of p. 4 of the miniature score.) The structure of this first piece, though fairly easy to follow after a couple of hearings, is very fine and is certainly too involved to attempt to describe except with copious quotations. Perhaps, however, it is worth while to refer to the figure that after its first quiet but slightly surprising brief incursion at the eighteenth bar, repeated 13 bars later, forms the basis of two strange and lovely outbursts (' outbursts ' is the word, although they are *ppp*) that come a little before the end. These outbursts, which are strayings into remote keys and involve the kettle-drum's only work in the piece (two long rolls, each marked ' *ppp* . . . dim. possibile '), are themselves dovetailed between eloquent ejaculations by divided violins of a thematic fragment that has made its first appearance some while earlier and is, indeed, derived from a passage in the phrase that answered, after some delay, the opening one (Ex. 56): a typical specimen of Sibelian movement-building.

No. 2, *The way of the lover*, begins as Ex. 57 and goes on just like that almost throughout, with only the simplest modulations and virtually no change of general texture. The entry—pizz., *pp*—of the double-basses, more than half-way through, is extraordinarily effective and, one might almost say, beautiful. The triangle comes in only twelve bars from the end, when the music after its long insistence on B flat (alternations of minor and major) suddenly moves through A major into D minor, still preserving the same kind of texture and movement. After six bars of that, however, with six taps of the triangle, come the final six bars of the piece, Ex. 58 : an ending comparable, for abruptness and apparent inconsequence, with that of the second movement of the Fourth Symphony. It is a delightful movement, and one that cannot be played too softly.

The third is the most elaborate and extended movement of

*Rakastava.* The plaintive violin-solo tune that enters over the rather strange ostinato accompaniment soon leads to a poignant little climax that is more or less a quotation from the first movement. This material occupies about the first quarter of the piece and ends with the utmost abruptness and simplicity. The next quarter consists of a brief modulating ejaculation, thrice repeated sequentially, the speed being indicated as ' Doppio più lento '; followed by a stretch of vivace, largely in semiquavers, largely chromatic, with very soft timpani rolls, and punctuated by a couple of pauses; followed by nine bars, allargando poco a poco, purely declamatory in character and including references to the ejaculation with which this section began; leading (and for the first time the transition is not abrupt, but is the culmination of a simple, direct modulation) to the lento assai that fills the latter half of the piece. The harmony now is fundamentally a very simple alternation of the dominant and tonic chords of D minor, though with some finely expressive diversions. The texture is full and simple, the movement steady and straightforward. The whole section is one of simple, eloquent chanting, in great contrast to anything heard previously in the entire work, except perhaps in odd bars or parts of bars. . . . So described, this finale would appear to be formless, episodic, thoroughly unsatisfactory; yet the aural effect is the very reverse. So much for verbal descriptions!

*Rakastava* is really like nothing else in all music. Perhaps its nearest kinship is with Sibelius's own Fourth Symphony, a fact that emphasises the improbability of its dating from 1893 instead of 1911. It is a very remarkable and very lovely work. Alone among Sibelius's smaller pieces it is fully worthy to be named with, say, the Fourth, Fifth and Sixth Symphonies, *The Oceanides* and *Tapiola*.

The other work of 1911 for string orchestra, the Canzonetta, Op. 62a, is a different matter. It is quite a minor affair, though not unpleasant. Perhaps its most notable one feature is its quietly sombre colouring. Its key is G sharp minor. The instruments are muted. Even the first violins only go as high as the first leger-line above their clef—and momentarily, at that. The closing bars, Ex. 59, give an excellent sample of the flavour of the whole thing as well as the particular effect of the sombre low final thirds. It is an amiable piece of work, without much strength or distinction. Its writing is much more regular, conventional, than is usual with Sibelius, though of course perfectly effective. It is simple ' pattern ' stuff, with only a trifle even of variation in the phrase-lengths, but that trifle very attractive. This Canzonetta has a strongly characteristic flavour; the melos and harmony are, in fact, fully impregnated with what one might call ' basic Sibelius '.

The other part of Op. 62 is the *Valse romantique*, for small orchestra (2 flutes, 2 clarinets, 2 horns, 2 kettle-drums and strings), which is the exact realisation of all that its title promises. It is written with every conscientiousness of craftsmanship. (All the same, the horn parts must be about the dullest ever written; out of the Valse's 200 ' romantique ' bars they are only silent for 29 in all, of which 9 are the last 9 of the piece; yet only 5 of their bars contain anything but holding-notes.) The *Valse* cannot be reckoned a very pleasing specimen of Sibelius's powers.

The Canzonetta and *Valse romantique* are for some undivulged reason referred to by Ekman as ' two orchestral pieces, *Sisters of " Valse Triste" '*: and then he gives the separate titles of them as they appear on the published scores. He says they were composed in January 1911, and makes it clear that they were produced *during* the work on the Fourth Symphony, which had begun in the spring of 1910 but did not come to an end until the spring of 1911. Between finishing the Symphony and presenting it for the first time to an audience Sibelius composed *The Dryad*, which received its première in the same concert as the Symphony, at Helsingfors on April 3rd, 1911, together with the Canzonetta, *In memoriam* and *Night-ride and Sunrise*. In more ways than the obvious one an amazing programme!

The *Dance-Intermezzo*, Op. 45, No. 2, *The Dryad*,[1] Op. 45, No. 1, and *Pan and Echo* (Dance-Intermezzo, No. 3), Op. 53, present us with another little puzzle as to dates. Gray and Ekman place both the Op. 45 works in 1910 and *Pan and Echo* in 1906, though Ekman mentions that the last-named was revised in 1909. The point has little importance, however. Whether *The Dryad* is to be considered as the other ' dance-intermezzo ' we do not know, but its character would make us believe so.

Op. 45, No. 2 is laid out for a very unusual orchestral force, viz. 2 flutes, 1 oboe, 2 clarinets, 1 bassoon, 4 horns, 2 cornets, castanets, tambourine, 2 kettle-drums, harp, strings. It begins with a 4-bar introduction, andante, comprising a held-on chord for the horns, short up and down glissandi (arpeggio, not scale) for the harp, kettle-drum rolls and (during the last half-bar) an upward arpeggio rush for clarinet. The harmony is a static dominant-ninth of the B flat minor into which the music then proceeds, commodo e tranquillo.

1 Not to be confused with the earlier piece of 1894.

Over a very simple accompaniment of held notes (3 horns and 1 flute, the latter in its bottom register) the oboe sings a very simple 3/4 tune. The rhythm is quite four-square, but for the fact that the final (eighth and sixteenth) bars are silent, each a ' G.P.', the tonic having been reached on the last crotchet of the seventh and fifteenth. The answering subject, in E flat minor, low on clarinets and, subsequently, strings, leads, through a dominant chord on F and a double bar-line marked ⌒, to con moto in B flat major—still 3/4. After four bars of simple pizzicato accompaniment, the cornets, staccatissimo and rhythmically doubled by the tambourine, introduce a perky fresh subject in the perkiest possible manner. One cannot pass over unnoticed an astounding stroke of orchestration here. The two ' voices ' allotted to the staccatissimo cornets are doubled at the unison in sustained notes on the flutes (e.g. a staccatissimo crotchet, four quavers and crotchet on a cornet, all on the same note, doubled by a dotted minim tied to a crotchet on a flute). Before long we come to a complementary section, using the same pugnacious rhythm, on wood-wind with castanets. Then both these sections are repeated with first violins playing a cantabile counterpoint on top of them. Next a brief, closely-related summing-up leads to a new, short section signatured in B flat minor but having a pedal E flat bass. Then back from that we go very briefly into B flat major—a couple of short references by oboe to the cornet tune and eight bars of *very* conventional coda. A strange work : likeable, perky, adequate, infectious (as is said of certain tunes), well-written, memorable in its at times perhaps slightly cheap way—but utterly unlike anything else in Sibelius's orchestral music.

Both in spite of and because of its special character, the Dance-Intermezzo, Op. 45, No. 2, provides an ideal example of something very important in the art of Sibelius. And something very important in all the greatest musical art : a something that is often overlooked by theorists and historians and technicians and the like. That something is nothing more nor less than notable, striking motives. Even in his last period, when they are brief and subjected to much transformation, Sibelius's themes are usually memorable in themselves. And prior to that period, of course, he sprinkled his output with one fine, memorable, highly-individual (however apparently simple) tune after another. He himself perfectly understands, probably has never dreamt of doubting, the basic importance in music of striking themes. As an old man he included among some *obiter dicta* that found their way into the Press a conjuration to aspiring composers to take great care of the ideas (the motives) that come to them when they are young, as they are a composer's most precious stock-in-trade, and ideas that the composer fails to use properly when young may very likely, if preserved, be welcomed by him and find adequate treatment when he is mature. The *practical* accuracy of that may be doubtful, but at any rate it shows Sibelius's attitude to thematic material *vis à vis* musical composition. His attitude is also shown by the following quotation by Ekman from one of the composer's letters: ' The idea of both *Night-ride and Sunrise* and *In memoriam* came to me a long time before. The principal motive of *Night-ride* was conceived during the spring in Italy in 1901, when I made a trip to Rome in April. The motive of *In memoriam* occurred to me in Berlin in 1905.' Even—this is the relevant point just here—even in the modest and structurally very uncharacteristic Dance-Intermezzo, Op. 45, No. 2, we are struck at once by a clear-cut theme, simple yet making an immediate conquest of ear and memory.

*The Dryad* is called, in the score, a *Tonstück*, but its character is, in a quite different way, just as dance-like as that of the Dance-Intermezzo. It employs piccolo, 2 flutes, 2 oboes, 2 clarinets, bass clarinet, 2 bassoons, 4 horns, 3 trombones, tuba, tambourine, castanets, side-drum, big drum and strings. For the second time in his known creative career Sibelius omitted the timpani (of which no composer has ever made such copious and varied and essential use as he) from his orchestra. Quite exceptionally among his works, *The Dryad* has small notes cued-in to make possible, if desired, performance by a small orchestra (the constitution of which is given at the head of the score). Despite, or perhaps because of, its greater elaboration and pretensions it is, all in all, inferior to the Dance-Intermezzo, Op. 45, No. 2. Structurally it must be the most restless piece of music Sibelius ever wrote: Lento—12 bars, Meno lento—6 bars, Poco stretto—4 bars, a tempo—4 bars, Un pochettino con moto—8 bars, allarg.—2 bars, a tempo—3 bars, G.P. ♩ 1 bar, Lento assai—8 bars, Un pochettino con moto—4 bars, allarg.—2 bars, a tempo—3 bars, Un poco lento—3 bars ' 2 bars, Poco stretto—2 bars, Poco lento—2 bars ' 6 bars, Stretto assai—8 bars, ♩, Commodo—20 bars, Poco a poco string.—8 bars, Vivace—44 bars, Risoluto e meno vivace—8 bars, Largamente—3 bars ♩ 2 bars, Poco stretto—3 bars, rit.—1 bar, Lento ed allarg.—11 bars. It is also much more chromatic than most of Sibelius's music. In fact, in all ways it is, while entirely different from the Dance-Intermezzo, Op. 45, No. 2, very nearly as different as that work from the rest of his output. It cannot be called good or pleasant music. This dryad seems rather to have been the habitué of the painted grottos of Paris or Buda-Pesth cabarets than of any natural groves.

The *In memoriam* funeral march, Op. 59, which also figured in that phenomenal concert at Helsingfors of April 3rd, 1911, is probably Sibelius's worst work of any dimensions and pretensions. And both dimensions and pretensions it certainly has, being scored for 2 flutes, 2 oboes, English horn, 2 clarinets, bass clarinet, 2 bassoons, double bassoon, 4 horns, 3 trumpets, 3 trombones, tuba, 3 kettle-drums, side-drum, cymbals, big drum and strings—and comprising 36 pages of grave e maestoso. With its ostinato rhythm and string melodramatics, Ex. 60, it suggests a blend of the *Eroica* and *Götterdämmerung*, but a blend that has lost all the virtues of either. It clearly aims at expressing the utmost tragedy and grandiosity and menace, but unfortunately the actual terms in which it is couched are conventional, containing very little of Sibelius's magic. No doubt it can sound impressive, in a rather physical way, in performance, but really its musical value can justly be said to be in inverse ratio to the elaboration of its almost desperately melodramatic phraseology. It is even less recognisable Sibelius than *The Dryad*. Yet Cecil Gray, who says that Sibelius ' was impelled to compose this work as the result of a genuine bereavement, a personal loss, a great affliction ' (though Ekman gives us Sibelius's own explicit declaration to the contrary), considers it first-class Sibelius, ' a profoundly moving work '.

*Night-ride and Sunrise*, Op. 55, is another matter. Superficially as conventional as *In memoriam*, it is in reality a fine work, strikingly inspired. After a brief, furious introduction it sets off on a not quite onomatopoetic but clearly suggestive career of precipitate and unremitting trochees that lasts for 300-odd bars. The rhythm, at the pace of a life-and-death gallop, is thrown from one group of strings to another, with plentiful splashes of side-drum. The effect is extraordinarily realistic, as if one were passing rapidly through a dimly-seen and quickly changing terrain, now high, now low, now up, now down, now in the open, now in a narrow way roofed with trees; one can almost hear the varying textures upon which the hoofs are beating their headlong tattoo. But, of course, realism though to be relished, does not constitute musical value. High musical enjoyment, however, is precisely what we in this case simultaneously receive. The harmony is very characteristic, and especially reminds us of, say, the Third Symphony (which is not unnatural, seeing that the Symphony dates from immediately preceding years). The structure, in a large sense, is simple. After the strings presently, following something of a climax, have been joined in the rhythm by the side-drum, the wood-wind add a series of high, long-drawn-out melodic phrases. Later the strings, low down, have those same phrases while the wood-wind, above, are weaving the same patterns as the strings had done in their ♩ ♪♩ ♪ rhythm but are in even notes, ♫♫ . For the moments when—this constant movement having been at length broken off, and two minute twirls on solo oboe and solo flute respectively having been heard, followed by a loud, high, single, prolonged note on the strings—the lower strings give out slow pizzicato thrummings, a sort of hesitant preluding, one can only use the paradoxical but accurate epithets of ' breathless ', ' motionless '. And then in come the horns and wood-wind with slow, religioso (as one might say) material, taken over rather beautifully after a while by the strings. (The best parallel to this passage that comes readily to mind, so far as the character of the material is concerned, is the first extended section of the Seventh Symphony.) This sinks into a pianissimo string chord and drum roll, with high wood-wind playing gentle roulades, prior to the entry of new material, rather brisker and brighter, through which trumpet and trombone pronouncements make their way before long. (Again, as in the Seventh Symphony, much of the actual musical substance is noticeably undistinguished in this ' sunrise ' section.) Next comes a striking change of key, and then a dumbfounding upward arpeggio on the clarinet ends in a high tremolo of violins, which is followed by terrific brass chords with electrifying modulations. The coda consists of a relapse into the previous, quasi-religioso, material. Such a relation in words of what happens in this piece of music, while almost useless in conveying the musical effect, accentuates the realistic methods employed to interpret the title. Cecil Gray, however, is absolutely right when he says of the ' sunrise ' section that ' it gives the impression of having been inspired by actual experience . . . is felt and directly observed *en plein air*.' Since a dawn can be a very beautiful and awe-inducing phenomenon, and since the effect of music—other things being equal—is in itself to heighten impressions of beauty or awe (or whatever the feeling may be), the effect of this work is quite overwhelming. Its neglect is to be deplored.

E

*Pan and Echo*, Op. 53a, called ' Dance-Intermezzo No. 3 ' but both composed and revised before the *Dance-Intermezzo* and *Dryad* that constitute Op. 45, is an odd little unimportant work, not unpleasing in parts but with little characteristic Sibelian power or beauty, in either its form or its material. It uses various alternations of remote tonalities that are at first agreeable enough but take on a rather trivial and mechanical aspect as the piece continues. It is all quite deft. It is a little strange (and significant?—but if so, of what?) that the composer drops into the Spanish dance-rhythm

♫♫ ♫♫♫ and some of the other material also, quite distinct from the bolero material, is very reminiscent of the *Festivo* (Tempo di bolero) in the first set of *Scènes historiques*.

*Pan and Echo*, revised in 1909, the year of *In memoriam* and *Night-ride and Sunrise*, was composed in 1906. And 1906 is the date given by Ekman to *Pohjola's Daughter*, symphonic fantasia, Op. 49. Gray has conjectured that it was actually written between 1903 and 1905. Not only is this piece, like a number of Sibelius's works both for orchestra and for voices and orchestra, based on literary ideas taken from the *Kalevala*[1] but it is, of all such works, his most elaborately, detailedly programmatic. Annexed to the score is a poem paraphrasing that *Kalevala* episode in which Väinämöinen, the magician, while on a homeward journey, encounters the Maid of Pohjola, the North Country, seated spinning on a rainbow. (Overwhelmed by her beauty he beseeches her to descend and join him, which she promises to do if he can perform various magic feats for her. The last of these, to make a boat for her out of the fragments of her spindle, is too much for him; he has to give up in despair; Louhi's daughter remains on her rainbow; and Väinämöinen jumps back into his sleigh and resumes the homeward trail.) It is a complex, colourful, very varied composition, first-rate music, and contains one of Sibelius's most ravishing motives. Like so large a proportion of his orchestral works, other than the symphonies, it is much too rarely played. It employs a large orchestra—piccolo, 2 flutes, 2 oboes, English horn, 2 clarinets, bass clarinet, 2 bassoons, double bassoon, 4 horns, 2 cornets, 2 trumpets, 3 trombones, tuba, kettle-drums, harp, strings.

Going backwards beyond 1905, out of Sibelius's forties into his thirties, we leave his first real maturity and enter the period when even his best works, magnificent as they were, contained flaws either

---

[1] An English translation of the Finnish national epic is published in Everyman's Library. The story of Louhi's daughter is told in Runo VIII.

in this or that detail or in their character as a whole. From that generalisation, however, there are two—perhaps three—exceptions, to which in due course we shall come. It is strange that the latest major work of this phase was in some ways the poorest: the Violin Concerto, Op. 47, composed in 1903 and revised in 1905.

On the whole, bearing in mind that we are engaged in an exhaustive and critical survey of Sibelius's work, it is not unjust to describe his Violin Concerto as the best concerto that Tchaïkovsky ever produced. Certainly its material has very distinctly Sibelius's own finger-prints, not Tchaïkovsky's, and certainly that material has charms and originalities transcending anything in Tchaïkovsky's concertos for violin *or* piano, but on the other hand its outlook technically, structurally, spiritually, is very much the same as theirs. No doubt when it was first performed, by Carl Halir, with Richard Strauss conducting, at Berlin in 1905, it sounded exuberantly original. Now, however, we can see it in perspective.

Its best pages are the very first: the rather languid, or at any rate meditative, slightly groping entry of the first subject over the violins' slow tremolo accompaniment. That is first-rate, and there is nothing quite so good, quite so worthy of Sibelius, afterwards. Apart from the fact that, as in several of his earlier works, the tunes have some-times a not quite palatable vulgarity or obviousness, the main root of the trouble in this work seems to have been its rôle of concerto. Especially in the first movement a lot of sequential writing and, in general, not very purposeful wandering (involving changes of key that take us nowhere worth going, which in their turn involve even less inevitable, though perfunctorily-imperative, return journeys) seems to be traceable to the concerto character of the task the com-poser had set himself. Not to speak of the solo part itself (especially, but by no means only, the deplorable cadenza—Sibelius's own, but one that could just as well be Sarasate's or Vieuxtemps's). Nothing could be more remote from the continuity and close-knittedness of his later works, or even from the splendid, sweeping consecutiveness of earlier ones. As a specimen of very cheap-tragic material, consider pp. 10–12 of the miniature score: those plangent flattened melodic thirds and that relapse by the soloist into double-stopped sixths—how effective and how second-rate! The abrupt changes of mood and texture and movement hereabouts are all instances of the stock, late-romantic-concerto, school of thought, so opposed to Sibelius's own structural tendencies. Some of the transitions, if such they can be called, are helpless jumps. This first movement has a full-dress recapitulation, of course, followed by a brief, fiery coda—equally of course.

The second movement opens promisingly; in fact the whole of the eloquent cantilena that somewhat inconsequently follows is, if just what we (we admirers of the stereotyped late-romantic concerto) expect as to mood and style, nevertheless quite beautiful and quite original within its limits of stylistic and structural conventionality. But what a deplorable second subject! It might surely have been as conventionally diverse in character from the first without being so diverse in quality? The student of the score will note its relation to the movement's introduction. And then we come to the jolly, tearing finale. With its two subjects, this time really complementary, a characteristic (Sibelian) switching between D major and D minor (cf. the finale of the Second Symphony, for one example), it is in some ways the most satisfactory movement of the three, if the emptiest.

The whole Concerto teems with technical difficulties for the soloist. The orchestra used is the standard late-classical one, with no 'extras'. Having noted all its faults, and accepted that it is a long way from being best or typical Sibelius, we can lean back with a self-indulgent grin and admit that it is very enjoyable.

From about the same time as the Violin Concerto dates a little work for string orchestra that has become quite popular in England of late, the Romance in C, Op. 42. Its popularity is well-deserved; indeed, in its way it is a perfect composition. It starts with a magnificently original harmonic stroke, an unaccompanied melodic announcement in E minor complete with C sharp and D sharp, which comes to rest on E and is immediately underpinned with a resounding C natural major 6/3 chord. (Like so much in Sibelius, it looks rather more daring than it sounds.) The whole of its opening section is ideally varied in inflection, and finishes with a cadential phrase that gathers itself repetitively for its final chord and then leaves that final chord unsounded, the music plunging instead into a fine canonic, modulating passage based on the opening phrase and leading after a while to the next, and middle, section of the work (Ex. 61). The middle section, a broad swinging chant in considerable contrast to the dramatic and ejaculatory first section, begins in E major (note, by the by, the favourite sharpened fourth) but subsequently works up excitingly into a closing fragment in C major, which then (nicely balancing the former passage, as quoted) breaks off and is followed by a plunge into the canonic, modulating passage (now inverted); this leads into an impassioned, broadened restatement of the opening bars, followed by a gradually quietening recapitulation of the whole first section, whose cadential phrase does now receive its final, tonic chord. In the brief coda the opening phrase is imitated by the 'cellos against a sustained chordal background, and the piece ends pianissimo. The string writing is a model of effectiveness and of unextravagant and resourceful variety. On close acquaintance the work tends to wear a little thin, and the explanation can perhaps be found in the fundamental character of some of the material, which is of the slightly cheap and obvious dramatic order already referred to.

In or about 1901, two years before the *Romance* for strings and the Violin Concerto, Sibelius had written a couple of orchestral works that have remained unpublished and unknown, *Cortège* and *Portraits*, the latter for strings only, and before that we have to go back seven more years for another purely orchestral piece: the *Spring Song* (or, as the French version added in the score has it, ' La tristesse du printemps '—' The Sadness of the Spring '), Op. 16. At least, 1894 is Ekman's date; Gray says 1891. It was first performed on June 21st, 1894, under the composer's bâton, with the title, *Improvisation for Orchestra*. It is a fairly ambitious work, scored for 2 flutes (both alternating piccolo), 2 oboes, 2 clarinets, 2 bassoons, 4 horns, 3 trumpets, 3 trombones, tuba, 3 kettle-drums, bells and strings, and lasting some seven or eight minutes. The mere aspect of the orchestration, on the printed page, with its doublings, its fullness, its ' block ' appearance, and its use of accompaniment backgrounds consisting of reiterated chords and elementary ostinato figures, is in startling contrast with anything yet discussed. The gap between this type of writing and that found in the orchestral works of ten years later was bridged by the first two symphonies and by certain very remarkable stage or quasi-stage compositions to be examined presently.

The *Spring Song*, whether or not it is spring-like or has anything of *tristesse* in it, is certainly song-like, being in fact, after four bars of prelude (accompaniment), an unbroken stretch of melody. Not, of course, one long-drawn-out melody such as some super-Berlioz might have produced, nor even a rhapsodic wandering like Sibelius's own *Swan of Tuonela* (only in that there *are* breaks), but a regular 8-bar phrase, made into a sentence by another 8-bar phrase; and then another 16 bars, matching the former 16; and then an additional 8; leading straight into a reprise of the initial 16; and so on and so on— for no fewer, in all, than 215 bars. Everything is so four-square that one is surprised to find the total an odd number, wondering where that bar can have been elided. ' Four-square ', indeed, is perhaps not quite the right epithet, for Sibelius has used a main theme that pauses at the seventh bar and fifteenth bar, the eighth and sixteenth being mere iterations (Ex. 62) (cf. the oboe theme at the beginning of the Dance Intermezzo, Op. 45, No. 2). This composition is, in fact, something of a tour de force; for Sibelius performs that apparently simple but nevertheless unheard-of feat of piling sentence on sentence of melody in an unbroken, steady-moving stream for more than two hundred bars with the utmost resource, nowhere spectacular, nowhere very far from—shall we say?—' Kapellmeister ' methods, yet varying his orchestration and introducing his rare, brief excursions into foreign keys with great skill and actually, as a result, making the thing tolerable, even rather better than tolerable. The orchestration, though conventional, is far from unelaborate. There are passages for solo viola and solo 'cello (the first statement of the theme starting on those two instruments in unison with the first clarinet, though the viola soon drops out, and a horn joins in for the second half). For a long stretch two piccolos are used. At one place all the strings except double-basses have quadruple stops, pizzicato. The first violins go as high as the top D. The bells have their mellow say, in the big G flat major climax just before the end. . . . A pleasant, not very important piece, whose several peculiarities are much more apparent to a close student of composition or of Sibelius's development than to any general listener.

Although Ekman so precisely gives the spring of 1894 as the date of the *Spring Song*, Gray's 1891 is certainly lent some colour by the character of the work, in comparison with that of *En Saga*, which was written in 1892 (but revised in 1900 or 1901). Even allowing for the different aims and scopes of the two compositions, *En Saga* is decidedly the more advanced-seeming product. It is, in fact, the possible third exception to the generalisation made just now : that no work from Sibelius's pen prior to 1905 fails to show flaws. (The other two exceptions are, of course, *The Swan of Tuonela* and *Lemminkäinen's Homecoming*.)

*En Saga* was written in response to a request from the conductor, Kajanus (Sibelius's friend and champion from the first) for a work suitable to put into the regular repertoire, likely to make readily a successful appeal to his audiences at the concerts of the Helsingfors Philharmonic Society. That it was a response that staggered him, and was decidedly less ' popular ' in spirit than both he and the composer had intended, is highly probable. That it is, in its own right, a masterpiece is undeniable.

It employs the usual full orchestra, including tuba and third trumpet, except that the percussion group contains no kettle-drums. What we should expect to find the timpani playing is given to the big drum, and there are also parts for cymbals and triangle. Whether Sibelius substituted big drum for timpani because he wanted that particular colour for this particular occasion, or whether it was because he had some old-fashioned and unfounded apprehensions about using kettle-drums (as freely as he would want to use them) in a work so full of modulations, is not known. The big drum figures as nothing else than an indefinite-pitched kettle-drum throughout the work, has a kettle-drum kind of part, and is played with kettle-drum sticks.

*En Saga* is so well-known that it hardly needs analysis or description here, and the factors that make it a masterpiece in its own right can be shortly enumerated : (1) themes of great vigour and beauty and distinction, (2) a masterly exhibition of academic form, as it stood at that period, (3) superb academic orchestration, (4) a number of amazing originalities that, while never disturbing the homogeneity of style and technique or the structural unity, take us straight from Sibelius's 'prentice days into those of his ripest maturity. The solid, academically sound craftsmanship need not detain us, except to comment that never again was Sibelius to write such canons and imitations and sequences, such wood-wind backgrounds, such ostinati, or to cover with such terrific force and beauty the conventional ' key-relationship ' frame. Here indeed were the conservative ashes rekindled with youth's flames! It is the fourth ingredient, the cluster of forward-looking innovations, that is worth notice in detail.

One simple little magic stroke of originality is the opening chord, an A minor triad with one pizzicato low E in the first bar but thereafter the bottom C of the 'cellos as its bass. The unforgettable passage, Ex. 63, that makes its solitary appearance directly that chord is relinquished is of a peculiarly Sibelian type of wood-wind colouring, a colouring that then must have been very novel, but is very familiar to anyone to-day acquainted with the bulk of Sibelius's music. (The changes of key all through this introductory portion of the work are tremendously powerful and lovely, but they cannot be included among the features that look forward to Sibelius's mature work; on the contrary, their only very close parallels are to be found in other early works, *The Swan of Tuonela* and *Finlandia*. Nor were the interminable *ppp* rolls on the cymbal, with kettle-drum sticks, original as they were, an effect afterwards used by Sibelius.) The writing for the brass, so strikingly effective in itself, so powerfully related to the whole general scheme, and so uniquely careful in its practicality of detail (especially as to breathing), as found in full swing in *En Saga*, was to be a distinctive trait in Sibelius's orchestral writing throughout his career. Is it fanciful to point to the fact that the brain responsible for the A flats that make so persistent a clash in the passage beginning with Ex. 64 in *En Saga* was also responsible for the high C sharps that so startle anyone hearing the middle movement of the Fifth Symphony for the first time? (The way that A flat–G—itself derived by simple inversion from the early wood-wind passage mentioned above—is worked into the design of *En Saga* later is another matter, not pertinent here but nevertheless admirable.) Note, in any case, the immediate fate of the A flat–G motive : after 32 bars of that shape it turns into Ex. 65 et seq. and then into Ex. 66 etc. There indeed is the embryo of one of Sibelius's favourite procedures in later life. In Ex. 67 and its later variants in *En Saga* we have an almost exact parallel to, say, the first entry of the second subject, the one on strings and horns in thirds, in the finale of the Fifth Symphony. Here, in fact, was Sibelius at 27 already at his own special game of dovetailing themes and textures! Then there is, of course, the long, ' buzzing ' passage for strings (here ' sul ponticello '), precursor of another frequent feature of subsequent Sibelius scores and strikingly paralleled in *Tapiola* itself. (The amazing, the unique, the simple, the perfectly adapted, and very beautiful, long clarinet solo, accompanied by *ppp* cymbal roll and muted string chords just before the end cannot be left unmentioned; though here, again, is a passage without noticeable descendants in Sibelius's music.) Finally, one must note the fact that *En Saga* was revised. As we have already seen, Sibelius revised many of his works, sometimes more than once. Such ability to revise is always, for a number of reasons both technical and spiritual, the hall-mark of the very finest creative metal.

An instructive exercise of an order very different from, but aptly complementary to, the foregoing is to compare the long motives of *En Saga* with the very brief ones of, say, *The Oceanides*.

Between the ages of 22 and 26 Sibelius wrote for orchestra a brace of overtures, in A minor and E, and a Ballet Scene—all remaining in manuscript. *En Saga* is the earliest of his published scores, unless indeed the *Spring Song* ante-dates it; and between 1893 and 1896 he added to the never-to-be-published ones a tone-poem called *The*

*Dryad*, based on the 'melodrama' of the same name, Op. 15, Cassation for small orchestra, Op. 6, and *Tiera*[1] for brass band.

Immediately after *En Saga*, however, he wrote the first of the series of stage or quasi-stage works that constitutes so interesting a section of his output throughout his career. (Outside opera, no major composer, except perhaps Purcell, has written so much dramatic music.) The *Karelia* overture, *Karelia* suite and *Swan of Tuonela* all date from 1893. Actually they are not, indeed, quite his first dramatic compositions; for in 1888, as a student, he had collaborated with his tutor, Wegelius, in the incidental music to *The Watersprite* (a dramatic fairy-tale, by Gunnar Wennerberg), and the performance of that play at an academy concert was the occasion of Sibelius's first appearance (in Ekman's words) 'as a composer before a larger audience than the teachers of the academy and his nearest relations and friends'.

The *Karelia* overture and suite, Opp. 10 and 11, are the published portions of a quantity of music written by Sibelius for a pageant, a series of historical tableaux, got up by the students of Viborg University. A generation ago the overture was reasonably familiar, but it seems now to have dropped right out of the repertory. It is typical early Sibelius. It has vigorous, distinctive themes, simple but unlike anyone else's. It has a *Kapellmeister*-ish lay-out, with plenty of canonic treatments and pedal-points. Its form is, of course, entirely 'pattern', with (by the way) some very bad joins. It is scored noisily and heavily for full standard orchestra, including piccolo and tuba. It is inappositely swollen by a quite unwanted intrusion of the theme of the Intermezzo (from the suite). It contains a considerable number of the kind of things, perhaps, that Sibelius himself (as quoted by Bengt de Törne) meant to deprecate when he spoke of 'dead notes': iterated horn chords, iterated figure backgrounds on the wood-wind, and so on. In every way the work is a startling contrast to *The Swan of Tuonela*, its coeval. It is obviously out of the same stable as *En Saga*, but not at all—like that—a masterpiece.

The *Karelia* suite contains considerably more attractive music than the Overture. Familiar as they are, its three numbers have features that bear closer scrutiny than one perhaps gives them in the course of ordinary listening. The Intermezzo, written for standard full orchestra including third trumpet and tuba, is a gem. It is delightful and exhilarating to listen to, and it contains nothing that one could possibly want altered. It is a perfect example of a thing Sibelius has

[1] Tiera was one of the heroes of the *Kalevala*, comrade-in-arms of Lemminkäinen.

always been good at : the application of very simple methods (simple, that is, in *effect*) with the utmost unostentatious artistry. The plagal cadence at the end is beautiful, especially because of the high horn E flat. The piece deserves note, too, as perhaps the earliest instance of what was to be Sibelius's characteristic attitude to the orchestra : each family dealt with separately, very little doubling. The continuous rapid broken-chord background of the strings is likewise notable, but that was not quite so unprecedented (cf. *En Saga* and the *Karelia* overture, not to speak of works by certain other composers, such as Wagner), though the way it is used here was quite novel. The treatment of the percussion, throughout the work never silent, is very happy : 52 bars timpani roll; 69 bars ostinato pattern for big drum, cymbals and tambourine (the latter having a brief break halfway through), while timpani intermittently double the rhythm of the trumpets; 11 bars of what one might term thematic rhythm on timpani; and 25 more bars of *pp* timpani roll.

The Ballade employs only 2 oboes, English horn ('ossia corno in F'), 2 clarinets, 2 bassoons and strings. It is very well instrumented and laid out, with lots of variety and of pleasant sounds. The thematic material, while not uncharacteristic, is a trifle uninspired and becomes boring with repetition. Structurally it is peculiar. The preliminary foretaste of the main theme, on clarinets and bassoons, is quite successful. The ensuing treatment, mostly on strings, of that main theme with its counter-subject is ingenious in a rather stereotyped way and, as I have just said, does not quite guarantee us escape from boredom. The tailing-off of this section, after a modulation, through 20 bars of a low mediant pedal is not ineffective in itself, but is found to be a slightly unsatisfactory link with the next section, a new theme in the new key. Further, the new key is only the relative major of the previous one, and the new theme is rather similar to the previous one (in both its rhythm and its conjunct movement) and is moreover interrupted by a major version of the actual first theme, and so boredom is again in the air. Then we come to a dead stop, a two-bar 'G.P.', after which an entirely *new* theme, but in the original key, is played by the English horn to a pizzicato accompaniment. Both English horn and pizzicato (apart from double-basses) are being heard for the first time. After this new theme has been dealt with for 26 bars, with a quite beautiful tonic close, a final 8-bar statement of the original theme, in the original key, in attenuated orchestration, provides the piece with a conclusion that sounds well in itself but is unsatisfactory from the structural point of view. (The nearest parallel in Sibelius to this work's structural peculiarity is perhaps the Dance-Intermezzo, Op. 45, No. 2.) Of course it is possible that the piece originally accompanied pageant-action to which it was suited and which concealed the weakness of its musical design and the sameness of its material.

With the Alla marcia we return to the orchestra of the Intermezzo, plus a piccolo; and we return, too, to music that can only be described as ' delightful and exhilarating '. The craftsmanship is beautiful—full of resource, original, essentially (but not too) simple. Nothing could be more effective than the absolutely abrupt change from A major to F major and the absolutely abrupt change back. The percussion is again used in the happiest possible way.

It was in 1893, the same year as the *Karelia* music, that Sibelius accepted the suggestion of a literary man, J. H. Erkko, that they should collaborate in an opera, *The Building of the Boat*.[1] He started work on the music, and indeed on the libretto too, but quite soon became persuaded that the operatic medium was not, after all, congenial to him. The idea was abandoned, and all that survives to commemorate it is the piece that was to have been the prelude to the opera. That piece is published, as No. 3 of Four Legends for orchestra, Op. 22, and its title is *The Swan of Tuonela*.

The ' programme ' of the opera-prelude manqué is expressed in an inscription on the score : ' Tuonela, the land of death, the hell of Finnish mythology, is surrounded by a large river with black waters and a rapid current, on which the Swan of Tuonela floats majestically, singing '.[2] It is also expressed, most eloquently, in the composition itself. The case is, in fact, an exact parallel to the product of thirty-two years later, *Tapiola*, and my remarks on page 41 about the relations between literary or pictorial ideas and music intended to convey them, apply equally to *The Swan*. The final strand of resemblance between these two compositions that form almost the extremities in time of Sibelius's output is that each is a stupendous masterpiece : *Tapiola* because of its absolute quality and because of what it is in relation to all other music whatsoever, *The Swan* because of its absolute quality and because of what it is in relation to Sibelius's age and development in 1893 and also to all other music in existence at that date. If the production of *Tapiola* almost cheek by jowl with suites *mignonne* and *champêtre* is dumbfounding, the

[1] Cf. Runos XVI–XVII of the *Kalevala*. This story is a sequel to Väinämöinen's adventure with the daughter of Pohjola.
[2] Runo XIV of the *Kalevala* tells how Lemminkäinen tried to shoot the Swan with his crossbow.

creation of *The Swan of Tuonela* side by side with *En Saga*, the *Karelia* music and the *Spring Song* is if anything more inexplicable. The one is a problem of an artist's more or less voluntary acts, the workings of his conscience; the other is a mystery of his involuntary manifestations, of his actual creative powers. In every technical respect but one *The Swan of Tuonela* is utterly different from any published work by Sibelius (or any one else, for that matter) dating from that period. The one respect is, of course, its finger-prints, which are Sibelian indeed—including the sharpened fourth degree of the scale, and the general modal leanings that Gray so astoundingly denies, and also the extraordinary metrical finesses that otherwise became prominent only later in Sibelius's career.

As every reader must know (the work being so often performed), *The Swan* is scored for oboe, English horn, bass clarinet, 2 bassoons, 4 horns, 3 trombones, 2 kettle-drums, big drum, harp, and much-divided strings. The violins are in eight parts almost throughout. Its harmonic idiom, not often used by Sibelius in such a wholesale way as here, is largely that of consecutive common chords of comparatively remote keys (nearly all in root position). This harmonic idiom—at any rate, as it figures here, the rhapsodic form (a minimum of ' pattern ' now), the extreme vagueness and elasticity of the rhythm, the orchestration : all are extraordinarily original. Simply by the fact of its *being* obviously original it is outstanding among Sibelius's works, very few of which were so iconoclastic in technique. It is, of course, not only remarkable and iconoclastic but fine and lovely. When towards the end the English horn takes up the broad, mournful tune that has just been played by the violins, violas and 'cellos in unison, the strings are subdivided into 14 parts (even the double-basses are divisi), of which 9 are double-stopping and 10 are col legno. The remainder of the accompaniment consists of a roll on the big drum, reiterated minor-third chords on kettle-drums, and a very striking ostinato in the lower register of the harp. Everything except English horn and harp is marked *ppp*.

The first two of the Four Legends, Op. 22, remain in the obscurity of manuscript.[1] The fourth is the fairly well-known *Lemminkäinen's Homecoming*. The relevant passage in the *Kalevala* (Runo XXX) describes the journey home from an unsuccessful expedition against Pohjola, the Northland, of Lemminkäinen, the hero (and, as Gray describes him, ' a kind of northern Don Juan '). The points made

---

[1] *Lemminkäinen and the Maidens* must be based on Runo XXIX, *Lemminkäinen in Tuonela* on Runo XIV of the *Kalevala*.

clear in the music are that the journey was an exciting and eventful one and that Lemminkäinen was hugely happy to be home once more. Although not so evidently, outstandingly novel, in its period, as *The Swan*, which in any case came two years before it, the *Homecoming* is really a staggering piece of work, a tremendous leap into the composer's future. Thus its motives are tiny fragments; its perpetuum-mobile framework is made not only tolerable but fascinating and transporting by the cleverest conceivable resources of subtle, unobtrusive variation; its harmony contains certain very prominent and striking phrases and a great many more originalities that make their effect without the listener being aware of them as such. To study the way in which its chief motive, short enough in its full form, grows by minute bit after minute bit from the bassoon's mere three notes at the very start is an education in what was later to be revealed as one of Sibelius's most distinctive methods of musical thought. It is hardly necessary to refer to the simply overwhelming energy and excitement of the piece.

Despite the fate of *The Building of the Boat,* the opera to have been written with Erkko, Sibelius did in 1896 compose an opera, a single-act one entitled *The Maiden in the Tower.* It was duly produced with no great success, remained unpublished, and has apparently been regarded ever since by Sibelius as a work of no importance. One refers to it only for the sake of accuracy and comprehensiveness. It is, of course, an indication of what must at least have been a quite strong leaning of Sibelius at that epoch.

In the course of his life Sibelius has contributed incidental music to stage productions of no fewer than ten plays. Gray expresses the view that Sibelius has something of an antipathy to the stage, but we can find many fragments of contrary evidence among the biographical particulars supplied by Karl Ekman and Bengt de Törne. Certainly as a young man he paid many visits to the theatre and was an enthusiastic member of artistic-cum-philosophic-cum-political coteries that included dramatists as well as other literary men. The point is perhaps to-day more one of casual interest than of real importance. A general question more worth scrutiny that is thrown into highest relief by Sibelius's theatrical music—by most of it, at any rate—is the one of ' pattern ' versus ' growth '.

Sibelius's incidental music to plays is largely ' pattern ' stuff of the clearest kind, and before proceeding to examine it in detail we may benefit from pushing an inquiry why a composer who in many of his works has revealed an unprecedented power of achieving organic growth, and of making that the main principle of musical design, should abandon that principle when writing for the stage. The reason, of course, is a very simple one. When a piece of music has unity, coherence, shape imposed upon it by its organic growth from bar to bar, phrase to phrase, section to section, it presents, *ipso facto*, a continuous line of thought, and a beginning-to-end curve of feeling. That line of thought and that curve of feeling are the music's thread of interest. A thread, moreover, despite the fact that we have to use, for want of better, words that are not specifically musical such as ' thought ' and ' feeling '—a thread of interest that is quite untranslatable into any other medium than the musical one in which it has its being. ' Growth ' music needs to be listened to with the closest attention, so that the thought is followed, the feeling experienced, unbroken from beginning to end. The thread of interest demands—and, if we are responsive, compels—concentration. The genuine and fundamental fallacy in, say, Massine's setting of choreography to such music as Beethoven's Seventh Symphony and Berlioz's *Fantastique* was that those works have, at any rate in most of their movements, threads of musical interest, created by the element of growth, that neither need nor admit of translation into the choreographic medium and from which the choreography merely forms an unwanted distraction. When Sibelius writes a piece of absolute music he opens to us undreamt-of worlds of ' growth '-design. When he writes music to accompany extra-musical material he very properly reduces the element of growth to a minimum, gives his composition an obvious ' pattern ' construction, and leaves the listener's mind free to devote its chief attention to other things. This is an analysis that tends, no doubt, towards over-simplification, but essentially it is correct.

The first play to which Sibelius put incidental music was *King Christian II*. Its author, Adolf Paul, turned to literature only after an earnest period of apprenticeship as a musician (in the course of which he was a pupil, in both Finland and Germany, of Busoni). It was in music-student days that he and Sibelius met and became close companions, and friends they remained in later life after Paul had deserted music and become a substantial writer of novels, plays, journalism and what not. Among Paul's widely varied output (indeed, it was his first book) was a volume called *A Book about a Man*, a typical product of youth, based on autobiographical material, in which he drew a portrait of Sibelius as he had known him in their student friendship. *King Christian II* is a historical play dealing with the passion of Christian II, King of Denmark, Norway and Sweden, for Dyveke, a Dutch girl of low birth, and her eventual murder. It was first performed on February 24th, 1898, and has remained in obscurity since. The music, composed for that production and conducted then by the composer, has, on the contrary, taken from the start a regular place in the orchestral repertoire. Three of its numbers were actually written only in the summer of 1898 : the Nocturne, Serenade and Ballade. It has the further importance of being the work with which Sibelius, egged on by Adolf Paul, made his first approach to German publishers. He took it to Breitkopf and Härtel, who in the sequel became publishers of a great deal of his output. The *King Christian* suite was one of Sibelius's most frequently performed compositions during the days when his music was still making only very slow headway with European audiences. The Elegy from it (conducted by the composer in person) was among the works played at the funeral of Martin Wegelius, Sibelius's old tutor and friend, in 1906.

The Elegy, scored for strings only, is indeed a quite beautiful little piece. In the stage performance it served as a prelude to the play. The Musette has obvious charm. It was played simply by 2 clarinets and 2 bassoons in the production of the play, where it figured as a serenade under the heroine's window by street musicians, but for the concert version string parts were added. The latter part of its middle section is deplorably commonplace, one of the worst patches in all Sibelius; otherwise it is delightful. The Minuet is very pleasant indeed and so, too, though not altogether innocent of triviality and triteness, is the Nocturne. The former is written for 2 flutes, 2 clarinets and strings, and the almost equally attractive *Fool's Song* for voice, harp, triangle and strings. The Nocturne is a quite elaborate piece of conventional music, employing the full standard orchestra, with tambourine and 2 kettle-drums. The tambourine's part is noteworthy : 5 bars of independent iteration (marked *f,* in a tutti at a climax) of the rhythm of an accompaniment figure previously established on wood-wind. One of the most notable aspects of the Serenade and Ballade, the two other numbers added some months after the play's production, is their resemblance to parts of the First Symphony, to which, of course, they are closely related in date. They are both written for full orchestra. The Serenade is a rather beautiful piece of music, elaborate and eloquent, even impassioned, very typical basic Sibelius with strong melodic and harmonic reminders of the big tune in the finale of the Symphony. The workmanship through-

out is exquisite. A lovely curtain rise is provided at the change to
'Tempo di minuetto' 28 bars from the end. The Ballade is ambitious
in lay-out but trite in substance, and over-full of repetitions. It
reminds one very strongly of the other, the rumbustious, part of the
Symphony's finale. It uses, at 'allegro molto', the rhythm
♩. ♪│♩ ♩ ♩│♩ ♩ ♩ ♩│♩ ♩ ‿ and has lots of quaver work with
Ex. 68 as a typical shape.

In 1899 Sibelius once again wrote a quantity of music for some
historical tableaux, which formed the climax, at a gala night in the
Swedish theatre of Helsingfors, to what were known as the Press
Celebrations and were, in fact, a demonstration of patriotism, of
political feeling, of rebelliousness against the Russian régime then
established in Finland. Sibelius, it may be mentioned, had already
made himself known as a champion of the Finnish nationalistic
aspirations and his recent *Song of the Athenians* (for male voices,
men's and boys', seven saxhorns and percussion, Op. 31) had been
hailed as being, behind its ostensibly antique and remote façade,
something of a contemporary and Finnish war-song. The tableau
music furnished the material for the *Scènes historiques*, Opp. 25 and
66, and also included the one work of all by which the composer
became most widely known : *Finlandia*. Not that it was so named at
first. When it had been revised, in 1900, its performance in Finland
or any other part of the Russian Empire under any title that betrayed
its patriotic motive was still forbidden, though in Germany, for
instance, it was played as *Vaterland* and in France as *La patrie*. So
late as 1904 it was given at Riga and Reval as an Impromptu.

*Finlandia* is perhaps worth scrutiny precisely because it is so familiar
to most of us that our perceptive faculties have been in danger of
lapsing. The truth is that it is a rather mixed piece of work. The
opening is melodramatic, though in the highest class of that
category and very individual. The type of harmony—partly
chromatic, partly jumping into remote keys, and partly conventional
—and the concomitant slow-moving strenuousness, tension, drama,
are very characteristic Sibelius, though not his finest vein; the second
movement of the Second Symphony contains perhaps the best music
that he ever wrote of this kind. In *Finlandia*, even in the prefatory
andante sostenuto to which these remarks refer, he drops every now
and again into atrocious obviousness and rhetorical repetitiveness.
Then, in the allegro that is eventually reached, could anything be
more trite than the four bars before letter G (p. 13 of the minature

score)? For anyone capable of dissociating it from its extra-musical significance the hymn-tune section beginning at Letter I is surely quite intolerable. In fact, the opening, not quite beyond censure as it is, is the best part of this work, which certainly exemplifies all one's worst conceptions of what a very popular, hackneyed piece is likely to be.

The *Scènes historiques* are, oddly enough, a very different matter. Although the second set constitute Op. 66 and are dated, by Gray and Ekman, 1912, they are numbered in the printed score IV, V and VI—just as if Opp. 25 and 66 were one single suite of six pieces: *All' Overtura* Op. 25, No. 1, *Scena* Op. 25, No. 2, *Festivo* Op. 25, No. 3, *The Chase* Op. 66, No. 1, *Love Song* Op. 66, No. 2, *At the Drawbridge* Op. 66, No. 3. It is undeniable that they are all in the same style, a style that, although more mature than one would have expected from the composer in 1899, is hardly as mature as one would have expected from him in 1912 (between the Fourth Symphony and *The Bard*). However, the Op. 22 *Legends* had already shown that he was capable of remarkably anticipating his own development, as one might say; and the fact that the first three *Scènes historiques* are known to have been revised in 1911 is perhaps enough to clinch one's belief that the six pieces did indeed originate at the same time.

The very *aspect* of the score of the *All' Overtura* (using the same orchestra as *Finlandia* but for the absence of a tuba) takes us straight into the characteristic mature Sibelius and very far from the period of *En Saga* and the *Karelia* works. And the texture and construction of the work are likewise in his later style. Such lay-outs and over-lapping lines, as we find at, for example, letters C–D could easily be mistaken for some passage out of *Tapiola* or the Seventh Symphony. We may observe here one of the most assertive of all Sibelius's uses of the sharpened fourth in the major scale (outside the Fourth Symphony), which appears both in the introductory theme (the 10 bars of alternate 2/2 and 3/2 in E flat, grave) and in the first subject of the allegro, which is in G and where the sharpened fourth is given great prominence from the very start, where it stands as a high D flat held by clarinet from the end of the previous section (where it had intruded in that last bar as a flattened seventh of the E flat tonality). As the main theme of the allegro progresses we get the melodic C sharp clashing against the C natural of the subdominant six-four chord (Ex. 69). There is a very characteristic second theme, hovering between B minor and A major, in thirds on flutes, later on violins and violas low down, with off-beat pizzicato chords on 'cellos. Its rhythm takes us straight to the Third Symphony, first

movement:

The *Scena*, for the same orchestra plus piccolo and a lot of percussion, is again very much the serious Sibelius. Of all the *Scènes historiques* this is the one that by far the most suggests its origin as the accompaniment of stage happenings. First there is a beautiful little minuet section, the tune on the high register of the bassoon and then the middle one of the oboe. The key is E flat minor. Then there is a striking transition over a pedal B flat to allegro moderato, where above the held B flat we have C major harmony. There is a big, fanfare-like tune for the three trumpets in unison. After that has been spaciously dealt with the speed increases during a remarkable passage (Ex. 70) that is in the same class as some of the Fourth Symphony. At the climax of that working-up passage (during which, by the way, the side-drum has a series of short soft rolls ' am Rand ', ' on the edge '), note the figure, Ex. 71, into which the strings relapse, not only because it is such a finger-print of Sibelius (cf. *Lemminkäinen's Homecoming*, first movement of the Third Symphony, Ex. 68, etc.) but because it is here presaged just before in wood-wind developments of the end of the trumpet tune, Ex. 72. Then, against ostinati on strings, horns, clarinets and bassoons, the trumpets and trombones sing forth a nobile melody, at the culmination of which we have one of Sibelius's uses of *two* piccolos.

For the *Festivo*, Op. 25, No. 3, castanets are added to the orchestra, and the movement is marked ' Tempo di bolero '. It is an extended composition and only in certain sections dance-like. Bustling, solidly built, full of craftsmanship, it is on the whole enjoyable but a good deal less individual than its two predecessors. Perhaps the most distinguished touch is that it ends very quietly and simply, although one would have anticipated the reverse.

The first of the Op. 66 *Scènes historiques*, *The Chase*, is almost a second *Lemminkäinen's Homecoming*. It has much verve, but just fails to reproduce that other work's magic. Nevertheless, nobody can call it anything but a good specimen of early-mature Sibelius.

The last chord of *The Chase* is Ex. 73a; the first of *Love-song* is Ex. 73b. It is difficult to imagine just how beautifully the latter, simple-looking chord falls on the ear. This piece would hardly merit quotation for its beauty, however; though it does for its typical unexpectedness of technical detail. Take the opening melody, with its long sweep (Ex. 74); look at its metrical construction. Then, again, examine the lay-out of the reprise of that passage (Ex. 75). This is superlative bravura of workmanship; getting the last ounce out of the material. And the way in which the appogiaturas and the triplets of the basses are gradually spread over other parts of the orchestra during the remainder of the work, with its lovely example of ' extension ' mechanism, is masterly.

Just as the best point of the *Festivo* is its unexpected quiet ending, so the worst of *At the Drawbridge* is its unexpected loud and conventional one. Otherwise the last of the *Scènes historiques* is an admirable piece, economical and interesting, full of characteristic material and methods. In it, by the way, is Sibelius's other tam-tam part, comprising four *pp* notes.

The only surviving part of the music Sibelius wrote in 1903 for *Kuolema* (Death), a play by his brother-in-law, Arvid Järnefelt, is the ubiquitous *Valse triste*. Although so different a work, it has just the same kinds of faults and virtues as *Finlandia*. The originality and effectiveness of some of the harmonic happenings are surely incontestable. On the other hand, the cantabile at Letter E, with its cheap, obvious lay-out, its vapidity, and its double grace-notes, is one of the worst things Sibelius ever perpetrated. Even taking into account its merits, one can hardly imagine the *Valse* to be more than a piece of hackwork. Originally it was for strings only; subsequently (and as published) parts for flute, clarinet, 2 horns and kettle-drums were added by the composer.

The years 1905–9 saw the composition of incidental music to no fewer than four plays, plays of extreme diversity in style and subject-matter: *Pelléas and Mélisande* (Maeterlinck), *Belshazar* (Procopé), *Swanwhite* (Strindberg) and *The Lizard* (Lybeck). The last-named was for some reason given the early opus number 8, but never published. It is unknown, yet Sibelius at the time described the music as ' among the most full of feeling that I have written ' (in a letter quoted by Ekman).

The *Pelléas and Mélisande* music was collected into the published suite, Op. 46, for small orchestra, which contains preludes to six of the scenes in the play, two pieces of melodrama and the song of *The three blind sisters*. It is not, on the whole, Sibelius at his best. Nor is it very much in tune with Maeterlinck's fantasy. Sibelius's idea of Mélisande, for instance (the prelude to Act I, Scene 2, bears her name) is a very slow waltz, mostly English horn melody with stereotyped accompaniment on muted strings. Several of the pieces are, indeed, quite beautiful little specimens of ' pattern ' work. For example,

*A fountain in the park* (Prelude to Act II, Scene 1), which is another waltz, a quick one, with pleasant material quite exquisitely worked out. Note the last melodic phrase given to the low register of the flute, and then the divided basses, pizzicato, Ex. 76. The 'cello phrase makes its lovely former appearances in this piece (when it is a pendant to a broad tune played by massed strings in unison) on a bassoon. Or there is the *Pastorale* that is to be played during the end of Act III, Scene 4. Here is a lot of very attractive wood-wind work; the string parts are entirely ostinatos or sustained chords. Anyone interested in the subject of Sibelius's affection for the low register of the flute will note the beautiful trills here. Again, there is *Mélisande at the spinning-wheel*, the prelude to Act III, Scene 1, a beautiful specimen of the ' pattern ' genre as such, delightfully and originally scored and laid-out, and something of a tour de force, in its simple way, in its ostinato aspect—a viola trill representing the spinning-wheel. Only Sibelius could have written the last four bars, Ex. 77.

Yet these neat, polished, artistic trifles are not, one is forced to reflect, the ideal music for such a play as *Pelléas and Mélisande*. So far as the ' pattern ' style is concerned, it might pass perhaps for the preludes and entr'actes, but the character of the mood created by, for instance, the *Pastorale*, played during actual dialogue, is not quite compatible with the atmosphere on the stage. Self-contained, fully worked-out music, whether ' pattern ' or ' growth ', is not wanted, but something quite subordinate and, so to speak, impressionistic. Impressionism of another kind we do encounter, by the way, in the melodrama for the end of Act I, Scene 4, *At the sea shore*. Here we have chromatic harmonies on the low strings, divisi, double-bass tremolos ' sul ponticello ', tremolos on very high harmonics for all the strings. (Note the final wood-wind phrase, played by piccolo and clarinet four octaves apart, *pp*.) Above all, perhaps, the prelude to Act V, Scene 2, *The death of Mélisande*, strikes us as simply *too* patterned and neat and even trivial for the occasion. It consists in the main of a longish melodic flow, but with a brief and very impassioned climax in the middle. (Fauré, one must admit, in his incidental music to the same play, was much more in touch with its atmosphere while still writing in the ' pattern ' genre.) The truth about the *Pelléas and Mélisande* music is that while Sibelius remains, in one sense, too much himself, in failing to mirror Maeterlinck's quiet and fragile otherworldliness, at the same time he is not sufficiently moved to give even of his own, personal best. The comparisons to be made with his next two play-settings are interesting.

In the *Belshazar* suite, Op. 51, Sibelius did quite evidently, and successfully, aim at local colour. The music is not in the least profound, but it is both in keeping with the play's atmosphere, at least superficially, and agreeable in itself. For once Sibelius, instead of spontaneously breaking into modal implications in the flow of his most powerful and personal musical impulses, deliberately resorts to them for descriptive purposes. Thus we find him decking this Eastern play with such passages as Ex. 78. One must, however, also quote from *Khadra's Dance*, beginning as in Ex. 79, which fits very well into the pseudo-oriental context and yet is very characteristic of the natural Sibelius—so much so, in fact, that it is a striking reminder of, and improvement upon, an idea in the *Valse triste*. In the *Night Music* one may happen to note the acciaccatura ' sob ' found in so many similar places in Sibelius, for instance in the first number, *At the castle gate*, in the *Pelléas* suite. The *Belshazar* music may not seem of very much account, but it does possess considerable individuality and charm as well as serving its avowed purpose excellently.

We come to *Swanwhite*. Strindberg's strange fairy-tale was written in 1901 and published in 1902. Sibelius wrote his incidental music in 1908, and very copious incidental music it is, exceeding by a good deal what can be actually accounted for by the various musical prescriptions in the text of the play. Like the two just discussed, this work is described as ' for small orchestra ', but the actual orchestra required contains the usual double wood-wind and 4 horns plus strings (a good deal divided), not to speak of harp, kettle-drums, castanets and triangle.

The mere aspect of the first chord of the first section (*The Peacock*), Ex. 80, suggests that this was a work into which the composer put much earnestness and enthusiasm. Equally fastidious is the lay-out of the pedal point for oboes, clarinets and harp that lasts through the entire section, after the two-bar introduction (Ex. 81). This is an extremely original piece of music, for all the extreme sim-plicity of its materials; in other words it is quintessential Sibelius. If in some moods, in the concert-hall, one might find it sound dull, ordinary, monotonous, that would certainly be an impression put into correct perspective if the music were heard in its proper context. Ex. 82 is a brief, typical excerpt from this peculiar study in iteration.

The same label, extremely original use of extremely ordinary materials, is appropriate for practically all the other sections. The second, *The Harp*, quiet, unostentatious, is an excellent specimen. So are No. 4, *Listen, the robin sings* (with its striking finish) and No. 5, *The prince alone*. No. 3, *The girl with the roses*, is rather different. It is in effect a very slow waltz; it is marked, and should be played; ' lento assai ', and has a certain dreamy, gossamer charm. If taken too fast it loses badly and sounds vapidly, commonplacely pretty and wistful. No. 6, *Swanwhite and the prince*, is a remarkable blend of Sibelius's symphonic style and certain ' pattern ' elements that in fact do, after all, dictate or mould its form; it is a fine piece of poetic and even passionate music. Only the last section, *Hymn of praise*, is a failure. Unlike its predecessors, its appearance of being ordinary and thick is not belied by its reality. The virtue of those sections here dismissed in a mere word or two can hardly be exaggerated. They are absolutely first-class. And what it amounts to is that Sibelius was this time writing music for a play that was of his own spiritual world, that Strindberg was a Swede and so, quite a large proportion of him, is Sibelius.

In 1911 Sibelius was again working in harness with his old friend, Adolf Paul. *The Language of the Birds*, however, is a very different play from *King Christian II*. It is a subtle, witty, urbane version of an episode in the life of King Solomon and has earned its author comparisons with Bernard Shaw as well as with Strindberg. It was first performed at the Burgtheater, Vienna, and subsequently seen at Prague and Buda-Pesth. The music, published without opus number, is quite unknown in concert-halls, but was considered an integral factor in the play's success on the stage. A dramatic critic found it ' charming'.

It was in 1913, the year of *The Bard* and of the beginning on *The Oceanides*, that Sibelius put music to *Scaramouche*, a melodrama by Poul Knudsen. As here the music is a continuous accompaniment to action and dialogue, from start to finish of the play, it is a very sizeable work; even the piano score runs to seventy pages. It does contain a good deal of characteristic Sibelius; but as a whole it is certainly not a typical product. It keeps on reminding one somehow of Richard Strauss, the Strauss of, say, *Der Rosenkavalier*; and also it brings into one's head a very unexpected speculation about what Sibelius might have done as a composer for films. Besides obviously following the action and dialogue with every conscientiousness, the score shows Sibelius interested in his music *as* music. Whether or not one finds them good, whether or not they are true to the composer's temperament, there is no denying the questing spirit so far as Sibelius is concerned, of such passages as Exs. 83, 84 and 85. For the third time in our study of Sibelius we have our attention drawn, by this work, to the bolero; for that is the dance for which the lovely Blondelaine, the wife whose passion for dancing is the immediate cause of her catastrophe, calls.

The incidental music that Sibelius wrote for Hofmannsthal's *Everyman* halfway through the 1914–18 war, and in the midst of the Fifth Symphony period, has the opus number 83, but was never published. Like *Scaramouche*, it is described as ' for small orchestra ', but we have seen how elastic that term can be when Sibelius uses it. Probably its remaining unpublished, unplayed, unknown, may be put down to the fact that, unlike all the earlier incidental music except *Scaramouche* (and that, after all, was not ' incidental ' music at all), it followed the stage happenings closely and was in the main a series of small pieces dependent almost entirely on the dramatic context for their effect. In fact it could hardly be more completely in contrast to the next and last of Sibelius's stage compositions, the music for Shakespeare's *The Tempest*.

It is true that the published *Tempest* music (Op. 109) contains eighteen separate items. Numerous as are the occasions for music specified in the text of the play they are outnumbered by Sibelius's music, and the Copenhagen production in 1926 for which it was composed must have been an elaborate ' producer's version '. Even so, however, some of the play's integral demands for music—the songs for instance—are not covered. Above all, the music is not closely related, bar by bar, to the action. On the contrary, each number is a very highly finished piece of musical patterning, so far as it goes entirely complete and self-sustaining.

The Prelude is conceivably the most thoroughly onomatapoetic stretch of music ever written. By this is to be understood not simply that it is more verisimilitudinous than any other composition but that it has far less than any other composition of anything *but* verisimilitude. Its opening bars, Ex. 86, give a good sample of the basis of the piece. The whole-tone harmonic scheme is comparable in monotony only to Skryabin's *Poem of Ecstasy*. A very big orchestra is used. Until they play pianissimo chords, tremolo, during the last couple of pages, the strings are exclusively occupied with chromatic-scale passages. The brass build up slow ladders of whole-tone chord and the wood-wind divide their time between holding notes and up-and-down chromatic-scale rushes (in which at one point even the horns join). That is all. There is no further material, thematic or otherwise. It makes quite an overwhelming effect in performance, but is scarcely to be cited as a specimen of any great musical value. Apart from the rather hypnotic grip it can take of one's ear it is chiefly notable, on the contrary, as a specimen of phenomenal patience on the part of the composer, the patience required to write so many repetitions or near repetitions of a mere handful of elements and to write so many accidentals and so many double or treble lines for the interminable chromatic scales in semi-quavers or demisemiquavers.

The two suites into which the remainder of the music is assembled for concert purposes contain between them 17 numbers, of which one, however, *The Tempest*, is a sort of abbreviated rehash of the Prelude. Quite inexplicably, this time, the title-page of the score describes the suites as ' for small orchestra '; actually they demand an orchestra of as vast dimensions as the Prelude does. A performance of the complete work requires 3 flutes and 3 piccolos (3 players in all), 2 oboes, 1 clarinet in E flat and 2 in B flat (2 players in all), bass clarinet, 2 bassoons, 4 horns, 3 trumpets, 3 trombones, tuba, 3 kettle-drums, big drum, side drum, cymbals, triangle, xylophone, harp and strings. This incidental music, then, is comprehensive in the situations it covers and the resources it demands (omitting only the songs from the first and the human voice from the second). Further one may say that it is written with the utmost supple and at times elaborate craftsmanship but that it amounts to nothing very much as music. One realises with slow astonishment as, recovering from the initial delightful impact of their deftness and verve, one scrutinises these pieces, that they completely lack any single touch of Sibelius's personality. They are utterly impersonal, cold : inhuman exhibitions of composing virtuosity. They only interpret the play loosely and at a superficial level. Their gambols are pastiche; their sentiment is sentimentality (cf. for example, the opening of *Miranda*). One can quite safely assume that no passion and no soul-searching went into their creation. Like the *Scaramouche* music they make us think of the film world, but beside them *Scaramouche* is a work of integrity and depth.

Heaven knows that Sibelius all his life has been a superb technician. The unconventionality of his methods has been matched not only by their absolute rootedness in his natural creative ego but the adequacy, the unfailing expertness, with which he has handled them. The performer, once he understands what Sibelius's intentions are, finds that a straightforward rendering of just what the composer has put on paper is certain to produce a perfect realisation of them. Not a note, not an inflection, scarcely a marking is wasted or misconceived. It is also true that, as he developed and matured, his spiritual growth, his access of depth and power and subtlety, was accompanied by a technical growth, so that although *En Saga* at the beginning was a very brilliant exposition of a standardised technique on to which were grafted a number of perfectly assimilated innovations, the Sixth Symphony and *Tapiola* at the end were dazzling displays (if the word may be used) of a technique so personal and so assured that its very achievements were hidden in its mastery and in its entire synthesis with its subject-matter. But the virtuosity of this incidental music of 1926 is something different, new and disturbing. Perhaps the point needs stressing, though dispassionate appraisal cannot fail to reveal its accuracy, that in the Seventh Symphony Sibelius did, in fact, more than anything else address himself to a purely technical problem. Weakest and most uneven of all his symphonies in its material, it is as obviously an attempt as it is obviously a failure to impose Sibelian unity and all-throughness on a single movement containing widely diverse tempi and containing a disposition of subject-matter similar to what one would have found if it had, in fact, been written in three or four separate movements. After not only the beauty but the unsurpassable mellowness and fluency of the Sixth Symphony (1923) Sibelius completed the heroic failure, a failure which the very indifference of some of the material proves to be the failure of a primarily technical feat, that 1924's Seventh Symphony is. After the masterpiece *Tapiola* (1925)—after, also, all the minor by-products of this period that have been mentioned earlier—the chance of the Copenhagen *Tempest* commission was a switch that released a cascade of almost exhibitionistic virtuosity at last uncoloured by any tincture of creative impulse. In *The Tempest* Sibelius gave the world the fruits of all his purely technical experience as a writer of orchestral music and a manipulator of ' pattern ' formulae, but included nothing whatever of what the whole of his career as an actual composer, a man who thought and felt and created in music, had comprised. No musician could take seriously, or believe that Sibelius took seriously, the *Suite caractéristique* or *Suite champêtre* and so on, but the music for *The Tempest* bears many indications that the composer did take it seriously, and the musical world has certainly taken it seriously. Taken seriously, and at the same time judged carefully and with discrimination, it is a rather horrifying phenomenon. Viewed in conjunction with the Seventh Symphony and, as after all it must to an extent be, with the *Suite caractéristique* and its kind, it makes a student of the composer wonder what that incredible silence of his since 1926 really does conceal. What is the Eighth Symphony really like? What other works are lying shelved until the composer's death? Are his survivors to be the happy discoverers of successors to the Sixth Symphony and *Tapiola* or to the Seventh Symphony or to *The Tempest*? The speculation is after all, one realises, not wholly a yearning one. Anxiety and even dread are difficult to exclude.

# 4

## The Chamber Music

### By

### Scott Goddard

SIBELIUS'S CHAMBER MUSIC has particular interest in regard to the history of his own music. The larger part of his early compositions, mostly unpublished and probably destroyed, was chamber music. This preponderance of work for a small array of instruments may have been a matter of choice; or it may have arisen from circumstances which, making chamber music consorts most readily available, caused the music to take that texture. It should be remembered also that Sibelius learned the violin when young and was therefore himself a chamber musician.

What the nature of this early chamber music may have been it is difficult to determine precisely, though a general estimate of its style and quality may be arrived at from the large number of short pieces that have appeared since. It becomes apparent that from those earliest times onward the chamber for which Sibelius's music was designed, as much as being a room set aside for intelligent or even intellectual converse, was the drawing-room, the salon, the living-room where 'company' was welcomed, where the family would naturally assemble for relaxation and music would form part of the accepted social scheme of domestic entertainment. This would account for the accumulation of compositions in the shorter forms and simpler constructions in the work of a boy studying in that kind of communal circle. That was presumably his social atmosphere and there he must have found his audience. If their critical standards, based partly on affection, partly on inattention, were the first he took account of after his own, there will have been sufficient cause for a style suited to the more simple-minded audience, a general homophonic structure of tunes unambitiously accompanied, the absence of contrapuntal ingenuities or much in the nature of abstract devices. That, in fact, is the average character of his published chamber music; and there is no cause to doubt that it was so from the beginning or that the reason for its having this peculiar quality arose from the special circumstances in which Sibelius's earlier chamber music came into existence. It is an expression of nothing more profound than the contentment and the easily appeased distresses of domesticity.

There is one exception, so extreme in differences in quality, character, style, from the rest, indeed in all that raises mediocre work to levels of high intelligence and great beauty, that this work—the String Quartet *Voces intimae*—stands alone. Not only is it Sibelius's sole extant string quartet; it is the only chamber music that a listener, hearing it for the first time and knowing the orchestral music already, would realise was the work of the same man.

The Quartet is in five movements. There is cross-reference (indicated in the musical examples by square ties) between the first and second, the second, third and fourth, and again between third and fourth. These links are tenuous, carrying nothing from one movement to the next but an outline. The character of such an outline is often much changed by alterations of rhythm, by being placed differently in the surrounding texture, by harmonic alterations; and it soon disappears among the changed material of the new movement into which it has been transported. Into such a new movement it introduces nothing of its original character. It is no leading-motive but a purely constructional link from movement to movement carrying with it none of its original mood.

The five movements are therefore distinct in character one from the other. Cross-reference, though undoubtedly deliberate since it is too definite to be otherwise, serves no more serious purpose than to recall from time to time to a sufficiently alert listener the realisation that the five movements are not only separate entities but parts of a greater whole. The scheme becomes clearer with analysis.

I. Andante. This consists of eight bars of introduction, in the form of a dialogue between the first violin and the 'cello (Ex. 87). The 'cello theme is the more important for the part it has in the development of the movement as a whole; but both parts of the dialogue will be heard again. The lay-out between only two of the four instruments should be noted. A more romantic composer would have given the first phrase to the viola, the second to the 'cello, the third to the second violin, the fourth again to the 'cello; thus the start of the allegro in the ninth bar would have had extra significance when for the first time the one remaining instrument, and that the first violin, came into play. But that is the kind of deliberate artifice Sibelius often discards for a less sensuous manner of presenting the material he is to work upon. Hence the directness of this introduction.

As the pace suddenly quickens with the allegro molto moderato of the first movement proper it is seen that the opening melody (Ex. 88) is an extension of the first phrase previously announced by the 'cello. Note the descending fourth; there is a remarkable re-appearance of it, with the intervening steps filled in, at the opening of the last movement (Ex. 99). The music remains in or near the main key (D minor) and upon that tonic are based the first subsidiary theme (Ex. 89) and the second, more important, subsidiary (Ex. 90). The second subject (Ex. 91) is in the dominant, according to classical procedure. It is in the major mode and has a more gentle motion than any of the first-subject group. It has just time enough to make its quieter mood felt; but the whole movement is quickly displayed and these niceties of changing mood are liable to escape the listener. There is, for instance, a change soon after this to G minor and some reference to the first subject (Ex. 88). It is a constructional point which must be noted, for it marks the end of the exposition (of that we may be certain) and thus by inference the beginning of some sort of development. This section is in the nature of a short (31 bars) discussion mainly to do with the first subject (the descending fourth notably) which veers to a distant range of keys, reaches at the climax a diminished chord of which any one note could be a pivot to a new key, and then proceeds by a series of enharmonic changes to return to the original D minor. So the short development ends and the recapitulation begins with the dialogue (Ex. 87) now in quick time and accompanied by the rest of the quartet. This final section is the longest; there is development as well as re-statement of the themes in the first group. The second subject is plainly re-stated. The coda (più moderato) is founded on this material, but its climax is the descending fourth, and so the movement ends affirming that that was always its chief aim.

II. Vivace. A flutter of semiquavers, extremely soft, ushers in the main theme, based on the second subject of the previous movement but altogether transformed (Ex. 92). This feathery writing for strings in staccato repeated semiquavers, at once rapid and soft, recalls the storm in *En Saga*. But the likeness is not complete, for there the parts are in similar motion, while in the Quartet there is much contrary motion with abrupt leaps and accents. It is a style that has its counterpart in the Fifth Symphony at that point in the first movement where the dance section begins to develop over a horn pedal. Out of this shimmering motion in the Quartet a melodic figure, Ex. 93, comes to the surface and recalls a subsidiary unit of the previous movement (Ex. 90). On this material the movement is founded; as it progresses it becomes at first wayward and ejaculatory with sudden bar-long pauses. At length it gets fully under way, reaches a towering climax with the opening figure in octave quavers and then begins once more to decrease in volume. At the end there is a sudden outburst (Ex. 94) which is expressed in a figure that is to appear again, inverted, in the next two movements.

III. Adagio di molto. The mood changes to a profoundly lyrical utterance. The design is spacious; fourteen slow bars is the length of the opening melody alone. Even the shorter phrases (Ex. 95) of the subsidiary subject are built into a large pattern. This is the most eloquent of all the five movements, indeed one of the most passionate movements in all Sibelius's symphonic writing, a masterpiece of construction with every detail relevant, the thought guided by the closest reasoning and logically concluded.

IV. Allegretto (ma pesante). A true allegretto, never quickening until the final, very short stretto, and that pulled back at the finish into the normal heavier pace. It is direct expression, beginning immediately with the melody (Ex. 96) which dominates the movement and is to re-appear in the next. Before the first announcement of this melody there is a phrase (Ex. 97) based on the inversion of the cry at the end of the vivace (Ex. 94). This becomes a subsidiary theme and leads to the second main theme (Ex. 98). This material is developed and the texture is lightened somewhat. The movement then gathers force again. Broad rhythmic patterns founded on the subsidiary phrase (Ex. 97), the main theme implicit all the time, carry the music through to the allargando which ends the movement.

V. Allegro. An abrupt semiquaver figure opens the movement in something of the shattering style of the opening to the vivacissimo third movement in the Second Symphony. On this follows the passage, starting on the first violin's high D and descending stepwise a fourth, the point already mentioned in the analysis of the first movement (end of Ex. 88) and then begins the main subject (Ex. 99). There is next a passage which sounds like boisterous humour and one of a contrasting fineness; these now alternate and between them give rise to others. The pace increases and the work ends in a climax of intense energy.

The date of *Voces intimae* (1909) is two years after the Third Symphony and two before the Fourth. The String Quartet has certain affinities with both symphonies in style (the way the thought moves, the sequence of ideas and their development) and in material (length and compass of themes, relative proportion between conjunct and disjunct motion). Harmonically it shares the more unclouded diatonic manner of the Third. With the exception of the *In Memoriam* funeral march it is the sole abstract work to appear between these symphonies. Among post-Beethoven quartets it draws nearer to the unaffected lyricism of the Russians and Czechs than to the heavy expressiveness of the Germans and Austrians; the slow movement has neither the serenity nor the intensity of the later quartets of Beethoven. The mood seems untouched by that type of introspective melancholy. There is in it a dramatic fervour that can naturally go over into melodrama, a quality Beethoven never allowed in his string quartets though Tchaïkovsky did. But this adagio is too bare and terse for any but a hint of Tchaïkovsky to exist for long in its bracing atmosphere.

The general atmosphere of the rest of the chamber music can be suggested by considering certain works from early, middle and recent dates in Sibelius's career. Among early works there is *Malinconia*, Op. 20, for 'cello and pianoforte (1901). It is an extended lyrical out-pouring, in construction a free fantasia, in method relying on abundant pianoforte arpeggios and strong formations of double octaves, all of this a foil to the 'cello's solo voice. It is obsessive music; it lives up to its title. There is some grandeur in the 'cello's opening phrase and in its impassioned themes accompanied by syncopated pianoforte chords. But as a whole the work lacks that distinction which is now associated with Sibelius's name. It is sound work of an admirable late nineteenth-century romanticism.

In the middle period (1915) the Romance for violin or 'cello and pianoforte, from Op. 78 is a pleasant piece, still having about it an air of rather facile melodiousness. Nevertheless it is a more distinguished work than the Op. 20.

In the same year appeared the Six Pieces for violin and pianoforte, Op. 79. They have more individuality and are of a stronger character. The *Tempo di minuetto*, the finest of the set, is uneven in quality but shows traces of a manner of thought certifiably that of Sibelius. Its neglect by players is regrettable. Next in importance in this set is the *Danse caractéristique* which again could only have come from this composer, as is felt immediately the violin enters in C major against the pianoforte's sharpened leading note in A minor.

Another admirable chamber work belonging to this year is the

Op. 80 Sonatina for violin and pianoforte. It starts as though there were some remainder of a memory of Debussy's *Tierces alternées*. It continues quite differently in mood and manner. Note the craftsmanship in the first movement where the thirds are heard again, inserted with perfect tact into the general texture of the movement. The Sonatina is in three linked sections; the second has a particularly remarkable atmosphere created by a lilting slow accompaniment full of vague hesitations where the sound is carried on by the sustaining pedal.

Also to this year belong the Five Pieces for violin and pianoforte, Op. 81. Of these the mazurka has some character and could be heard again with pleasure. The valse should be looked at by connoisseurs of that dance (by them alone) for the hint it gives of the progress of that type from Austria through Russia to Finland; and for the signs it offers of the interaction of temperature and temperament.

Finally, the Four Pieces of Op. 115 and the Three of Op. 116, all for violin and pianoforte. These date from 1929 and are the latest known chamber music. In Op. 115, *On the heath* is disappointing. On the other hand, the Ballade, though it is harmonically jejune, has a certain dignity and grace.

In Op. 116 the first two, called *Scène de danse* and *Danse caractéristique*, are indubitable Sibelius, with a turn of phrase and a whole vocabulary that are his alone. These are strange little movements with a curious quality of concentrated thought throughout them. The idiom is derived from some essentially personal type of utterance, the last refinement of years of thought. These two pieces, on a different level from that of *Voces intimae*, produce an even stronger feeling of being the creation of a powerful mind. They afford the fascinating spectacle of such a mind filling a movement of an inherently slight nature with concentrated meaning.

# 5

## The Piano Music

### By

### Eric Blom

DESPITE HIS VARIED OUTPUT, Sibelius is almost as exclusively a master of the orchestra as Wagner is of the stage, Chopin of the pianoforte and Wolf of the song—and I put him in such great company of specialists deliberately. No other category of his work is really important, and the one exception, the String Quartet, is hardly in itself a category. Even his songs, which at one time promised to lead a life in their own right, have after all not shown very great vitality, and the most tenaciously favoured of them, it is curious to note, are those showing a strong inclination to court a wide and not particularly discriminating public. *Svarta Rosor* and *Flickan kom*, which are the most frequently sung, had very much the same kind of success as the *Valse triste*, *Finlandia* and the Romance in D flat in other departments of his art.

The Romance, which is relevant to this chapter, is representative of quite a large proportion of Sibelius's smaller piano pieces, and again, small pieces predominate vastly among his keyboard works. There are about 120 of them, a great many nothing more than the suavely lyrical things one may find in profusion among the piano works of Scandinavian composers like Gade, Kjerulf or Sjögren, or indeed among the lesser and not strongly characteristic Grieg. As for the more strikingly individual or national Grieg, there is little among the Sibelius pieces to match it. A large number of them may be said to be potboilers, if that term will be accepted as implying nothing more shameful than the supplying of pleasant recreation for the leisure hours of amateur pianists and providing a composer with an occupation which, though doubtless lucrative, is innocent of anything worse than agreeable trifling for the sake of harmless triflers. Certainly no worse accusation can be levelled at Sibelius for spinning a hundred and one innocuous yarns for the entertainment of those who would probably be worse occupied, at the piano or elsewhere, if he had devoted the time given to these pieces to an Eighth and Ninth Symphony instead—which is about what the saving of labour on the piano music would have represented in orchestral work. What he can decidedly not be reproached with is either scamping or skimping : his craftsmanship is perfectly adequate to small-scale work, so far as it needs to be called upon for that purpose, and his invention is never ungenerous even when it is unadventurous. Not that he writes for the piano as though it were congenial to him. A violinist by his youthful training and a composer who obviously has as little recourse to the keyboard for his orchestral music as Berlioz or Elgar had, he was rarely quite at ease when he felt called upon, whether by inspiration or practical expediency, to make the pianoforte his medium.

The question of Sibelius's keyboard-writing as such, which raises some quite interesting points, may be deferred for discussion when the smaller piano pieces come up for consideration. They could not possibly be dealt with one by one without imposing a severe trial on the reader's patience, but will be quite useful in a general way as material for the study of various matters. But first of all a closer investigation of the three most important works may be embarked on, after which the sets of smaller pieces may be left to take what chance they can.

These important works are the early Sonata in F major, Op. 12, the suite *Kyllikki*, Op. 41, and the three Sonatinas, Op. 67, all of them remarkable things enough and progressively more so as the opus numbers mount higher. The Sonatinas are undoubtedly the peak of Sibelius's achievement as a pianoforte composer—or rather as a great composer who happened just then to choose the keyboard instrument for his medium. After them there is a relapse into relative triviality, with one or two notable exceptions, such as the two Rondinos, Op. 68, which still reflect, as it were, something of the peculiarly choice quality that distinguishes their immediate predecessors.

The F major Sonata is in some ways a tentative but by no means an immature work. It is as orchestral as Greig's equally early Piano Sonata and has other Griegish qualities and defects, such as the static but harmonically flavoursome passage quoted in Ex. 100, a good deal of tremolo filling where a true pianist would have devised some more vital figuration, and an embarrassingly hesitant halt at the beginning of the first-movement working-out section. One can almost see Grieg, with pen lifted, waiting for the next idea to pay him a call, at the very juncture where one expects something to happen immediately. That working-out is very much protracted, but it does not sprawl, for it makes interesting use of the material stated in the exposition, even of some subordinate accompanying matter. Still, it is for that very reason not characteristically Sibelian : the developments are, though not exactly academic, too literal for that. Yet a passage jumps out at us from the middle of what is otherwise not very enterprising harmonic writing which points straight to the later symphonic manner (Ex. 101).

The recapitulation balances the exposition pretty symmetrically, except that what was a codetta at first becomes a coda of modest dimensions at the end. The key-sequence, on the other hand, is original. The transition to the new key for the second subject is made by the rather crude but quite ingenious device of suddenly letting the restatement of the first subject jerk down a semitone, and for the second subject Sibelius may be said to adapt the classical procedure for sonata-form works in minor tonalities to a sonata in a major key. A classic writing conventionally in the minor would have let his second subject appear first in the relative major and then in the tonic minor; Sibelius, writing in the major here, gives the second subject first in the dominant major and then in the tonic minor.

The middle movement alternates between slow and quick, thus representing both slow-movement and scherzo elements. The latter is good : a kind of lean and impish country dance, written almost wholly in two parts and a transposed Phrygian mode—C sharp with 3 sharps at first and later F with 5 flats. The slow portion also begins in the latter tonality, but is more indefinitely modal, for the G flat is immediately contradicted in the second bar and the melody later turns decidedly towards D flat major, a key that suits its character, for it is in that rather thick-blooded melancholy vein of the familiar *Black Roses* type which some people seem to like in Sibelius, but which is not to everyone's taste. At its restatement after the first quick episode the composer falls into the delusion common to many not especially pianistic writers (and even some particularly pianistic ones, like Rakhmaninov, for instance) that elaboration by means of arpeggios will be acceptable as development. It is, of course, nothing of the kind, for arpeggios merely amplify without intensifying. At the last return, on the other hand, the treatment of the tune is too much simplified to sustain the hearer's interest, or even the player's. Two pages of block chords in slow time spell dreariness.

The finale, in spite of a good deal of orchestral writing, is the best or at any rate the most characteristic movement. It is like a good and effective transcription of a symphonic piece in the *Saga* or *Lemminkäinen's Homecoming* manner, much shorter and less thrilling, but admirable in its way. The broad melody on chords alternating in syncopation that comes in at 'l'istesso tempo' (fortunately 'l'istesso tempo', for any slackening would have been disastrous) threatens for a moment to become as disconcerting as the slow section in the scherzo of the Second Symphony; but just as the latter is saved on being found to be relevant to the finale, so here an apparently incongruous lyrical incident is made valuable by being satisfactorily integrated into the structure.

*Kyllikki* is simply called ' three lyrical pieces' by the composer, but it is justifiable to describe it as a suite, because it is unified by the subject indicated in the title and obviously intended to hang together musically, both the first and the second movements ending inconclusively, so that an incomplete performance would be unsatisfactory. The work as a whole is clearly in a key scheme of B flat minor and major; but the first number ends in C sharp major (not, it is true, as far from the tonic as it appears on paper, the concluding key being merely the relative major—D flat—in enharmonic notation), while the second (a slow movement) finishes on a B flat minor chord in the first inversion. The music then goes into B flat major for the finale.

The subject, like so many of Sibelius's programmes for his orchestral works, comes from the *Kalevala*. It will be found in the eleventh Runo, dealing with Lemminkäinen and Kyllikki, and perhaps the opening of the twelfth, which is concerned with Lemminkäinen's first expedition to Pohjola. The arguments summarising the relevant portions of the poem may be quoted here from the Everyman edition of W. F. Kirby's translation of the Finnish national epic cycle :

> Lemminkäinen goes to seek a wife among the noble maidens of Saari. At first they laugh at him, but afterwards become very friendly. But Kyllikki, on whose account he has come, will not listen to him, and at length he carries her off by force, drags her into his sledge and drives away with her. Kyllikki weeps and especially reproaches Lemminkäinen with his fondness for war, and Lemminkäinen promises not to go to war if Kyllikki promises never to go to the village dances, and both swear to observe these conditions.
>
> Kyllikki forgets her oath and goes to the village, whereupon Lemminkäinen is enraged and resolves to divorce her immediately, and to set forth to woo the Maiden of Pohjola[1]. . . .

It would be unprofitable to try to fit the music closely to this tale; but there is no doubt that it wonderfully suggests the atmosphere of a story which turns primitive passions into a crude yet compelling poetry, and there is no harm in seeing in the three pieces a reflection

---

[1] The lady who has already played such tricks on Väinämöinen.

of three phases of the brief Kyllikki episode in Lemminkäinen's career, which is one of gallantry in both senses of the word, half heroic, half amorous.

The first piece frames within slow and emphatically declamatory phrases a darkly passionate and agitated movement written mainly in a manner which might be that of a very effective transcription of a welter of orchestral tremolos into pianistic figures that lie well under the hand and pass at least one test of good keyboard-writing by sounding more difficult than they are; Ex. 102 is a specimen. But there are also broken octaves and arpeggio passages demanding virtuosity and capable of sounding richly brilliant if they get it. The tale of a violent wooing and an abduction fits the music well enough.

The slow movement may be regarded as a troubled love scene with gloomy forebodings at the back of it and disturbed by agitations suggested by double and quintuple tremolos like shrieking trills distributed over a group of wood-wind instruments. The finale may very well be taken to represent Kyllikki at the dance. It is light and graceful, yet by no means carefree, and the tranquillo episode in the middle is another of those strange Sibelian lapses into a kind of sluggish gloom in the course of an animated movement. The conclusion is abrupt and utterly simple : as usual, Sibelius disdains to perorate; he just stops when there is nothing more to say.

There is a marked resemblance, in manner and often even in expression, between *Kyllikki* and the Violin Concerto, which, although it bears a later opus number (47), dates from 1903, whereas the piano suite was written in 1904. The same distance of about a year separates the Sonatinas (Op. 67, 1912) from the Fourth Symphony (Op. 63, 1911), and here again there is a strong resemblance. The A minor Symphony is still the least familiar, still the most mysterious and fascinating, of Sibelius's seven, though it is absurd to excuse its neglect by pretending that it is obscure and impossibly difficult to grasp; and mysteriously fascinating in much the same way are the Sonatinas. But there is a difference in size and importance. Sibelius's best piano work is very slender. In that respect, if any comparison must be made, it has to be sought elsewhere. One's first thought goes to late Beethoven, and reflection confirms that for apparent slightness combined with concentrated significance nothing else in pianoforte music resembles these Sonatinas so much as the two sets of Bagatelles of Beethoven's final period.

The simplicity of the Sonatinas may be illustrated by the typical opening of No. 1 (Ex. 103). A single stave is used here for convenience of quotation, but it is astonishing to find, on looking through the first Sonatina with a view to such simplification of notation, how much of it could be thus reduced without confusing the eye or resorting to many leger-lines.

The publishers, seeing three sharps in the key-signature, calmly describe No. 1 as being a Sonatina in A major. A glance at the work as a whole shows quite plainly that it is in F sharp minor, all three movements of it, though the second ends in the major. True, the opening of the first is not in that key, nor indeed even in A major : it is plain D major; but although the key-signature leads one to expect a transposed Lydian mode and the next key glanced at actually is A major, there is no doubt about the predominance of F sharp minor, for all that initial mystification. The slight tonal vagueness and the deliberate evasion of clear tonic-and-dominant implications result in the kind of subtlety that often makes Gabriel Fauré's piano music so alluring; and although, except for the finale of the third Sonatina (Ex. 104), Sibelius here never suggests anything remotely resembling Fauré's often elaborate and sometimes too uniform figuration, there is in these works something not by any means unlike the French master when he is purposely simple, as for instance in the adorable song *Lydia* or in some of the equally adorable *Pièces brèves* for piano. French critics, who have so far never had the least use for Sibelius and whose stock adjectives for their ideal music are *dépouillé* and *pudique*, might do worse than favour the Sonatinas with some attention.

If *dépouillé* means ' stripped ', that is certainly what these three great little works are. Their bareness is not one of texture merely : it is also formal. Every statement is direct and to the point; the demarcations between exposition, working-out and recapitulation are deliberately blurred; there are in fact no conventional stages, much less conventional developments. Yet, while the musical discourses are never labelled as premisses, arguments or conclusions, they proceed none the less logically—in fact more so, for the composer treats us to pure cogent musical thinking without relying on the oratorical paddings that pass for eloquence but are too often only empty phrase-making kept going while the speaker tries to think of the next significant thing to say.

There seems to be a deliberate intention to concentrate on the key-centres of each of the three Sonatinas and thus to hold in leash rather than give free rein to the creative forces at work on them. It is doubtless not by accident that No. 2, which is in E major, also keeps its three movements in the principal key. The third, again, remains in B flat minor—with plenty of incidental excursions into other keys, of course. This work, however, has not, strictly speaking, three movements but only two, the second being a sort of gradual progression from a march-like andante to a kind of condensed rondo made of the same material, transformed by a process of acceleration (see Ex. 104).

So much for the three principal pianoforte works. The pity is that more cannot be said about them and that not sufficient space remains to discuss a few of the smaller pieces with some thoroughness. It is tempting, in particular, to give a good deal of attention to the two Rondinos, Op. 68. Not only because they follow Op. 67 immediately, but also because they continue in something like the same vein, one may quite easily imagine them to be final movements of two more incomplete sonatinas, in G sharp minor and C sharp minor. The fact that the first is marked andantino does not, when Sibelius is in the exploratory mood shown at this stage of his career, disqualify it from being a finale; neither is the slowish pace and 9–8 time against its displaying the character of a rondo, though the brisk 2–4 motion of the second Rondino accords far more closely with the classical notion of what a rondo should be, considered as a last sonata movement rather than as a form. The second piece is harmonically piquant; the first is the more appealing of the two and beautifully written for the instrument in a spare, economical yet richly satisfying way. One thinks of a Chopin prelude looking some way into the future.

To claim for many of the other pieces that they are beautifully written would be extravagant. Sibelius's catalogue shows that most of them were composed in sets, some containing as many as ten and one even thirteen numbers. This suggests inescapably that on the whole he did not compose for the pianoforte spontaneously, because his fancy often took him that way, but that he regarded the turning out of keyboard pieces as a task, not indeed to be undertaken without pleasure merely because it happened to be expedient, but principally a duty nevertheless. What follows? Clearly the realisation that he was not irresistibly drawn to the pianoforte by having something to say that could not be expressed in any other terms, but that he went on inventing a number of small things without always being in a particularly pianistic frame of mind, and then, having found his ideas, proceeded to present them as adequately as possible in terms of the instrument. The results of this cart-before-the-horse process of creation (which *mutatis mutandis* is rather like Tennyson's or Browning's writing for the stage) could not fail to be sometimes uninspired and occasionally trivial in his case, and there is nothing inexplicable about the fact that while some of the inventions adapted themselves quite satisfactorily to the medium chosen by or imposed on the composer, others had to be more or less arbitrarily adjusted to it. Hence, no doubt, the inequality not only in the musical value of Sibelius's small piano pieces, but also in their pianistic lay-out. He simply is not a born pianist-composer. Let us think again for a moment of his Violin Concerto : it sounds as if he could not have avoided writing it even if he had tried to prevent himself. On the other hand, a pianoforte concerto from his pen just cannot be imagined.

Now there is no need to pretend that only truly pianistic piano music is ever worth playing and hearing. Such a notion would dispose, for example, of Schubert's sonatas and Mussorgsky's *Exhibition Pictures* at a stroke of a rashly critical pen; and there is no need to insist on the appalling expense of mediocrity in a waste of polished keyboard phraseology that has amassed mountains of unplayed and forgotten rubbish ever since the harpsichord gave place to the fortepiano—not to mention the rubbish that is remembered and played. After all, the pianoforte is not just an instrument intended to display nothing but itself and the music ideally suited to its peculiarities. It is an instrument not only in universal use but of universal utility : it can do many things, and much of what it cannot do it can suggest. There is no good reason why all its resources, including even those of compromise, should not be exploited by its performers, who would be very much the poorer in musical experience if they were never to touch any music but that by composers who happen to have made a speciality of it. No amateur pianist could claim to be much of a musician who had not studied many operas and oratorios at his instrument from vocal scores and who had always declined to play arrangements of symphonic and chamber music for two or four hands. And almost as poor in spirit would be the player who refused to have anything to do with original keyboard music without first making strict inquiries about the composer's bona fide as a purveyor of good keyboard-writing rather than of music that is good of its kind, whatever that kind may be.

The way to approach Sibelius's smaller piano pieces is to search them for good music, not for ideal piano music. Even so they will not be found very rewarding, and when the trivialities have been weeded out and the agreeable trifles found to have worn thin after being given the fair chance of repeated trial, not much will remain. But the process of judging will itself have been worth while as an experience, and the discovery will have been made that the piano—which is nothing if not a generous instrument—has sometimes made a Sibelius piece valuable enough to cherish for some length of time, even where the composer did not go out of his way to make himself congenial to it. For it is not always when he is most pianistic that Sibelius is musically most engaging. The eight pages of arpeggios of which the fifth of the Impromptus, Op. 5, consists, comprising more than half a page of concluding B minor common chords, are nothing if not good piano music—unless they are still better harp music; but the piece is tiresome beyond words. The Waltz in D flat, Op. 34, No. 1, could not have been better devised for the instrument if it had been by Durand or Chaminade, but it is musically no improvement on such drawing-room writers, save for just a spice of something more in one or two places, including a clash of E flat and E natural so daring in such a context that one wonders for a moment whether it is not a misprint. On the other hand, some of the best things, musically, are hardly pianoforte music at all in any technical sense. The five curious, strangely modal tree pieces, Op. 75, for instance, such as *The Aspen* (sic), which is Phrygian in G sharp, contain things that would sound far more perfect in a string orchestra; and one almost feels sure of having heard the very typically Sibelian phrase, Ex. 105, from *The Birch Tree* in some orchestral work, scored for flute and two bassoons with violas or a horn sustaining the B flat in the middle.

Sometimes one is aware of a conflict between musical and instrumental claims, as in the five charming flower pieces, Op. 85. Here and there arpeggios or chord-groupings make excellent effects, and so does such a passage as Ex. 106 in *The Snapdragon*—almost a Schumannesque *Blumenstück*. But elsewhere, in *The Iris* for example, the composer just happens to have something very characteristic to say that will not adjust itself happily to the keyboard. Nevertheless he says it, and one should be grateful when it is as individually flavoured as here.

These tree and flower pieces often have a distinctly Finnish character, or what Sibelius has accustomed us to regard us a Finnish character, though it may be much more peculiarly his own. This emerges even more strongly in his pianoforte arrangement of six Finnish folksongs, published without an opus number and dated 1903. They are especially interesting, not only on that account, but also because they compromise admirably between three claims—that of the spirit of the originals, that of music as an art and that of the piano as an instrument. One of them, entitled *Fratricide*, is remarkable moreover for its curious resemblance to Bartók's arrangements of

Hungarian folk music, where, as in Sibelius's case, one is never quite sure how much is national and how much is personal. Can it be that this unexpected contact between two otherwise quite different composers has something to do with the affinities between the Finnish and the Hungarian languages, which both belong to the Finno-Ugrian division of the Ural-Altaic group? For words obviously influence the metres and cadences of folksong.

Except in some of the best things already mentioned, the ' Finnish ' Sibelius—which may be to say the most personal Sibelius—rarely emerges in the piano music, which often aims at a kind of cosmopolitan suavity and deals with topics likely to be discussed and understood in drawing-rooms all over the civilised world. We have already met pieces that might be French; well, the delightful Humoresque, Op. 40, No. 3, might be a Czech polka by Smetana, the Mazurka, Op. 34, No. 3, and the Polonaise, Op. 40, No. 10, could just as well be genuinely Polish, and so on.

Sometimes the small pieces are too simple to hold the musician's interest for long and technically too easy to entice the accomplished pianist; but there are a few very pretty things among those that remain fairly easy all through, such as the *Dance Air*, Op. 34, No. 2, a captivating little gavotte with a winsome interrupted cadence (Ex. 107) near the end. Such attractive trifles will always endear themselves to those who cannot master great difficulties and do not ask for much significance or great depth. But there are many pieces in which Sibelius seems to be unsure about the kind of player he addresses, or appears not to care whether the appeal he makes has any sort of consistency. He will often begin very simply and keep going for two or three pages in a vein that cannot be expected to hold the interest of any but technically modest players; and then, in order to build up a climax, he will suddenly confront these players with difficulties they cannot possibly overcome, while those who can will not keep their patience during the first and last simple pages. The Idyll, Op. 24, No. 4, has, for once, more than a surface charm so long as it remains simple, but it becomes quite incongruously over-elaborate in the middle, and much the same is true of No. 8 in the same set, a Nocturne that is easy enough to play until it reaches a climax which does not disdain even the meretricious virtuosic effect of ' blind octaves ' (Ex. 108). These over-steep climaxes seem to be altogether a special fault of Op. 24. It will be remembered that the cadenza in the familiar D flat major Romance, which is No. 9 of that set, is a particularly bad example of it.

However, it tends to disappear in the later pianoforte works, and there is not a trace of it in the very best of them, the Sonatinas and Rondinos, which on the contrary state what they have to say with extraordinary economy and point. The originality of these, and of such things as the tree and flower pieces, occasionally begins to come out earlier—in the quite easy but strikingly individual Andantino, Op. 24, No. 7, for instance, or the capricious, spoilt-child Scherzino, Op. 58, No. 2. And when all is said, a number of very attractive things will be found scattered up and down the Sibelian pianoforte catalogue, in which the reader whose curiosity has, it is hoped, been sufficiently whetted by this all to brief survey, must now be left to browse alone.

# 6

## *The Songs*

### By

### Astra Desmond

SIBELIUS AS A SONG-WRITER is inevitably dwarfed by the greatness of Sibelius the symphonist; so that it is difficult to avoid some disappointment upon a first acquaintance with his songs. This is not to deny that some of them are masterpieces, but it is true that they are very uneven in quality and do not show the wide range of expression we are used to in the orchestral works. Certain weaknesses mar many of them, such as a tendency to end a song too abruptly with the last word of the poem, without any postlude or suitable rounding-off; a poverty of invention in much of the pianoforte writing; and a rather too frequent use of orchestral devices. He is also too fond of using the lower registers which, so effective in his orchestral writing, sound heavy and turgid on the pianoforte (cf. *Till Frigga*, Op. 13, No. 6, and *Vattenplask*, Op. 61, No. 2). But these faults are counter-balanced by the deep sincerity, the intellectual grasp of form, the rhythmic invention and the outstanding power of creating atmosphere and colour which mark his best songs.

If his songs are to be judged fairly, it is essential that we clear our minds of all preconceived ideas of song as exemplified by the German *Lied*. Whereas the German *Lied* has evolved from the *Volkslied*, Sibelius seems to have gone back to some ancient declamatory style, such as the bards may have used. It is, therefore, inadvisable to study or sing the songs in German translations, for, excellent though many of these are, we are liable unconsciously to try and fit them into the familiar *Lied*-form, and the better the songs fit that form the less good they generally are. Also, though superficially Swedish and German are very similar, the rhythm of Swedish is quite unlike the rhythm of German, and a melodic line that suits one often sounds awkward in the other. That songs do not take the high place in his general output that Schubert's, for instance, do in his, must be admitted, but that there is much to be found in them worthy of admiration and study, it is the task of this chapter to show.

In the place of pure melody, Sibelius has evolved a kind of declamatory recitative (not in any way to be confused with what is known as *Sprechgesang*), which is singularly beautiful and expressive and quite peculiar to himself. As often in Sibelius's music one feels he has tapped some primeval source of inspiration, so here one feels he has gone back to a rhapsodic style that ancient minstrels may have used; indeed many of his accompaniments can be equally well played on a harp. His vocal line sweeps over the whole range of the voice with great freedom and is capable of dispensing with any accompanying harmony for long stretches at a time. One of the most striking examples of this is *Höstkväll*, Op. 38, No. 1. His unusual style does not always appeal at a first hearing, but his best songs grow upon one more and more. They are exacting, as they need a voice of wide range and the use of the original text for their full effect, for Sibelius sets his words very sensitively, and his style changes completely according to whether he is setting texts in Finnish or in Swedish, in which latter language the bulk of his songs are written.

To anyone familiar with his orchestral music it will not be surprising that his best songs are concerned directly or indirectly with Nature and her moods. Love lyrics do not seem to attract him unless there is a secondary Nature theme, such as in the lovely *Langsamt som kvällskyn*, Op. 61, No. 1, where the fading colours and sounds of sunset provide the main interest for him. The popular love song *Var det en dröm*, Op. 37, No. 4, would be rather ordinary but for the intricate cross-rhythms with which he has disguised his lack of inspiration.

A few of his songs have achieved wide popularity, notably *Svarta Rosor*, Op. 35, No. 1, and *Flickan kom*, Op. 37, No. 5, and are consequently despised by ' the few ', but they illustrate the forthright common sense of the composer and his complete lack of musical snobbishness. These songs are direct in their appeal and more or less contradict all that has been said above about his style.

Sibelius's opus numbers contain such a mixture of good and bad songs that it is pointless to attempt to trace his development as a songwriter chronologically. It seems better to deal first with those opus numbers (37, 35, 36, 38 and 50) which fall into the particularly prolific period between 1895 and 1905, and which include so many of his most famous songs. The others will then be dealt with in order—with certain gaps, inevitable through inability to procure copies in present world conditions—leaving the two great songs with orchestra, Op. 33 and Op. 70, to the last.

Op. 37, No. 1. *Den första kyssen* (*The first kiss*).

On the edge of a silver cloud sat the Evening Star. From the grove a maiden asked 'Evening Star, what think they up in heaven when love's first kiss is given?' Heaven's pale daughter answered, 'The angel hosts look down and see their own bliss reflected—only Death turns away his eyes and weeps' (Runeberg).

This simple and lovely song is worth study not only for its beauty but because it offers several examples of points of style that will be found in other of his songs. The phrase quoted as Ex. 109, which occurs in the introduction and in the voice part, is a favourite one to convey a question, or a feeling of uneasiness, as in *Höstkväll*, Op. 38, No. 1. Here it beautifully expresses the upturned questioning gaze of the girl. The spareness of the accompaniment, in unison with the voice, gives a feeling of coolness and clarity. The wide span of melody which carries the question and the star's reply foreshadows that melodic line which reaches its highest perfection in *Höstkväll*.

The heavy chordal accompaniment in the second half of the verse is also very typical (cf. *Men min fågel*, Op. 36, No. 2) and here seems to be used to contrast the majesty of the starry sphere with the simplicity of the young girl. A curiously dead-sounding chord precedes the sentence 'Only Death . . .', modulating with poignant effect on the word 'weeps', and then lingering on the leading note before coming to rest on the already resolved chord beneath it—a device that will be met with over and over again.

Op. 37, No. 2. *Lasse liten* (*Little Lasse*) (Topelius). This curious lullaby is an example of a song marred by the excessive lowness of the accompaniment, which is almost exclusively in the bass clef. Presumably the composer wishes to convey an idea of the grim dangers that await the child should it stray from its mother's arms, but it is not very convincing.

Op. 37, No. 3. *Soluppgång* (Sunrise).

It is dawn; sea and snowy lands lie still beneath the rosy sky. A knight stands at the window listening for sounds of battle and paces the floor. Then a tiny snow-white hand cools his brow. He blows his horn; and golden-red the sun slowly rises (Hedberg).

A rhythmical figure accompanies the description of the still frosty dawn. A short trumpet-call is followed by a restless arpeggio as the knight paces the floor. Gentle arpeggios accompany an exquisitely tender passage as the 'snow-white hand' steals over his brow. After the blast of the horn the echoes die away, and the opening figure returns as quiet settles upon the scene and the sun rises in a softly-rising vocal phrase. This otherwise beautiful and dramatic song suffers from an excessively abrupt ending, a fault we find only too often in the songs. The beautiful effect of the slow soft rising of the sun is subtly conceived but it needs something more than the rather banal ' Amen ' close to make it effective.

Op. 37, No. 4. *Var det en dröm* (*Was it a dream?*) (Wecksell) is for some reason one of the more popular of Sibelius's songs, perhaps because it is one of the few love songs and has a warm and grateful voice part. Its rather conventional nature is disguised by the highly intricate rhythmical pattern of the pianoforte part. This complicated accompaniment seems to rob the song of much of its spontaneity, though admittedly some singers do not let it trouble them, and get over the difficulty by ignoring the accompaniment and leaving the pianist to follow as best he can.

Op. 37, No. 5. *Flickan kom ifran sin älsklings möte* (generally known as *The Tryst*).

> The maiden comes from the tryst with reddened fingers and lips, and to her mother's questions she replies with excuses of rose-thorns that have scratched her and raspberries that she has eaten. The third time she comes with blanched cheeks and bids her mother make her grave and write thereon how her lover, who reddened her fingers and her lips, now has blanched her cheeks by his betrayal (Runeberg).

This is one of the best known of the songs and deservedly so, for it tells a very human story—a story that might well be a folk tale—in a very moving and dramatic way. The fine passionate phrase with which it opens is very ingeniously used to represent the girl's true feeling. It appears in the accompaniment only in the verses where she is making excuses to her mother, and not until the last verse, when she tells the true story, does it appear in the voice part. The pianoforte opens with this phrase, but before it finishes, the voice interrupts with the narrative; short urgent snatches of melody in the bass belie the girl's pretended calmness, and each time she has given her excuse the pianoforte completes the interrupted phrase. The third verse opens very quietly over a sustained chord, and then quickens as the terrified mother questions her daughter for the third time and the girl gathers all her strength for her answer. Now the true facts are given out with the opening melody in the voice part, and voice and pianoforte end together with the completed phrase. Here the song rightly ends without any postlude—none is needed.

This song is sometimes underestimated by musicians in this country, perhaps as a result of the banal translation in which it is generally sung; and also because of a fatal tendency in singers to drag and sob the last phrase instead of finishing it at white heat.

Op. 36, No. 1. *Svarta Rosor (Black roses)*.

' Say, why are you so sad to-day, you who always are so gay? ' ' Never am I sadder than when I appear to be gay—for sorrow bears black-petalled roses.

A rose-tree grows in my heart and its thorns fill me with pain and bitterness.

My rose-tree will bear a wealth of roses, whiter than death, redder than blood. It grows, I faint, it wrenches my heart and slays me. For sorrow has black-petalled roses ' (Josephson).

This song rivals the previous one in popularity and also suffers badly in translation. But as the original poem is not a very good one that is not surprising. However, Sibelius has used the ballad style with considerable effect. Over a simple arpeggio accompaniment in C major the voice enters; a change into E major enhances the effect of gaiety ('Who always are so gay ') and a sudden return to the C major with the flattening of the G sharp to G natural has a curiously damping effect as the sufferer replies with her tale of tragedy. In the second verse the vocal line takes on a wider span and then changes to a recitative on a single note against a tremolo and chords in sixths, rising chromatically in the bass to a climax, after which the voice drops to the refrain, ' For sorrow has black-petalled roses '. The third verse is similarly treated with increasing intensity until the refrain reappears an octave higher than before and marked fortissimo.

Here a small advantage that the original text has is worth observing. The last word is ' rosor ' (roses)—and the two syllables appear on the first and third beats of the bar. This perfectly conforms to the rhythm of the Swedish word but causes an undue stress on the weak syllable of ' roses ' (or ' Rosen ' in German).

Op. 36, No. 2. *Men min fågel märks dock icke (But my bird is long in homing)*.

The birds are all waiting for the call of spring. She comes and entices them with sunshine and warmth.

I, poor maiden, long to dispel the darkness of longing, to be friendly as the spring and light as a summer's day. And I laugh while sorrow gnaws me, but my bird does not return (Runeberg).

This song has a curiously square-cut melody, moving in even crotchets for long stretches, while the accompaniment doubles the voice for much of the time : yet there is a haunting poignancy, expressive of the girl's deep sadness. Two bars of heavy chords in sequence accompany 'entices them with sunshine' at the end of the first verse. The second verse works up to a climax on 'summer's day', followed by the same chord sequence as ended verse one; but this time with the voice singing the same melody full voice—only to break off suddenly before the pathetically simple 'but my bird . . .'. This is one of the songs that call for a voice of wide range, as it must be effective from low B to top A.

Op. 36, No. 3. *Bållspelet vid Trianon (Tennis at Trianon)* (Fröding).

This setting of Fröding's rather macabre poem is in strong contrast to the other two songs of this set of three. A charming little minuet played in the treble clef and a graceful melody in the voice describe the elegant lords and ladies chattering and playing in their rustic costumes. Suddenly the music stops after a quick descending chromatic scale on the pianoforte. An unkempt head appears from behind a tree. Consternation and alarm reign for a few moments, the gentlemen try to go on with their tennis, but jerky staccato chords show that the Vicomte is missing the ball— and everyone is asking questions. Then, inconsequently, all is forgotten and the minuet is resumed, while the ladies turn up their noses and click their heels. Again the music breaks off and after a pause the narrator, in a serious voice, unaccompanied, save at the end, sings, 'But silently, with heavy tread goes the headsman's son, Jourdan Coupe-tête!' In this song Sibelius displays an unusual lightness of touch which makes it useful as a contrast in a group.

Op. 36, No. 4. *Säf, säf, susa (Sigh, sedges, sigh)*.

Sigh, sedges, beat, ye waves! Ye tell me whither young Ingalill has gone. With a cry like a wounded bird's she sank into the lake. They were cruel to her in Östanålid, she took it so to heart. They pierced a jewel with thorns, they besmirched a lily's dew. Sing your dirge. Sigh, sedges, beat ye, waves! (Fröding).

Here we find fully developed the Sibelian quasi-recitative style which is typical of his finest songs. Over a harp-like accompaniment of rising arpeggios the voice enters sostenuto in a falling phrase to words the sheer beauty of which cannot be reproduced in another language: ' Säf, säf, susa; våg, våg, slå '. A sudden crescendo leads to a high tremolo which accompanies the account of Ingalill's death, given in a vivid recitative. A swift down-rushing arpeggio bar leads into a largamente section, ' they pierced a jewel . . .' backed by heavy chords which sound like a denunciation, followed by a quick uprush of notes like a flash of anger. Then sudden silence, as if to say, ' Of what use is anger now she is dead? ' and the song closes with a reprise of the sighing movement with which it began. Here Sibelius had the double attraction of a romantic story and an opportunity for creating atmosphere and the result is one of his most beautiful and successful songs.

Op. 36, No. 5. *Marssnön (March snow)*.

> The cool snow falls and lies in whorls upon the ground. Keep shut your eyes, O Spring, sleep softly in the kindly snow, so more glorious may be your blossoming, more rich your death (J. J. Wecksell).

Written in 5/4 time, the melody of this exquisite little song winds on and on as if there were no barlines—giving an effect of ' the smooth monotony of snow ', to quote Alfred Austin. Then it takes on a more definite character at the call to Spring and rises to a majestic climax and a change to 6/4 time at ' more rich your death '. This is a most valuable song which deserves to be better known.

Op. 36, No. 6. *Demanten på Marssnön (The Diamond on March snow)*.

> On the snowdrift a diamond gleamed. In longing she gazed at the rising sun. At the foot of his ray she lay and worshipped, and melted into a teardrop. O happy fate to love the highest, and to die when most sweetly he smiles! (J. J. Wecksell).

This song is a companion piece to No. 5 and though not as perfect as the latter it is very lovely and is a great favourite in Scandinavia and Finland. It is strophic in form and set to a beautiful melody over a simple accompaniment, decorated with a little phrase like an extended turn which suggests the sparkle of the little snowflake. A charming touch is the change of the last note of the second verse from the fifth, as in verse one, to a rise to the keynote above it on the word ' smiles '. The chord which accompanies it is also spread to enhance the bright effect.

We now come to Op. 38, two songs of which mark the highest point to which Sibelius has brought his individual style.

Op. 38, No. 1. *Höstkväll (Autumn Evening)*.

> The sun is setting, clouds wander sadly above the lake. Sea-mews are crying and the falcon wearily hides her beak in her downy wing. The sun has set; darkness falls; the sound of rain and the beating of the waves are like voices of anguish in the storm. A wayfarer stands, entranced, he listens and is content.
> Does his soul feel harmony with the night?
> Does his sorrow die with the sorrows of autumn? (Rydberg).

This wonderful song, to which reference has already been made, exists also in an orchestral version, and it is interesting to see how certain orchestral devices on the pianoforte appear in orchestral form, the latter being apparently later than the pianoforte edition.

The song opens with a full chord of D minor which is sustained through the bold opening statement, ' The sun is setting . . .', after which the voice continues, unaccompanied for five bars, rising and falling in the melodious recitative. Two very typical phrases appear; the one that was quoted in the first song discussed, *Den första kyssen*, Op. 37, No. 1, and another consisting of a drop of a fifth which gives a most pathetic effect. The sense of desolation is heightened by the eerie note of the sea-mew suggested by D double sharp against D sharp in the bass. The hiding of the falcon's beak is accompanied by a passage of fluttering minor seconds alternately rising and falling. On comparing this with the orchestral score we find a favourite Sibelian device—a tremolo in the strings, so divided that they play in contrary motion, resulting in a kind of shimmer (cf. a similar device in *Tapiola* where the divided strings sweep up and down with a throbbing effect).

The sun sets and darkness falls: note the curious hush obtained by a piano F sharp minor chord instead of the unaccompanied top A in the voice of the previous verse. The rain falls to an octave tremolo, and as the storm begins to gather, the voice sweeps in great ever-widening phrases, reaching a climax on top B; then the octave tremolo slows down to a single note and we become aware of a wayfarer standing engrossed in the scene. His spirit is drawn into harmony with the landscape, and on the word ' njuter ' (lit: ' enjoys ' or ' finds satisfaction ') the voice holds a D natural on the first syllable for a bar and a half against a crescendo of arpeggios in C sharp major before coming to rest on the C sharp, and it seems as if the man were holding back the whole force of nature before allowing himself to be drawn into unity with her. The first of the two questions is sung fortissimo over massive chords and the song ends on a note of quiet resignation.

There is hardly a bar in this song that could have been written by any other composer and it stands out among the songs as *Tapiola* does among the smaller orchestral works.

Op. 38, No. 2. *På verandan vid hafvet* (*On a balcony by the sea*).

Mindest thou the sigh of the waves as they seek in vain the shores of eternity; or the pitiful gleam of the endless stars?
Ah! that all must perish at last!
Mindest thou the silence of earth and sea and sky as if in the fore-knowledge of God? (Rydberg).

In this song the desolation is not physical but spiritual, and in its way it is as expressive as *Höstkväll* is. It is built upon Ex. 110, followed by a falling of sighing thirds with which the introduction begins, like a question left unanswered, and the voice enters in a typical recitative. Voice and pianoforte repeat the original theme in other keys with ever greater urgency, till finally, over a crescendo tremolo low down in the bass, the voice returns to the declamatory style and ends in a great fortissimo which rings out high in the voice with terrible poignancy. Sibelius has here achieved a remarkable effect of spiritual loneliness combined with great beauty.

Op. 38, No. 3. *I Natten* (*In the Night*).

> Silence reigns and evening shimmers on the temple hill,
> > silently dreaming.
> Silently fade the stars, the wind sighs in the myrtle wood,
> > silently dreaming.
> Weary the Naïad sinks to sleep by the basin's edge,
> > silently dreaming.
> She sees the stream of life stand still, and all the world
> > asleep in All-Father's arm,
> > silently dreaming.
> > > (Rydberg).

This is not quite such a good song as the other two, but is remarkable as a study in silence and darkness. This is achieved by a long winding melody in the accompaniment, both hands playing single notes in unison, an octave apart, low down in the bass clef while a flattening of the sixth adds a touch of mystery. The voice then enters in canon. A second section opens with broken chords accompanying a warmer and more lyrical melody in the voice part. The second verse is almost identical with the first and one cannot help feeling that the composer's interest has flagged a little before the end of this rather long song and one wishes he had made rather more of the last lines of the poem and not finished off quite so abruptly. The fine opening section calls to mind Handel's ' The people that walked in darkness'. Both composers use a moving unison, and while Handel's line is perfect for his purpose so is that of Sibelius which curves in on itself, a subtle modification conveying stillness as well as darkness in contrast to Handel's which had to convey movement.

Op. 38, No. 4. *Harpolekaren och hans son* (*The Harper and his son*) (Rydberg), and

No. 5, *Jag ville jag vore* (*I would I were*) (Fröding), are neither of them in the same class as Nos. 1, 2 and 3.

The Harper has a square-cut melody somewhat like that of *Men min fågel*, Op. 36, No. 2, but though it has a certain charm one gets a little weary before the end of a rather long song, and the very solid arpeggiando chords which form much of the accompaniment are heavy and dull. No. 5, *Jag ville jag vore*, is more interesting and shows some enterprise in the pianoforte writing, though here again Sibelius's passion for the lower registers rather detracts from the exuberance. In Fröding's exotic poem the singer dreams of ' a magic palace on India's strand, of a dusky beauty who whispers of Karma's strife and Nirvana's repose '. Here with a few sustained chords he subtly suggests an organ tone, somewhat in the way Hugo Wolf does in *Auf ein altes Bild*.

An interesting comparison can be made with a later song *Vårtagen*, Op. 61, No. 8, another song expressing vain desires which has a very similar vocal line.

In Op. 35 we find two magnificent songs.

Op. 35, No. 1. *Jubal*.

> Jubal saw a swan flying—swiftly he drew his bow. Clang! The bird fell, dying, into the waves. The sun was just setting in a rosy glow, a soft melodious wind caressed Jubal's cheeks and ruffled the waves. The swan sang: ' How sweet was the note that rang from your bow when you brought me to earth! String to string shall you bind, and sing to all the world your Maker's praise! '
>
> Jubal sang: ' White swan, every evening will I sing of your death, for you have laid on me the minstrel's task ' (Josephson).

In this superb song Sibelius gives his own individual style the freest expression. The voice is almost throughout unaccompanied, save where there is a background of shimmering octaves, and the matching of words with music is faultless. A single D in alt, preceded by the three octaves below as grace notes, begins the song. The voice then enters alone with a sweeping phrase which suggests the swan's lofty flight. The twang of the bowstring and the flight of the arrow are suggested on the pianoforte. Then follows a more lyrical section over a recurring octave figure (Ex. 111) to which short snatches of melody are added in the bass.

The words of the swan are set to the same notes as the opening phrase, which is subtly altered in time values and broken up into short phrases to suggest the dying bird's supreme effort. A brilliant scale passage precedes ' string to string shall you bind '. In high exaltation Jubal promises obedience; the key then changes to the minor and after an interlude Jubal, now sobered by the solemn charge laid upon him, accepts his lot and the shimmering octaves gradually die away. Like so many of Sibelius's songs, this requires a voice of wide range able to compass its great rhapsodic sweep.

Op. 35, No. 2. *Teodora.*

> A rustling of silk, a shimmer of rubies,
> The night is still and the full moon shines,
> She comes, the Empress, she approaches, Theodora,
> Now she approaches my pleasure-garden where roses of Orient
>     bloom and fountains plash.
> She comes with stealthy tread, with limbs trembling with desire.
> Theodora, I will kiss thy traitorous lips,
> Theodora, I will trust thy vows that are false,
> And forget the ruin that follows in thy wake (Gripenberg).

This, though technically a love song, is actually a brilliant study in atmosphere and quite unlike any other of the songs. For sheer unhealthiness it can only be compared with Strauss's *Salome*, but here the atmosphere is created with the barest minimum of material while Strauss uses the whole range of orchestral colour.

The seven-note figure Ex. 112, played pianissimo and una corda forms, with but slight variations, the only accompaniment for nearly three pages, conveying a feeling of secrecy. The voice enters mezza voce in monotone, then rises in a stealthy scale from low C double sharp to the keynote B, followed by a drop of a diminished fourth, three times repeated, with strangely enervating effect. The seven-note figure quickens to one of ten notes with the approach of the lustful Empress, and the voice rises to the high G in suppressed excitement, and still mezza voce, on the word 'Teodora'. Then as the lover describes his garden and the Empress's stealthy approach, the voice moves up and down the scale in intervals never more than a second apart, over a rippling and cascading accompaniment, after which the first theme returns, as the lover gloats over the pleasure to come, and the only forte in the whole song comes on the word 'ljuga' (false) as he defies the knowledge of her falsehood and his own doom.

Obviously the full effect of this song can only be appreciated in the original language by an audience that understands Swedish. But with English audiences it would have a better chance if sung in Mrs. Newmarch's English version.

The six songs of Op. 50 are all settings of German texts. Sensitive as Sibelius is to the rhythm of language, we find, as we should expect, a decided change of style, though it must be confessed that the most successful of the set are the two songs where he has changed least and written more in his usual style. Unfortunately, when a foreigner essays German lyrics the ghosts of the great Austrian and German song-writers arise to invite comparison, and though these pianoforte accompaniments show a distinct advance in some respects, they mostly suffer from Sibelius's old habit of setting them too low on the keyboard with a resultant heaviness and inability to blend with the voice. Op. 50, No. 1, *Lenzgesang* (*A song of Spring*) (Fitger), suffers from this defect, which is a pity because it has a very warm and exuberant vocal part of considerable charm. So does Op. 50, No. 2, *Sehnsucht* (*Longing*) (Weiss), which is the greater pity as the voice part is very attractive and more lyrical than usual.

Op. 50, No. 3. *Im Feld ein Mädchen singt* (*In the field a maiden sings*) (Susman).

In the field a maiden sings, perhaps her lover is dead that her song sounds so sad? The evening red fades, the fields are still, and ever strangely sounds the sad song. The last note sounds. I would I might go to her, surely we would understand one another. The evening red fades, the fields are still.

This is undoubtedly the gem of the set and worthy to stand beside the best Swedish settings. It is significant that Sibelius has reverted to a style more suited to Swedish than German both in this and in his other only slightly less successful song, No. 5. Over syncopated chords the voice has a melody of haunting beauty, somewhat in the style of Op. 36, No. 2 (*Men min fågel*). Again this rather square-cut type of melody gives a singular pathos, and very expressive is the descending phrase to ' the fields are still ' from the high light of ' the evening red ' and the pianoforte repeats the end of the phrase till it dies away. This is an exquisite little tone-picture achieved with great economy of means.

Op. 50, No. 4. *Aus banger Brust* (*O wert thou here*) (Dehmel).

This is a more ambitious song and quite effective but, perhaps because his type of melody does not really suit the German language, especially in quick-moving songs such as this, the result is a little laboured. It is nevertheless a useful song in a group and worth singing.

Op. 50, No. 5. *Die stille Stadt* (*The Silent Town*) (Dehmel).

Like No. 3 this lovely little tone-picture sounds much more like a Swedish than a German song. It has been unkindly compared with Schubert's *Die Stadt*, but such a comparison is unfair, for one cannot liken this poem to Heine's. The town here has not necessarily any special connection with the traveller as Heine's has, so Sibelius is justified in giving a more external impression of the misty stillness, broken only by the little light and the children's voices singing. Sibelius uses again the type of melody used in No. 3 over a slow, continuous arpeggiando background, broken only at the words ' Kindermund ' (children's mouth) to suggest the hymn being sung.

Op. 50, No. 6. *Rosenlied* (*The Song of the Roses*) (Ritter).

The last song of the set is in much lighter vein and has a distinct lilt like that of the Strauss waltzes for which Sibelius has such an affection. It is written in 3/4 time, and the crochet first note of the phrase seems to ask to be lingered on while the two bars of quavers lead to a bar of crotchets unmistakably reminiscent of Vienna. The pianoforte part is very light and attractive in a slightly Schumannesque manner.

This collection of songs, though useful for the non-Swedish-speaking singer, is not, if we except Nos. 3 and 5, really typical of Sibelius at his best.

We turn now to the earlier songs, beginning with the earliest set of all, Op. 13.

Op. 13, No. 1. *Under strandens granar* (*Under the fir trees*) (Runeberg).

This is nearly a very fine song. It has a ballad-like subject of a water-sprite who tries to entice a boy into his power by assuming various disguises. At last he appears in the shape of a young horse. Unable to resist, the boy jumps on to his back and away goes the sprite with his prey. The mother then appears, seeking her son. The sprite tries various tricks upon her, finally assuming the boy's likeness, whereupon the mother rushes into the water after him and is likewise seized by the sprite.

So long as Sibelius uses the recitative style accompanied by a very expressive tremolo the effect is successful, but when he abandons it the weakness of his pianoforte writing becomes evident. Even the chords in triplets which imitate the tramping of the horse are too stiff and heavy and the climax of each verse, where the sprite carries off his prey is too abrupt and not sufficiently dramatic to sustain the interest in a rather long song.

Op. 13, No. 2. *Kyssens Hopp* (*The Kiss's Hope*) (Runeberg).

This charming fancy tells how a lover listens to the thoughts of the kisses which are waiting on his lips for the arrival of his beloved. It opens quietly with a staccato melody in the bass and syncopated chords in the treble, then when the kiss begins to speak the vocal part flows freely over a characteristic Sibelian shimmer of repeated chords in the treble (Ex. 113). As the maiden approaches, an accented chord seems to indicate the moment of the given kiss, followed by a quick waltz-like passage slightly reminiscent of the *Valse Triste*. The kiss then tells how the maiden will fear to eat or drink all day lest she lose it. A return to the shimmering accompaniment brings the song to a close. Though not a great song, it has much charm and is useful as a contrast to weightier songs in a group.

Op. 13, No. 3. *Hjertat's Morgon (The Heart's Morning)* (Runeberg).

This again just misses success by being overloaded with heavy chords low down on the key-board. The poem recalls the darkness of life before love entered it and filled it with warmth and light. A man's voice with plenty of weight in the lower notes should be able to make use of this song, though he must be capable of a good high G in the centre section.

The songs of Op. 13 were written when Sibelius was in Vienna and we are told that Brahms expressed admiration for them. One can fancy he would have admired this one, because although the accompaniment is pure Sibelius, the vocal line has a type of melody which is less characteristic and more in the accepted *Lied* style.

Op. 13, No. 4. *Våren flyktar hastigt (Spring is flying)*.

> Spring flies swiftly, summer more swiftly still,
> Autumn lags slowly, winter yet more slowly.
> Lovely cheeks will fade and never bloom again.

> The boy replied: ' Even in Autumn Spring memories can gladden, and Summer's harvest lasts through the winter. Let Spring fly and let cheeks fade! Now let us love and kiss! ' (Runeberg).

This is an excellent little song, the words perfectly set and the witty pianoforte part exactly right. One wonders how it found its way into so early an opus. A whimsical little tune in the right hand has an impudent air and the voice of caution enters with wise warnings. A jaunty figure introduces the boy's reply, a moment of regret appears at thought of fading cheeks, followed by a complete abandonment at ' let us love ' and a catch of the breath at thought of the kiss, while the piano whisks away up the scale with an air of finality.

Op. 13, No. 5. *Drömmen (The Dream)* (Runeberg).

This is not very interesting. Sibelius is evidently groping after certain effects which do not quite succeed. Little falling grace-notes, which look well on paper, fail to give the lightness intended, and it is difficult to understand the use of a solid cluster of reiterated chords at the words ' som en rök försvunnen ' (like smoke vanished). Op. 13, No. 6. *Till Frigga* (*To Frigga*).

The treasures of earth and sea allure me not
' Tis Frigga alone that draws me!
Mind and eyes swoon at her glance till a kiss from her lips revives me.
Where were you, smiling angel, before you came down to cheer my way? What bliss to hasten to your arms! Then life's load becomes a bubble and the soul sinks into divine repose (Runeberg).

This fine song is treated in a very unconventional way. There is something primitive and saga-like about the thrumming accompaniment (Ex. 114), the rhythm of which, added to an unusual melody which rarely moves by intervals greater than a second, produces a curiously hypnotic effect; a change to a rather massive chordal treatment at ' Mind and eye swoon ' makes one wish for a more lyrical form suited to the words; then the thrumming is resumed and, save for a brief tremolando passage, continues to the end. Judged as a love song it has shortcomings, but as a piece of music it is strikingly original.

Op. 13, No. 7. *Jägargossen* (*The Young Sportsman*) (Runeberg) is, on the contrary, neither striking nor original, though it has a mild Schubertian charm.

Of the songs in Op. 17, no copy of No. 1 being available, it is only possible to give its title : *Se'n har jag ei frågat mera* (*And I questioned then no further*) (Runeberg). No. 2. *Sof in!* (*Slumber on*) (Tavaststjerna) is a lullaby, full of charm and tenderness with a well-written accompaniment.

Op. 17, No. 3. *Fågellek* (*Enticement*).

Twilight falls on tree and lake, deep from my lungs I sing the throstle's love-call.
Perhaps it will be borne with the chorus of woodland sounds until it reaches her who will kindle the flame of love in my heart. Perhaps we shall fly together to the seventh heaven at eventide (Tavaststjerna).

This delicate song is written almost entirely in the treble clef : a welcome contrast after so many sombre songs. Alternating chords give a buoyancy to the light-hearted vocal melody, and then, as that becomes more lyrical and passionate, they change to rippling arpeggios. A return to the manner of the opening culminates in a rapturous upward sweep of the voice on ' sjunde himlen ' (seventh heaven) and the song ends in quiet ecstasy. The song is a miniature, in keeping with the idea of the smallness of the bird and shows Sibelius in a very charming and tender mood.

Op. 17, No. 4. *Vilse (Astray)* (Tavaststjerna) is a gay little song, quite attractive, but undistinguished.

Op. 17, No. 5. *En Slända (A dragon-fly)*.

> Pretty dragon-fly! You flew in to me bringing all the summer with you and I forgot my grief. Pretty dragon-fly!
> Then you flew away as you flew in.
> Magic dragon-fly, there was no bitterness in our parting.
> I felt blessed because once you were mine (Oscar Levertin).

Here we get a foretaste of the individual style which culminates in such songs as *Höstkväll*, Op. 38, No. 1, and *Jubal*, Op. 35, No. 1. For much of the song the voice is unaccompanied, the pianoforte just giving a few descriptive touches, such as the alighting of the dragon-fly and its flight, or supporting the voice with sustained chords or arpeggios. The recitative has not the wide sweep of the later songs and the central section is lyrical. Cadenza-like passages and trills on the word 'slända' (dragon-fly) cleverly suggest the hovering and flight of the insect. The song requires a good technique and a good trill, and needs the original Swedish to make effective the descriptive trill on the first syllable of the word 'slända', an effect impossible in English.

Op. 17, No. 6. *Illalle (To the Evening)* (Forsman).

This and the following song are among the few that are set to Finnish texts and it is interesting to note how the style is changed to suit the totally different rhythm of the language. Spoken Finnish has rather a level monotonous sound, except for a marked drop in pitch at the end of phrases. Being a very much inflected language the words tend to get very long in some of the cases and the frequency with which long vowels occur in unstressed syllables decreases the effect of the stress. So in the Finnish settings we find that many repeated notes followed by a short falling phrase are a marked feature of the melodic line.

> Hail, thou starry Evening! How I love thy dreamy solemnity! O that thou wouldst make a bridge with thy dark tresses and draw me to thee, who have not strength to fly to thee! Would I were the day that, when black-winged night has drawn her veil over hill and dale, can fly, exhausted, dear Evening, to thy side! (Forsman).

This lovely song is of extreme simplicity. The vocal line follows the pattern of the repeated note followed by a descending phrase, referred to above. The opening bars are repeated three times and followed by a similar section a tone higher, over a slow tremolo of chords an octave apart in the treble clef. With but slight variations this constitutes the whole song. One lovely effect is made where the accompaniment passes from A minor to D flat major, but the voice at 'kun mustasiipi yö . . .' (when black-winged night) retains the C of the A major bar right through the first D flat major bar, as if too weary to rise to the D flat until the next bar on ' yö ' (night). (Cf. a similar effect on the word ' njuter ' in *Höstkväll*, Op. 38, No. 1.) It is hard to explain why the song should be so lovely, but here Sibelius works the magic that we so often meet in his orchestral pieces when, somehow, he transmutes an apparently ordinary thing into something magical : here, an impression of that strange wavering light that comes just before nightfall.

Op. 17, No. 7. *Lastu lainehilla (Driftwood)*.

Whence come you little piece of wood, drifting on the waves at evening?
You come from the dwellings of the North. Thence, where a lover hewed a fir-tree and built his boat to bring home his bride.

(Calamnius)

This is another Finnish song with a similar vocal line over a syncopated chordal accompaniment. A change of key and the addition of an independent melody in the accompaniment enriches the second section from ' You come from the dwellings ' which ends with a charmingly naïve little phrase. The melody is a very haunting one and the song is all too short.

We now turn to the later songs, beginning with the eight settings of Josephson's lyrics which make up Op. 57.

Op. 57, No. 1. *Elfven och Snigeln (The Snail)*.

This is a disappointing song. It is the story of a snail which made its home in the rushing river, resisting all the water's efforts to dislodge it, until one day a boy came gathering mussels. He tore the snail away and found inside a gleaming pearl. Winter comes and the river freezes solid, but the pearl adorns a queenly breast. The accompaniment is meant to describe the torrent and takes the form of quick scale passages punctuated with sforzando notes in discord. It is the kind of writing that would be effective in the orchestra, with the quick scales on the strings, but it does not sound well on the pianoforte. The voice has a good flowing line and the words are dramatic, so that it is a pity the accompaniment is not more satisfactory.

Op. 57, No. 2. *En blomma stod vid vägen* (*The wild flower*).
The pathetic little tale of the flower that was picked by a maiden, who took the butterfly which was poised upon it and set him in a cage with her pet bird; and of how the butterfly fell in love with the bird while the poor little flower drooped in the vase, makes a charming little song. It is a little naïve, with a vocal line not unlike a folk tune; but the almost continuous repetition of one note whatever the rest of the accompaniment is doing gets a little tiresome.

Op. 57, No. 3. *Qvarnhjulet* (*The Mill-wheel*).

> Drenched in tar the mill-wheel goes. The old wheel that stands still is empty now. Overgrown with wild rose, worn by wind and weather, it thinks: ' Now I am tired '.

The song opens with a staccato figure which well suggests the turning of the mill-wheel while the voice takes up the figure legato and in half time, getting gradually slower, indicating the running down of the tired old wheel. There follows a silent bar followed by a tranquillo section and little snatches of staccato indicate the creaks which are all the worn-out wheel can now achieve, and which get feebler and feebler till they die away altogether.

Op. 57, No. 4. *Maj* (*May*), is bright but not very striking.
Op. 57, No. 5. *Jag är ett träd* (*The Tree*).

> I am a tree that would have been green with leaves had not the storm stripped me in my prime. Now I stand naked among my fellows. O, when shall I die? O, how I long for you, you cold white snow!

Here once more is the real Sibelius, not in one of his most striking songs, but in quite a good and typical one. After a short introduction, a syncopated rhythmical background is heard supporting the voice in a fine long sweeping phrase which forms a whole verse. The third and last verse has only sustained chords instead of the rhythmical figure, and they carry on in an unusually long postlude to the end of the song.

Op. 57, No. 6. *Hertig Magnus* (*Baron Magnus*).
This very long ballad telling of the enticement of the Baron by a mermaid has not enough variety to redeem it from dullness.

Op. 57, No. 7. *Vänskapens blomma* (*Friendship*).
This song has a very promising beginning but one feels that the striking tune with which it opens should not be repeated quite so often. A quiet unaccompanied section provides a welcome contrast and the song ends with the opening tune again.

## Op. 57, No. 8. *Necken (The Elf-King).*

Deep stood the shadows of fir-tree and stone upon the gold and silver foam. Upon a stone sat a ghost-pale boy and drew his bow across the strings. The watersprite struck up a dance upon his harp, the violin followed suit, and the boy lost all his sense before the Elf-King with
The boy was but my phantasy, the sprite was the torrent that splashed my cheek.

This fantastic song has a charming accompaniment descriptive of the splashing waters, the voice has a good if not striking part—and a good climax is made at the appearance of the Elf-King. Then follows a very odd treatment of the rest of the song from ' The boy was but my phantasy '. Marked lento assai and pesante the pianoforte has octaves in both hands, the right hand's lower note being a third above the top of the left-hand octave. What does it mean? Is it meant to convey a heavy depression which the man hoped to dispel by the phantasy? Whatever it means it comes as a shock and certainly makes a rather unsatisfactory finish.

On the whole, though there are good things in Op. 57, it is an unsatisfactory set, as if Sibelius were trying to write in a more conventional way, as he did in Op. 50 in setting the German texts. Mercifully, if this surmise is correct, he gave up the attempt and became himself again in Op. 60.

## Op. 60, No. 1. *Come away Death.*

This is a setting of the Swedish version of Shakespeare's words from *Twelfth Night.* With a few very minor adjustments it can be sung with the English text and makes a very valuable addition to an English singer's repertoire, for it is a setting worthy to stand beside even Arne's beautiful one. Unfortunately, the published English version quite unnecessarily distorts the text and does not even follow the Swedish words closely. The song is strophic in form and, as Sibelius himself has varied the time values to suit the words in the two verses, it seems justifiable to make such alterations to fit the English words also. For instance in bars 5 and 6, if the English follows the original Swedish, no alteration need be made and the dreadful false stress on ' me ' of the published version is shown to be quite unnecessary (see Ex. 115a). In verse two, bar 24, a similar adjustment can be made for ' let there be strown '. Again in bars 14 and 15 if we tie the first and second crotchet in each triplet of bar 14 we get the metre right (Ex. 115b); similarly in bar 28 (Ex. 115c) which is only doing what Sibelius did in the first verse (Ex. 115d).

A difficulty occurs at bar 33, ' Lay me, O where . . .' Arne himself got into difficulties here and does not solve the problem. The second English version in Ex. 115e preserves the words correctly but needs skilful breathing and the carrying on of the voice through the rest in bar 33. The first version is closer to the Swedish but necessitates the omission of ' sad '. The original Swedish text has been given in order to show how slight are the changes necessary. The song was intended to be accompanied by the guitar, and if played on the pianoforte the chords need to be well spread.

Op. 60, No. 2. *When that I was and a little tiny boy.*

This is also set to the Swedish version of Shakespeare's words but unfortunately the Swedish text has an entirely different metre from the English, so it is impossible to sing it to the original words. However it should be possible to make a better paraphrase than that offered in the translated edition. It is noticeable that we are told the name of the author of the French adaptations but not that of the author of the English ones, so one is led to believe that in both songs the English adaptations were made by a foreigner. This song, though not as fine as *Come away Death*, has a good swinging tune over a thrumming accompaniment and catches well the spirit of the poem.

Op. 61 opens with one of Sibelius's most beautiful songs, *Långsamt som kvällskyn* (*Slow as the colours*).

Slowly, as the colours of sunset fade;
Slowly, as the breeze falls asleep in the far distance;
Remotely, as the last echo of the fisher-girl's song dies away; so only, shall I forget thee, who once brought colour, spring breezes and music to my life (Tavaststjerna).

Though this is a love song, the interest for Sibelius obviously lies in the opportunity for painting an exquisite picture and he gives us one of his most satisfying songs. It is more lyrical than some of his other great songs and he does not use the recitative form. The accompaniment begins with a vague wandering single-note figure in the bass, later joined by a pathetic melody in the right hand which breaks off as the voice enters. The subtle cross-rhythms enhance the feeling of remoteness. Rhythm and tonality become more definite as the poet recalls the fisher-girl's song and then comes the tremendous outburst at ' skall jag dig glömmer ' (shall I forget thee) which recalls the climax of *På Verandan*, Op. 38, No. 2, but which is here supported by weighty chords and a great rushing arpeggiando before the word ' vårbris ' (spring breeze). Then as memories revive, the voice is hushed and in a phrase which rises, as if questioning, to the sixth, breaks off, leaving the pianoforte to answer with the dominant followed by the major chord, as it were confirming the impossibility of forgetfulness.

Op. 61, No. 2. *Vattenplask* (*Lapping Waters*) (Rydberg).
This is another of those songs that look wonderful on paper but are disappointing in performance. The pianoforte has an ingenious tremolando of accented triplets with an occasional watery gurgle followed by a series of swift chromatic ascending and descending scales, also in triplets; but the tremolando somehow is too heavy and the chromatic scales too brilliant to suggest gently plashing waters and one cannot help thinking regretfully of what Sibelius could have done with the idea had he had the orchestra at his disposal.

Op. 61, No. 3. *När jag drömmer* (*When I dream*).

Upon the silver fjord at even, an islet is seen, leafy and lovely. There I may unravel my thoughts from the tangle of heavy grief and prepare my dwelling-place. All the dreams and hopes that never had soil to grow in, now are blossoming, and victorious love has turned strife into fulfilment.

In the calm summer night I lie and build a bridge of song for the world to hear. Hark! That is the nightingale! (Tavaststjerna).

This lovely poem makes rather a long song which is a little unequal in quality. But there is so much to recommend it that it is well worth singing, and as it is even more important than usual that the words should be understood, singers are recommended to use Mrs. Newmarch's excellent version.

The song opens with rippling arpeggios which suggest the water lapping against the islet. Then in an abrupt change of key the singer begins to tell of his hopes and dreams. Sibelius achieves a very gradual climax by a swaying accompaniment which, beginning with single notes, increases in texture by the gradual addition of notes till full chords are formed, and in intensity, by a quickening from a single dotted minim to the bar to four crotchets to the bar. Thus a climax is reached without the feeling of repose being disturbed. Very lovely is the description of the calm summer night. A short vivid passage breaks off suddenly and the song ends surprisingly but very beautifully with ' Hark, the nightingale! ' where Sibelius makes use again of the lingering discord—here an A sharp in the voice on the word ' Hark ' against an E minor arpeggio leading to the inevitable B, as if to prolong the anticipation of pleasure before partaking of it.

Op. 61, No. 4. *Romeo* (Tavaststjerna).

*Romeo* is an attractive serenade. An ingenious twanging forms a background to the vocal melody which is repeated in a variety of keys. There is an amusing touch where the would-be Romeo asks his lady whether she intends to call her servants to throw him out of her garden and he impudently plucks the strings in imitation of her hand-bell. But, as so often, the song comes to an abrupt close and we are left with an unsatisfied feeling.

Op. 61, No. 5. *Romans* (*Romance*) (Tavaststjerna).

A captive prince sings from his prison to his princess. He bewails his lot and begs her to think of him and visit him with her sweetness. Sibelius in this ballad has very suitably adopted a troubadour style. The material for each of the five verses is similar but varies in pitch according to the intensity of the words and each verse ends with a rather archaic prayer to God. Again one can recommend Mrs. Newmarch's version, except that surely the ' sweet troubadour ' at the end of verse four is a little misleading? It is the prince who will reward his lady with his troubadour lay, not vice versa.

Op. 61, No. 6. *Dolce far niente* (Tavaststjerna).

This is another of the lighter songs, but it is not very interesting.

Op. 61, No. 7. *Fåfäng önskan* (*Idle Wishes*).

> Countless waves wander over the shining sea.
> O would I were one of them, careless, cold and clear !
> Yet were I a wave I should still have my heart.
> O were I heartless as they ! (Runeberg).

This is one of the most lyrical and vocally effective of all Sibelius's songs, but one longs to transfer the brilliant single-part accompaniment to the strings of the orchestra. For these wide-flung bravura passages—eight demisemiquavers to each beat of a 6/4 bar marked ' veloce '—which continue throughout the song sound just a little flashy on the pianoforte.

Op. 61, No. 8. *Vårtagen* (*Spell of Springtide*) (Gripenberg).

This begins promisingly with a rather more manageable arpeggiando accompaniment and a vocal line rather reminiscent of *Jag ville jag vore*, Op. 38, No. 5, both songs expressing the idea of vain desires. But this setting does not seem quite adequate for Gripenberg's very passionate poem and it tails off lamentably at the end.

Of the songs of Op. 72, 86 and 88 the writer has been able to examine only a few.

Op. 72, No. 5. *Der Wanderer und der Bach* (*The Wayfarer and the Stream*) (Greif) is a dainty little setting of a German poem, charming but not at all characteristic.

Op. 72, No. 6. *Hundra Vägar* (*A Hundred Ways*).

> Forgive me that in church my thoughts are so often full of him. A hundred ways my thoughts do take, but they always go to him and when most they turn to Thee then are they almost all of him.
>
> (Runeberg)

This is a much more characteristic song. It opens in 5/2 time quietly and prayerfully, but as the girl tells how all her thoughts lead to her lover, the melody becomes free and warm and the time changes to 3/2, returning with the more prayerful mood to the 5/2. At the end there is the ' Amen ' close to which I have taken exception elsewhere, but which here is eminently suitable.

Of Op. 86 only three songs have been available.

Op. 86, No. 1. *Vår förnimmelser* (*The Coming of Spring*) (Tavaststjerna) is a fresh and vigorous song, attractive, but not at all distinguished.

Op. 86, No. 3. *Dold förening* (*Hidden Union*) (Snoilsky).

> Two water-lilies, on the water, hidden every now and then from each other by the waves, yet are joined together by their roots below.

This delicate little song has much charm. It has one of those repeated, gently undulating figures beloved of Sibelius under a tender melody in the voice part that floats serenely over it.

Op. 86, No. 4. *Och finns det en tanke* (*And is there a thought?*) (Tavaststjerna) is another exquisite little miniature.

> If a thought remains when I go from hence it will be with a memory of summer warmth over trees and water that I go.

A tiny figure high up in the treble over a monotonous treble accompaniment in sixths and a long beautifully drawn melody in the voice, which is strangely haunting, give a general effect of dreamy limpidity.

Of Op. 88 only two songs, Nos. 1 and 6, have been available and they are in an English version only. They are settings of poems by Franzén and Runeberg. No. 1, *The Anemone*, is quite pretty and No. 6, *The Flower*, has a nostalgic waltz-like rhythm which does not seem to have very much to do with the sense of the poem, but neither song is of much importance, and neither can compare with some of those of Op. 90, of which the best is No. 1. *Norden* (*The North*).

Leaves are falling, the lakes are freezing; flying swans sail sorrowfully southward, longing to return. They plough those seas yearning for ours. Then shall some eye behold you, and from the palm-trees will ask ' What magic is there in the North? Whoso is discontented with the South surely longs for Paradise!' (Runeberg).

A steady rhythmical figure |♪ ♩ ♪♪♩ ♪| pulsates without intermission though with varying harmony throughout the song, while over it floats a lovely sweeping voice part, suggestive of the majestic flight of the swans; a little suggestion of the labour of ' ploughing' the seas is a happy touch, and throughout one feels the exiles' poignant nostalgia.

Op. 90, No. 2. *Hennes Budskap* (*Her Message*) (Runeberg) is a pathetic little song of a kind that is apt to appeal more to Northerners than to us. Use is made of two of Sibelius's favourite devices : repetition of a phrase in various keys and the suspended cadence in the voice at the end of the song.

Op. 90, No. 3. *Morgonen* (*The Morning*) (Runeberg).
A bright, fresh little song which might equally well have appeared in one of the early opus numbers, with its solid blocks of chords, and little grace-note effects such as we met in *Drömmen*, Op. 13, No. 5. However, if one can accept the tiresome ' Amen ' close, it makes a useful number in a group.

Op. 90, No. 4. *Fågelfängarn* (*The bird catcher*) (Runeberg).
If one were given no indication of the date of composition one would be tempted to assign this to the Vienna period and Op. 13, for it is much more in the *Lied* style. The poem tells of the lad who sets his snare, but has to confess his relief when no birds are caught in it. One snare, however, never fails, and at evening it caught a maiden, for the snare was his arms.

There is a charming accompaniment and the voice has an interesting and effective part; and what is not so usual in lighter songs, it has a good ending.

Op. 90, No. 5. *Sommarnatten* (*Summer Night*).

On the calm lake I sat all night and thoughtlessly paid out my fishing line. But a thrush was singing on the bank. I bade him keep his song till daylight, but the little devil bade me ' Put away your rod. If you looked about you you would sing all night.' Yes. I lifted up my eyes and saw the lights upon earth and sky and the thought of my sweetheart came to mind and I sang a song in that hour (Runeberg).

Sibelius is here in a gay mood and has given us some amusing effects. The rather angular vocal line quite well expresses the careless mood of the boy as he idly drops his line into the water. His mild irritation with the thrush and the bird's answer are amusingly contrasted and the bird's note imitated on the pianoforte. Heavy chords doubling the voice at ' I lifted up my eyes ' rather mar the song, but there is a change as thoughts of his sweetheart come to mind, and the song ends as it began—effectively enough perhaps, but one feels a dramatic effect has been missed.

Op. 90, No. 6. *Hvem styrde hit din väg* (*Who has brought you here*) (Runeberg).

This is a very touching song only marred by the inadequacy of its ending :

> Far away from here you were born, we grew up apart. Who guided you hither? How could you become my all who once were nothing to me?

The poem is set very simply; over a continuous chordal accompaniment the voice seems to be musing quietly to an inescapable rhythm that somehow suggests the inevitability of the fate that draws the two beings unconsciously together. Note that in some printed copies there are misprints in the Swedish text. The title should read ' Hvem styrde hit *din* väg? ' not ' *du* väg ', and in bar 9 ' di tåt ' should read ' dit åt '.

There are, if we treat *Höstkväll* as primarily written for the pianoforte, three songs with orchestra to be considered. One very early work appeared as Op. 3, and was first published in 1893, but was revised by Sibelius in 1913: the *Arioso* for voice and string orchestra.

> One winter morning the maiden walked in the frosty grove and saw a withered rose.
> Grieve not, poor flower, for you have lived and had your Springtime ere cold Winter came. Sadder is my fate for I have Spring and Winter together. My lover's eyes are my Spring, Winter is my Mother.
> Grieve not that thy happy times are gone (Runeberg).

This work is pleasing but, though there are certain touches that we recognise, it is not very characteristic. Of course, the orchestral score would probably reveal more of the composer's individuality, especially as Sibelius revised it in 1913, but unfortunately only a pianoforte score is available.

After an attractive opening a more characteristic cantabile section follows which faintly brings to mind the later song *Men min fågel* Op. 36, No. 2, and there is a fine moment when the voice rises to a top A on ' Spring ', while the orchestra departs from its former sustained character and colours it with a gay little motive, and then the voice drops suddenly an octave and a half for ' and my mother is

the Winter '. The effect is a little weakened by the whole section from
' Sadder is my fate ' being repeated. After a pause the last words are
sung low down in the voice while the orchestra brings the song to an
apparent close with an ' Amen ' in the minor, but then suddenly introduces the major third. In this work we find traces of Sibelius's
favourite habit of giving rhythmical independence to voice and accompaniment, but as yet he has not quite achieved his later felicity
in the wedding of words to music.

The other two orchestral songs are Finnish.

Op. 33. *Koskenlaski an morsiamet* (*The Ferryman's Brides*)
(Oksanen).

The ballad tells of Vilho, mightily skilled in seacraft, who takes his
bride, Anna, to witness his prowess in shooting the fierce rapids of
Pyörtäjä. Often has the river-nymph, herd-maiden of the river-god
Vellamo, watched Vilho with a strange feeling of love in her heart.
When she sees his boat approach she is filled with joy until she suddenly becomes aware of the maiden with him. Mad with jealousy,
she tears a rock from the depths and throws it into mid-stream. The
boat founders and Vilho and Anna are drowned. To this day the
maiden's rock remains and the nymph sits mourning for lost love.

Two themes, Ex. 116 *a* and *b*, keep recurring, the first associated
with the river nymph, the second with Vilho's death. The work opens
with Ex 116 *a* against a background suggestive of rushing waters.
Vilho then bids Anna not grow pale for ' the waters are powerless
against one who knows every rock '. The tempo quickens as they
enter the rapids. Ex. 116*a* is heard again in a short interlude which
leads into a tranquillo passage in which Anna tells of the beauty of
the night and in unconscious prophecy she sings Ex. 116*b* as she
says : ' How sweet to die on such a night with him one loves! ' The
orchestra repeats the theme and then a stringendo scale passage leads
into an allegro molto. After a climax a rather sinister hush descends
and, using Ex. 116 *a*, the voice describes the river-nymph's dwelling
place.

There follows a beautiful passage where the nymph, bewildered by
her own strange feelings of love, looks for Vilho's coming. Excitement reaches fever-pitch and then she sees someone—a human—in
the boat. Vowing vengeance, she hurls the rock into mid-stream.
This passage is not as effective as one would expect. Whether it is a
deliberate attempt to emphasise the fact that the catastrophe is being
prepared underwater, or merely as in some other dramatic songs,
shows a failure of dramatic feeling, it is difficult to say. Now Ex. 116 *b*

is heard again in the orchestra as the boat founders and Vilho and Anna are drowned. Once more *a* appears amid the rushing of the waters over the new rock, then a diminuendo leads to a return to *b* in which the voice joins and the song comes quietly to an end. It is a fine work, though a little long.

The other orchestral song is a mature work, *Luonnotar* (from the *Kalevala*[1]), Op. 70. It tells the story of the creation of the heavens from the union of the winds and waves with Luonnotar, the virgin of the air.

> Luonnotar, virgin of the air, slender and beautiful, is wandering solitary over the desolate wastes. She descends upon the waves. For seven hundred years she swam in all directions. Then a mighty wind arose and the waters swelled; in her distress she called upon Ukko, the God of All.
>
> Then came a wild duck seeking a place to make her nest, but wind and waves buffetted her and she cried out against them. Then Luonnotar stretched out her knee and received the eggs into her lap. A fire coursed through her frame and she shook the eggs into the water. Lo, the eggs were broken into myriad pieces and the topmost parts became the heavens, the white shone as the moon and the coloured parts became the stars in the sky.

This is certainly the most subtle and original of all Sibelius's vocal works. For an account of the remarkable qualities of the orchestral score the reader is referred to Cecil Gray's admirable book.[2] The vocal treatment is also unique. The composer has created an ethereal, strange atmosphere about the airy virgin in contrast to the more material treatment of the wild duck's music. Also he has approached the miracle not dramatically, but esoterically, as a supreme mystery —not externally, as just a picturesque legend, but in the spirit of his ancient forefathers.

A short wavering figure in the orchestra serves as introduction, then the voice enters, unaccompanied, describing the strange maiden; a short interlude of the wavering figure of the introduction follows, then another recitative, at first unaccompanied, takes up the story of her descent upon the waves. Against a tenuous sustained background the maiden's cry of woe is heard, marked misterioso, in long, faltering phrases such as Ex. 117, that rise and fall—culminating in one long cry on the high B double flat and faltering away again. A longer interlude follows, introducing the section dealing with the wanderings of the wild duck, and though we still have a fluttering movement and

[1] Runo I.
[2] *Sibelius.* Oxford University Press, 1931: see pp. 85-7.

a very similar vocal line, there is a thickening of the texture and a greater firmness in the vocal line, subtly differentiating the nature of the two distraught beings. A great climax is reached with the powerful cry of despair of the bird; then it subsides and the pale tints of Luonnotar's music return and the mystical hush persists to the end of the song. The moment when she feels the fire coursing through her is marked ' visionarico ', and throughout there is only the softest background in the orchestra, while most of the account of the miracle lies low in the voice, only rising at the extreme end with an octave jump and a slight crescendo at ' stars in the sky '. Any suggestion of drama has been rigorously excluded from the passage. Throughout it is treated in the same spirit that a Christian would approach the supreme mystery of the Incarnation : as something too sacred to be treated dramatically.

And so in justice to the sopranos whom Cecil Gray so fiercely denounces it must be said that the work is extremely difficult both to sing and to interpret, especially to an English audience who cannot enter into the mystical spirit of the song. Added to that, it is almost impossible to sing it properly in any language but Finnish, for the Finnish language has fewer consonants and more vowels than any other European language (with the possible exception of Italian) and of its consonants a large proportion of those are liquid l's and n's. It is impossible to think that Sibelius would have evolved the vocal line he uses here had he been using any other language.

To what conclusions then does this study of the songs bring us? That Sibelius as a song-writer is at his greatest when he abandons himself entirely to his own peculiar idiom, and this is invariably where his imagination is stirred by the moods of Nature. His best songs are, generally, sombre or tragic, though not without flashes of brilliant colour which lift them from an atmosphere of unrelieved gloom, flashes such as the end of *Långsamt som kvällskyn*, Op. 61, No. 1; the drama of *Säf, säf, susa*, Op. 36, No. 4, or the exultation of *Jubal*, Op. 35, No. 1. There are times when one feels him strangely insensitive to drama in the songs, which is curious in one who can write so dramatically for the orchestra. It is a pity that his imagination is so rarely stirred by more cheerful subjects, as it is difficult to get variety into a group of his songs without having recourse to inferior ones for the sake of contrast; and that so often his imagination is only partially caught by a lyric so that an inadequate song results. Or can it be that that great mind suddenly feels the inadequacy of the medium and impatiently finishes what he has begun so as to free himself for greater things? That many of such songs are to be regretted is true, but even so we should bear in mind that they were not written for our sophisticated ears. It is a fact that the Northern peoples find a charm in simpler things that may sound banal to us. It is certainly true that the songs of Grieg that are popular in his own country are not always those that appeal most to English people, and it is highly probable that Finnish or Swedish musicians will entirely disagree with the opinion expressed here upon many of Sibelius's songs.

However that may be, there is no doubt that Sibelius has created a new type of song, one that has already borne fruit among his successors, notably in the earlier and best songs of his countryman, Yriö Kilpinen, and that without the few superlative songs he has given us the literature of song would be definitely the poorer.

# 7

## The Choral Music

### By

### Scott Goddard

THE FIRST THING that strikes the foreign student of Sibelius's choral music to-day is the scarcity of available material. The second is the relatively large amount of this music that remains unpublished. It is known that the composer has deliberately withheld work that has ceased to satisfy him. His reported saying, ' The thing that has pleased me most is that I have been able to reject ', has been quoted in an earlier chapter of this book; it has to do with other works than his choral compositions, but it has special force in regard to them.

Among the unpublished works are a number that would appear, from their titles, to be considerable creations. Such are, for instance, a Coronation Cantata for chorus and orchestra (1895); and, still more fascinating, such ' lost ' works as the choral portions of the *Kullervo* symphony[1] (1892) and an Improvisation for recitation, male voice chorus and orchestra entitled *Islossningen* (*The Breaking of the Ice*) (1899). There is, too, the later cantata (1918) for chorus and orchestra, *Oma maa*, and another (1920) *Maan virsi* which, with the *Song of Vaino* (1926), from the *Kalevala*, also remain in manuscript. The fact that the four last-named works are included in the canon, each with an opus number, suggests that their present state is less the result of rejection by the composer than of failure by publishers to interest themselves in unusual and uncommercial works.

Such an attitude has this to be said for it, that judging by the material available (admittedly sparse) Sibelius's choral music has only an infinitesimal admixture of individuality and therefore the less interest in comparison with his symphonic music and the less right to persist. Probably the *Song of Vaino* being a late work is indispensable in any complete study of Sibelius's choral music. The present writer has been unable to obtain access to it and bases his tentative conclusions about the choral music mainly upon the *Kalevala*

[1] The adventures of Kullervo are told in Runos XXI–XXXVI of the *Kalevala*.

cantata *The Origin of Fire* (sometimes called *Ukko the Fire-maker*) (1902) and the choral ballad *The Captive Queen* (1906). Apart from these relatively significant works there is also the 1897 Promotion Cantata.

*The Origin of Fire* is a setting for baritone solo, chorus and orchestra of one of those episodes from the Finnish epic poem, the *Kalevala*, which had already inspired Sibelius to write the four legends connected with Lemminkäinen several years previously as well as *Pohjola's Daughter* three or four years later than this cantata, and other works. *The Origin of Fire* is occasional music, in that it was written for the opening of the National Theatre at Helsingfors. At the same time it is, as we know, the outcome of long acquaintance with the *Kalevala* tales. In style it is unlike any of the orchestral *Kalevala* works, not unexpectedly since the medium is quite other. Nevertheless, one is left with the feeling that only the composer of the Lemminkäinen Legends and indeed only the musician who had already written those works could have created this remarkable, if rather unyielding, unresponsive cantata. No quotation suffices to give more than a vague idea of the strange intermittences of originality of vision (Ex. 118) interspersed with material of a for-bidding ordinariness (Ex. 119) that characterise the cantata. Sibelius has never appeared to a foreign listener as a man who would shrink from the use of any material, however worn with previous use, if it served his purpose. His greatness has consisted in the magic with which he can invest such material. In *The Origin of Fire* that magic is present but does not always work the well-remembered wonders.

The tale[1] is of the return of sunlight to the dark dwelling of Kalevala, of Ukko, the chief god, brooding over the darkness that had come to the world of men and dispelling it by his power, thus bringing warmth and light to mankind. The first part of the tale is given to the baritone solo, accompanied by a rich orchestral texture that at times reminds the hearer of the more obvious passages of, say, the *Pelléas and Mélisande* incidental music and at times of the Lem-minkäinen Legends at their finest. At the climax, where the tale tells how Ukko struck light and fire from his sword as a gift to mankind, the male voice chorus takes over the recounting of the legend and con-tinues to the end. The work is thus divided into two sections, one for solo, the other for chorus. The two are not combined and the effect of their complete separation is at first disconcerting. The plan, which

[1] Runo XLVII of the *Kalevala*.

certainly results in a magnificent peroration for the chorus, has to be accepted on its own valuation.

*The Captive Queen* is interesting in the first place, and significant among Sibelius's choral works, for its political implications. There is, I think, no doubt that this is political matter. It is the work not only of a man pensioned by the State and therefore in some ways its mouthpiece; but it is the expression of a political faith held by Sibelius himself at that time. Finland, as a grand-duchy of the Tsar, was being ruled with completely autocratic tyranny. A work such as this cantata for full chorus and orchestra (still more the later version with male voices only) must immediately have been recognised by Finnish patriots for what it was intended to be and the message it was meant to convey must have been clear. The captive queen was Finland; the young man hearing the queen singing her heart out in the prison where she had been immured by a tyrant was the young and growing force of liberation in the country. Viewed from that standpoint *The Captive Queen* has its own strong significance. It is a manifesto, not easy for a foreigner to savour fully, though it can be understood for what it is: a call to revolt. Musically it is less important.

As soon as the trombones have announced, with a certain dignity and more than a passing remembrance of the finale of the Second Symphony, the stern figure of repeated D minor chords that informs the first part of the work, the male voices enter with the first strophe. The melodic line throughout is of the simplest; there is the feeling that this is deliberate, that the composer intended not only that the music should be understood by untutored masses but could be sung by them also. As the tale unfolds the music becomes increasingly dramatic, though always the voice parts move along simple, folksong lines. The full score shows ingenuity, some poetry and a remarkable sense of restrained embellishment; so that although the orchestra has infinitely more interesting music than the voices and palpably is intended not only to support but to adorn them, it never becomes the more important participant.

How far the special sentiments of the cantata and the peculiar circumstances of its production affected the artistic consciousness of the composer may be judged from the march tune which announces the coming of the hero who is to free the captive queen (Ex. 120). It will be noticed that even here the authentic Sibelius appears in the final bars. Such a work, occasioned by the heightened emotions of national sentiment, is part of the history of Finland. It was never intended, nor in fact should it be used, for export. But the explorer of Sibelius's creative mentality cannot afford to ignore *The Captive Queen*; it belongs to an honourable ancestry and to the same category as Brahms's *Triumphlied* and Elgar's *Pomp and Circumstance* marches.

There remains one work to be discussed, the set of what are presumably student songs listed under the opus number 23 as *Cantata for the Year 1897*. This was an occasional piece for the ceremony of the bestowal of degrees at Helsinki University, Sibelius being at that time a teacher of music there. This slight but rewarding exercise, appearing four years after the *Karelia* music and the first of the Lemminkäinen Legends, has little enough of what has come to be recognised as the true style of Sibelius. But there is a stark purity about the writing that is in keeping with the divided string chords in *En Saga*. The last but one of the nine songs is a remarkable study in effects of voices accompanied by percussion. The means, as usual, are extremely simple, but the unequal-footed strophes (Ex. 121) interspersed with percussion ritornellos compel attention.

# 8

## *Special Characteristics of Sibelius's Style*

### By

### David Cherniavsky

IN THIS CONCLUDING essay it is proposed to study the general characteristics and gradual development of Sibelius's musical style. At once it must be emphasised that the words 'style' or 'idiom' can here only imply an exceedingly broad generalisation since, actually, underlying the works of the masters, there is invariably an ever-changing growth in their expression and technique, a development bound to be concomitant with their unfolding personality and maturing approach to life. Furthermore, especially in the works of recent composers (and particularly in those of Sibelius) their idiom will also be conditioned by the nature of each composition, by whether it be in symphonic or operatic style, a tone-poem or chamber music, a song or perhaps a miniature for the piano. Indeed, in the case of Sibelius, as several of my collaborators have already pointed out, we often discover an extraordinary change of method even between works written in the same genre; and this is simply because the style of each composition, whether it be a symphony or miniature, is inherent purely in the individual conception of the work itself. In this way, it will be found more appropriate to the present essay to study Sibelius's music as one gradual stylistic development rather than as a static idiom, confining generalisations only to those few basic features fundamental to almost every work.

As has already been suggested, the spiritual growth of an artist, in personality and therefore also in style and technique, is ultimately bound up with his personal and exterior environment. Thus, in the music of those composers whose lives were comparatively undisturbed (for instance, in the works of Palestrina, Bach and Haydn) the development of their means of expression appears organic and gradual, whereas with later and more romantic composers, each one of their works can often be related to their further experience of life or to the changing spirit of their time. The stylistic development of Sibelius would seem to partake rather more of the attributes of this latter type. He is often considered to have had an uneventful life; yet in truth, it is doubtful whether any other composer has had a career of broader or of more intense experience, or has lived through a period of greater change and spiritual upheaval. And, as with Beethoven, Sibelius's music is especially rooted in his growing personality; therefore, in attempting to trace the really fundamental influences on his development, we should consider far more his environment and racial characteristics, his general culture and the changing contemporary spirit, rather than expect to find the seeds of his development so much in the works of other composers or in any aesthetic theory. These deeper, and less technical, influences we will consider first.

As a youth, Sibelius had been deeply impressed by Martin Wegelius, his teacher at the Helsingfors Academy. The Professor had always insisted on the great importance of attaining a comprehensive outlook and ever broadening range of artistic experience, for, as he had said, the wider a composer's horizons grow in general perception and understanding, the broader too become his boundaries in art. The young student soon became an exceptionally wide reader, interested in all the vital problems of his time, often discussing these subjects into the early hours of the morning with fellow artists and thinkers in Helsingfors. Moreover, through these stimulating contacts he became acquainted with the new movements in Finnish painting, poetry and philosophy, becoming more and more in touch with the rising spirit that was to inspire the Finnish people with new intensity in their deep idealism, their national consciousness and love of freedom. But this passion for freedom was as yet to remain but an unfulfilled dream, for it was not to be until after three decades of the hardest oppression—after altogether over seven hundred and fifty years of Swedish and Russian domination—that Finland at last regained her independence; and thus it is significant that there should be felt behind the most representative works of Sibelius written after this liberation (that is after the completion of his Fifth Symphony) some of the great exultation expressed by the Finnish race as a whole. Perhaps this is not surprising, for undoubtedly Sibelius owes much to the spirit of his people and to the inspiring landscape of his native land; he has even intimated that he could not permanently leave his home surroundings without thereby cutting himself off directly from the roots of his art. Yet it would be a mistake to infer, as some writers do, that he is primarily concerned with racial expression or merely with a search for local colour; indeed, in viewing his development as a whole, we shall find that he should hardly be placed in the category of a 'nationalist composer' at all. In the first place, he cannot be said to belong to a Finnish nationalist school in music, for his art is too individual to inspire the founding of such a school. Secondly, nowhere in his works can there be found the use of folk-music as thematic material (as we frequently find in the works of the Russian 'handful', or of the nationalist composers of Hungary, Spain, Czechoslovakia and England); nor can we find to any noticeable degree (apart from one important exception, *vide infra*, p. 167) the trace of the characteristic thematic inflections and rhythmic tendencies of his country's folksongs, or the general influence of their character on his melodic style (which reveal, for instance, the nationalism of Dvořák or Grieg).

So although Sibelius may be considered to be a patriot and perhaps even a nationalist in *sentiment*—and one or two of his works might further suggest this fact—he is not one by conscious deliberation and most certainly soon became broadly international in general outlook. However strongly he may feel a bond with the Finnish people and with his own surroundings, he has a keen appreciation of the other peoples and of other lands in which he has lived; and he has travelled frequently, perhaps more than any other great composer, in all the larger countries of Europe, as well as having visited Russia, England and America. Naturally the period in which we shall find his music to be most eclectic and cosmopolitan in spirit is that in which he was travelling most abroad.

In his literary taste too, there can be found a similar balance between Finno-Scandinavian and international influences; for, besides his fondness for both contemporary Finnish poetry and Scandinavian drama, and although in many of his most moving tone poems he has been intensely inspired by his country's national epic, the *Kalevala*, his later works reflect almost equally his lifelong appreciation of the art of Shakespeare and of the Greek and Latin classics. In his own words 'Homer and Horace had a significance in my development which I cannot value highly enough'.

It must also be remembered that, even by extraction, Sibelius is by no means purely Finnish, most of his ancestors having been Swedish in origin, only one or two having been pure Finns. Much of the duality of temperament inherent in his nature might be partly attributed to this fact, for he seems to embrace within his personality some of the most fundamental characteristics of both the Finnish and Swedish races. At times, he can be intensely moody, aloof, and happy only in solitude, or may show the staunch independence, the immense vitality, the vivid imagination and love of nature—and especially that of his native land—which so often are rooted in the Finnish soul. Yet this is not the only side to his personality. It is balanced by a more extraverted mood in which he may be rapt in the sheer joy of living, or may reveal an eclecticism of outlook, a natural affability, a calm poise and serenity which may well be attributed to his Swedish ancestry, for these are prominent characteristics of that race as a whole.

Naturally, these same traits are as evident in his music as in his personality, for with Sibelius the two are inseparable, indeed, are one. For example, the influence of nature, which can be so strongly felt behind nearly all his works, is revealed not only in the impressionism, in the colour and mood awakened in his tone-poems, but also in the organic growth, in the vitality and elemental power of the music itself—music which often seems to have been inspired by that same natural force from which the organic world itself draws its unceasing life and fertility. Sibelius's feeling for nature, which at times might seem to be almost pantheistic, not only extends to a love of the beauty of its contours, the harmony of colour and delicate detail, nor even is limited to a feeling for the lakes, the vast forests and lonely moors of his native land; in certain works it seems at the same time to penetrate far deeper, right down to the elements and roots within the soil, to the power and rhythm of the Northern winds and rushing torrents, ultimately, as it were, becoming one with the force of life itself. Indeed, his music when viewed as a whole—and especially such works as the Fourth and Fifth Symphonies, *Tapiola*, *The Swan of Tuonela*, *The Oceanides* and the prelude to *The Tempest*—is more truly elemental and deeply rooted in the organic world than that of any other composer; and, although we may sometimes find this very same quality to an almost equal degree in the works of Mussorgsky (especially in his *Night on the Bare Mountain*) and, to a lesser extent, also in Wagner and perhaps Stravinsky, we have to look to a sister art—surely to the work of Cézanne—to discover an equally intense elemental power and instinctive feeling for that organic vital force in nature as has inspired Sibelius. Certainly, the influence of the countryside, of the sea, and climate is to be felt behind the works of other composers too, but here it is nearly always of a very different order. In the music of Delius, for example, we are usually presented with an essentially anthropomorphic impression of nature, reflecting her more sensuous beauty, often exemplified in the luxuriance of the summer foliage, the fragrant scent in the still air and harmony of delicate tints and shades—an impression which has awakened in the composer a mood in which he may wander and dream. With Sibelius the response is fundamentally different; we are entirely, even disturbingly alone in *Tapiola*—as if immersed in the vast forest ourselves.

Besides this unique influence which the North with its emphasis on the cold and wintry side of nature, has had on Sibelius's music, his extraordinary originality can be traced to a further stimulus which has been perhaps even more important to his development. It was midway through the last century that Schumann, in an article on the music of the Danish composer Gade, first heralded ' the spirit of the North ' as a new voice within the language of music. Yet Gade's originality was soon to succumb to the excessive influence of the German school, and thus, it was left to Grieg, his former pupil, to arrive first at a truly Northern tone of voice, though his message was mainly restricted to purely *lyrical* expression. However much we may appreciate his Piano Concerto or even the Quartet and sonatas, Grieg remains essentially the composer of inspired songs, miniatures for the piano and of the immortal music for *Peer Gynt*; he never attempted symphonic form.

Thus, it is in Sibelius that we meet for the first time in music an all-embracing personality and *great* master from the North, one in whom there can be felt, not only the ethnical influence of the Nordic race and the austere grandeur of the Northern landscape, but also the vital stimulus of the new progressive spirit of Scandinavia and Finland in modern culture, and that most enlightened way of life and advanced outlook which has placed these countries in many respects ahead of all others as examples for the future. Here we have, in the main, the secret behind the great originality of his message, an individuality of utterance which, besides being invariably natural and unforced, is never based on reactionary or iconoclastic ideas. In fact, it might be said that he has been inspired by an entirely different *Zeitgeist* from that of his contemporaries in Europe.

This phenomenon is perhaps not so unusual as it might at first appear. ' The Spirit of the Age ' is in reality an exceedingly loose expression; indeed, it would be truer to say that each generation is inspired, not so much by one great spirit or *Zeitgeist*, as by the anti-thesis, and sometimes conflict, of several contrasted attitudes towards life. This seems to be true for instance of the period of the Renais-sance with its clash of political and of religious ideas, of the Romantic era, mirrored in music by the opposing schools of Brahms and Wagner and the various nationalistic tendencies, and more than ever true of the last epoch, in which a complete disintegration is to be seen, splitting up into contrasted camps, ideals in art, politics, creed and ethics—in fact, in every sphere of human endeavour. And, as must inevitably accompany this approach to life, the music also of the last generation shows an endless search for new means of expression, an enthusiasm for theory and experiment and the birth of such tendencies as atonality, polytonality, neoclassicism, and *Gebrauchsmusik*—to name only a few of the many contemporary movements.

Yet when we come to study the musical style of Sibelius, we are faced with a gradual progression towards more complete formal integration and directness of expression, a growing disdain for superficial brilliance and elaborate detail, and finally an insistence on unity of conception, not only between the various elements of composition—between content and form, together with texture, harmony and orchestration—but also between the separate ideas and movements contained in each major work. And while the prevailing mood in Europe was one of disillusionment and of nervous reaction to the materialism and excessive sophistication of the age, the later works of Sibelius reveal a profundity, a depth of conviction and spiritual repose, such as have been almost completely absent from all music written since the works of Beethoven's last period. It is not as if he were forced into a narrow world of his own out of touch with the revolutionary movements of his time—indeed we know from his own words that he has always been keenly interested in contemporary music; rather does he seem to embrace within his style all these contemporary schools of thought, not so much by showing allegiance to any single one, but, on the contrary, by assimilating into his own outlook and making wholly his own the vital truth contained in each. This process may have been almost entirely unconscious, or may even be largely a matter of independent development, yet we can point to passages in the works of his maturity in which there can be found the essential trend behind nearly every main technical advance of recent years. Nevertheless, as a whole, it might be said that Sibelius has forged his way along an entirely different path from those being followed, to their bitter end, by the majority of his contemporaries in Europe, and that such suggestive influences as he may have received from contemporary movements have been so completely absorbed into his own highly original style, as to have become entirely imperceptible unless we are definitely seeking to find them.

This capacity for making absolutely their own, and for infusing a new significance into, all outside influences, is one of the most valuable gifts common to all great artists. The originality of Sibelius, like that of all the masters, is founded, not so much on a deliberate search for new means of expression or on a narrow concentration on his own point of view alone, as on the spontaneous creation of a new synthesis from those past and present tendencies which appear to him (mainly subconsciously) to be vital, and at the same time to be conducive to further development; and naturally, it is dependent even to a greater extent on this power of individualisation, inherent in the sheer strength of his own unique personality and spiritual development.

Later it will be shown how synthesis is also the principle on which is founded his often noted development of symphonic form; it is furthermore the most prominent feature underlying the whole progression of his style. For although, for the purpose of analysis, we will divide this stylistic development into four distinct periods, in which new influences and fresh aspects of his personality gradually come to the fore, there can be seen running parallel to this advance a gradual selection, or rather, a spontaneous accumulation, of the most vital elements from each successive period which finally reach a culmination in the synthesis, in the complete mastery and breadth of outlook that inform the fourth and latest phase of his productivity.

It might be said that Sibelius's student days had been passed, and that he had reached the *first* stage within his stylistic development with the completion of the *Kullervo* Symphony (for solo voices, chorus and orchestra) and with the first version of *En Saga*, in 1892. Hitherto his music had been mainly bound by classical traditions (in which he had been receiving a strict training both in Helsingfors and abroad) although there soon began to appear evidence of his great enthusiasm for the works of Grieg and Tchaïkovsky and occasional signs of the startling originality which suddenly was to be revealed later on. With the completion of the *Kullervo* Symphony, however (a work which he has so far withheld from publication), he at once attained a real independence of expression and a style distinctly Finnish in character, so close is his idiom to the Karelian folk soul in expression, and so original in its orchestral colour. As it happened, it was only at a time *following* the production of this symphony that Sibelius visited the Karelian district and heard those folk-songs which so many had supposed to have been his models for this work. The real influence on his style at this time had been the performance of the *Aino* Symphony[1] of Kajanus which Sibelius himself admits to have been of paramount importance to his development. Although directly founded on Finnish folk music—an example which Sibelius was never to follow in his own works—it was the fresh spirit of the music which affected him so overwhelmingly and the light it threw on the rich possibilities which the *Kalevala* held in store for interpretation into music. The legends of this national epic have inspired some of the most vivid and imaginative works throughout his output, yet during this first period, lasting from 1892 till the turn of the century, they might be considered to have been almost the prime influence on his development; not only the *Kullervo* Symphony, but also his projected opera *The Building of the Boat*, the tone-poems *The Swan of Tuonela, Lemminkäinen's Homecoming* as well as *The Origin of Fire* are all directly inspired by the myths of the *Kalevala*; while the moods and atmosphere of the whole poem seem to have become deeply integrated into his romantic personality at this time. *En Saga*, with its bracing style and vitality, its rough-hewn harmonies, dark orchestral colours and incessant pedal points which give a curious impression of great spaciousness and power, would seem to owe much to the Northern landscape and rigorous climate. But the First and Second Symphonies and the *Karelia* suite, also belonging to this initial period, show the influence of the Russian school rather than any dependence on classical models. This affinity of his early symphonies with those of the Russian masters—especially with the works of Tchaïkovsky and Borodin—is revealed mostly in the similarity of their *approach* to the art form, in the intensity and brilliance of expression, the predominantly emotional appeal and in the importance of mood common to each master; although, already in his Second Symphony, Sibelius had also achieved a sense of unity, not only within each movement but throughout his work as a whole, such as had never been quite attained by the Russian masters. Nevertheless, the great formal conception of his first movement had, as Mr. Abraham has shown, already been initiated by Borodin in his First Symphony, and it is not as if Sibelius had as yet arrived at a vitally new attitude towards symphonic style as had the Russians of the previous generation.

It is with the second phase of his development—a period which

[1] Aino is a Lapp maiden who figures in Runos III-V of the *Kalevala*.

lasts approximately from 1903 till 1909—that the example of Beethoven, and classical influences in particular, at last assume real importance in his major works. No longer do they serve mainly as a force of outer control, but now correspond with a more mature state of mind, in which the perfection of form, the refinement of texture, the attainment of proportion, restraint, continuity, and the organic growth of his ideas gradually become matters of prime importance. His former inclination for rather personal and emotional expression now tends to give way to a more lyrical vein, a feeling which reaches its highest flights in the many beautiful songs of the period and in the fine slow movement of the Quartet *Voces Intimae*. Signs of this change of style already appear in his Violin Concerto (composed in 1903), but it is towards the end of the period, in the Third Symphony and String Quartet, that classical ideals and Sibelius's own expression are fully reconciled and become as one. Doubtless, the comparative classicism and eclecticism of these years, which stand in such striking contrast to his previous more Northern and romantic style, were influenced by his travels in Europe, where he had heard many performances of both classical and contemporary music, and also by his first contact with the very different culture and landscape of Italy during his two months' stay there. This catholicity of outlook is revealed, not only in the comparative impersonality of his style, but also in the versatile manner in which he now manages to identify himself with foreign cultures; with that of classical Greece in the orchestral intermezzi *The Dryad* and *Pan and Echo*, with Shakespeare in his two songs from *Twelfth Night*, with Maeterlinck in the incidental music for *Pelléas et Mélisande*, with Strindberg in his music for *Swanwhite*, with Hofmannsthal in his music for *Everyman*, and with the spirit of the East in the incidental music for Procopé's *Belshazar*.

With the arrival of the Fourth Symphony, however (that is in 1911), a fundamental change of style and outlook can be observed, providing an astounding contrast with that of the two previous periods. Thought and expression become intensely personal and concentrated, the sense of tonality, rhythm and harmony, abstruse and vague, whilst in place of the comparative serenity of his immediately preceding works, a strained, wintry and profoundly meditative mood now pervades the whole symphony, as also the tone-poem *The Bard* and, to a lesser extent, *Luonnotar* for soprano and orchestra, the symphonic poem *The Oceanides* and the Fifth Symphony. During these years, that is from 1911 till 1915, Sibelius spent several months in Germany, France and England, sometimes with the avowed intention of gaining fresh impressions by listening to as much music as possible; but the more basic cause of this abrupt change of style is rather to be found in the periods of deep melancholy and uncertainty which he was then experiencing owing to anxieties of various kinds. He imagined that he was living under the constant threat of cancer owing to the mistaken diagnosis of his doctors; he was besieged by severe financial worries—which lead him to write : ' I do not advise anyone without private means to become a composer. That way lies tragedy. . . .'—while in the outer world, Europe was embroiled in the bitter struggles of the First World War and his own country undergoing a period of the hardest Tsarist oppression, culminating in the civil war and declaration of independence in 1919. Nevertheless, with the completion this year of the *second* version of the Fifth Symphony, Sibelius's spiritual conflict seems to have reached a final and triumphant resolution, as had also—or rather, as seemed to have had—events in his own country and in Europe. In a letter of this time he speaks of the whole revised version of the symphony being ' a vital climax to the end. Triumphal . This work might be taken as being symbolical, as it were, of his return to life and new-found feeling of unbounded confidence and power.

Yet, a further five years were needed, in which he was only to produce smaller works, and while the conceptions of the Sixth and Seventh symphonies were slowly developing in his mind, for Sibelius gradually to transcend this transitionary mood and to arrive at the complete maturity and contemplative state of mind of his final period. As has been suggested, the key-note of this fourth and last phase of his development is one of synthesis, a mastery of style now embracing the predominant qualities of all his former works. Besides the perfect command of orchestration, the elemental power and vitality shown even in his earliest works, there now appears a universality of outlook and poise (which partly had been revealed during his ' classical ' second period) the extraordinary originality, concentration and depth of expression which characterised his ensuing phase (his Fourth Symphony in particular) and lastly, that great *formal* mastery and attainment of a sense of unity, not only within each movement, but within each work as a whole, which inevitably resulted from the stylistic development underlying the entire progression of his symphonies and other major works up to that time. Sibelius's Seventh Symphony, *Tapiola*, and to a lesser extent, the incidental music to *The Tempest*, are not only three of the very greatest works in his whole output, but notable masterpieces, each in its own formal category, within the entire literature of music; moreover, the Sixth Symphony, which is yet another great work belonging to this period, on close acquaintance, reveals a transcendental joy, a serene beauty and classical perfection, which must surely raise it to an equal stature and unique significance among his major works.

Perhaps the greatest influence on Sibelius during the composition of this work, and to a lesser degree also of the Seventh Symphony, were the works of Palestrina, whom he appreciated almost above any other master at this time; in fact, we shall find in these two symphonies, not only a certain affinity in spirit with the music of the Renaissance master, but also the direct influence of the modal tradition and, at times, even of the polyphonic texture of the sixteenth century style. And, as I shall show later in this essay when considering Sibelius's use of ' thematic germs ', Palestrina had laid an equal stress on the importance of achieving a sense of unity among the separate movements of any great work, and even had attained this cohesion, perhaps less unconsciously, by means very similar to those of Sibelius.

It is interesting that Beethoven also should have returned to the purity and modal tendency of the old masters in order to express one of the deepest and most inspired conceptions of his last period, the slow movement in the Lydian mode of his Quartet in A minor. Indeed this may be significant, for, in addition to this partial resemblance of his music to the style of the Renaissance and to that of Palestrina in particular, Sibelius's works now share many aspects in common with those of later Beethoven. He had always considered the Viennese master as being, for him, the musician above all; even in his student days, Sibelius had felt that ' Beethoven's quartets were to be appreciated as the Bible ', and naturally the music of the earlier master had been an important influence throughout his career. Fundamentally, both composers are in many ways representative of the same type of musician; each might be considered as being, intrinsically, almost as much a thinker and idealist as a musician—hence the fact that both Beethoven and Sibelius produced little of importance until after they had reached their twenty-fifth year, and both might spend many months, or even years, of extreme labour on the creation of one masterpiece. Moreover, it might be said that the most vital aim of each composer was to find expression for his ever more mature approach to life, embracing its deepest and most *unconscious* aspirations, united and integrated within a correspondingly unique conception of pure musical form. And Sibelius stands at approximately the same distance from the culmination of the Romantic movement as did Beethoven from its inception; thus it comes about that both composers in their later styles combine that formal mastery and austerity of the classical school with the freedom and originality of the Romantics, both maintaining a perfect balance between the opposing forces of traditional and innovatory ideals. In fact, in his later period, Sibelius was at last to reach a stage in which he could feel a real bond of unity with the Beethoven of the last quartets, the late sonatas and Ninth Symphony. Each had arrived, and not without intense struggle, at that same contemplative outlook and aloof detachment from the outer world, both their styles being characterised by a striking concentration of thought, a refinement and subtlety of expression. And even if Beethoven is inclined to be more esoteric and mystical in feeling (especially in his most intimate slow movements) and Sibelius rather more elemental and aloof, their symphonic writing (for instance, in their Choral and Seventh Symphonies respectively) is, in either case, characterised by a struggle for unity, a profundity and vastness of conception such as is quite unique in the entire history of the art form. And design and structure in the later works of both composers, far from being bound by any established procedures, evolve naturally and inevitably from the inner compulsion of their own ideas alone, their melody being equally free from traditional pattern, often consisting to a large extent of tiny pregnant motives or thematic fragments.

In mentioning, however, these rather incidental points of resemblance between the styles of their maturity, I do not in the least intend to overstress their similarity, especially as those elements which both composers share in common refer mainly to their symphonic writing alone. For actually, at this time, as also during the three other phases of his development, Sibelius's style bears witness to four quite contrasted aspects of his personality, all four of which are together unfolded *throughout* his whole development. In the most representative of these, we meet the universal thinker and inspired master of the symphonies, the String Quartet and the Violin Concerto—which doubtless constitute by far the most important expression of his genius. Second in importance, yet equally inspired and not less successful, there is the master of the tone-poems and the works for solo voice (sometimes with chorus) and orchestra, in which we usually meet a more distinctly Finnish and imaginative side of Sibelius, often inspired by the myths of the *Kalevala* or by the power and unique beauty of his northern surroundings. Thirdly, we must take into account the incidental music to plays and the best orchestral suites (consisting mainly of extracts from his incidental music) which together display a more eclectic and versatile aspect of his personality, now, on many occasions, able to interpret into music the contrasted moods and dramatic characterisation of plays from lands far distant from his own, at times, exquisitely inspired (as in the delicate *Rakastava* suite), on other occasions, producing works frankly popular in appeal (such as the *Karelia* suite, or the *Valse Triste* from the incidental music to *Kuolema*)—and yet in all its manifestations accompanied by a craftsmanship of quite indisputable mastery. Finally, there is a fourth and far less prominent group of pieces which seem to be quite apart from the rest, hardly anywhere, except perhaps in the most inspired of the songs, attaining to anything like the heights reached by his other works, and—most surprising of all—revealing little or no sense of progression from the earlier to the latest examples, although written periodically throughout the composer's lifetime. Within this category, there must be placed the majority of the songs and unaccompanied vocal works, practically all the miniatures for the piano and for various instrumental combinations (amounting to well over a hundred in number), the lesser orchestral suites (which often are surprisingly conventional and even banal in expression), and the remaining few miscellaneous works for orchestra. Sibelius himself has mentioned that most of these small pieces were written only in his free moments, presumably to gain relaxation and experience from work that poses no problems, and thus develop spontaneity and fluency of expression; while, no doubt, they also served in some degree to relieve his financial position. In this type of work, we must expect to find fluent but often facile expression, hardly ever distinguished by any particular qualities, rather than the inspired message of the symphonies or the exceptional originality and imaginative atmosphere of the tone-poems.

At least it might be said that this aspect of his style corresponds to a similar group of works within the output of nearly every composer, even if, in Sibelius's music, it may be more predominant than is usually the case. But when we realise that each one of his major works, or in other words, each separate manifestation of the three *main* aspects of his personality, possesses an individuality, and therefore also a distinctive style, absolutely its own, we then can understand how wide and varied is the range of expression covered by his output as a whole. There may be a certain limitation in his choice of medium, there may be few signs of humour in his music (except perhaps in the last movement of *Belshazar*), little of sensuous appeal, and never brilliant virtuosity for its own sake; moreover (and this is the only real point of weakness) he may only too seldom lay bare that deep personal sentiment—striving, as it were towards the depths of spirituality, yet always so profoundly human in feeling—such as illumines the most sublime slow movements of his predecessors.[1] But, despite this one shortcoming, his music, when considered in its entirety, is characterised by a breadth of appeal with which the work of few other artists can compare. As Cecil Gray has said in his admirable monograph on the composer : ' Sibelius, in fact, has provided a satisfactory answer to the question which has been debated so solemnly and for so long by philosophers, aestheticians, and art critics, namely, whether the artist should create for his own personal satisfaction like Flaubert, for an ideal audience of a " happy few " as urged by Stendhal, primarily for his own countrymen in accordance with the doctrines of the nationalists, for Mr. Newman's hypothetical " average intelligent music-lover ", or for the ordinary man in the street or simple peasant as Tolstoy would have him do; and he has solved the problem by writing music for all of them, of each kind, at different times, in different works.'

In the foregoing pages I have attempted to trace the general characteristics and development of Sibelius's style, together with the most important influences affecting that development. Now it remains to examine this evolving idiom in greater detail, and from a more technical point of view, studying in turn his struggle to achieve a sense of unity within each work as a whole, his gradual integration of form and changing attitude towards tonality, harmony, melodic style and texture, finally arriving at a consideration of his music in relation to that of his predecessors and contemporaries, together with a suggestion of his significance for the future.

Sibelius's progression in purely technical matters in many respects provides as interesting a subject for study as is offered by his stylistic and inner developments, for all three, in reality, are simply different aspects of the one basic evolution; his progress in technique is naturally to a great extent the outcome of his need for further expression, whereas this demand, in turn, is intimately bound up with

---

[1] For, with Sibelius, the only exceptional occasions are in the particularly fine slow movement of his Quartet, or in the first part of the Seventh Symphony.

his growing artistic personality and ever-greater experience of life. Furthermore, his general method of procedure—like that of every master—is never merely the product of academic theory, nor hampered (at any rate in his later works) by any forced reliance on past traditions inevitably rooted in a type of expression quite distinct from his own. We never find that fundamental incongruity between content and form, between essentially romantic expression and yet classical style, which so frequently weakens and disintegrates the symphonic works of his immediate predecessors, sometimes rendering symphonies even by Schumann, Dvořák and Tchaïkovsky quite imperfect in conception and—as it appears to some—rather ineffective as a final result.[1] Sibelius's utterance, on the contrary, is invariably inspired by sufficient strength and vitality to embrace within each major phrase of its development its own stylistic independence together with its own advance in technique; thus, we should always keep in mind this utterance—that is the vital music itself—even when examining the purely technical aspects inherent in its expression.

This may be especially noticed while studying the means by which Sibelius gradually attained to an ever greater sense of unity within each whole work, arriving in his later masterpieces at that unique coherence, at that oneness of conception, which is revealed in *Tapiola* and the Sixth and Seventh Symphonies. Without doubt, this advance, together with his gradual integration of form and progress in orchestration, is a feature of his style which is uppermost in importance, not only on acount of its great intrinsic value in his own works, but because of its vital contribution towards the evolution of musical form and its special significance for future composers. For unity of conception is not only a requirement of taste or merely an additional aesthetic quality; it is an attribute which is absolutely essential to the natural integrity and to the final beauty of any creation, whether appertaining to art, to creed, or to nature herself. In the realms of music, for instance, unity within diversity is the ideal, indeed is positively indispensable, to the perfection of any melody, of any form (or separate movement) or of any work that would achieve greatness in its complete conception.[2]

---

[1] Dvořák's Symphony No. 2 in D minor is, of course, an important exception to this generalisation.

[2] In fact it is precisely the capacity of comprehending a work—or at any rate, each movement—*as a whole* that is the supreme gift of the creative, the executive, and appreciative musician alike (distinguishing him from those whose emphasis or appreciation is primarily focused on the individual melodies or episodes from which the work is built).

And thus it follows that, however perfect its themes may be when considered individually, the poetic idea and the beauty of a movement in its entirety are bound to be lost, unless it be conceived as one organic whole. (In this way, perfection of form becomes a first essential in music, as indeed it is in every other artistic or intellectual achievement.) And even should all its movements be perfect when regarded as separate pieces, the conception of a work *as a whole* still cannot rise to true greatness and power, indeed, even be considered a single entity, unless a real coherence exist between its constituent movements. Without this coherence, a work may possibly attain to such perfection and relative greatness as might, for example, a composition, consisting of a study, a nocturne, a polonaise and a ballade of Chopin placed together in an attempt to create one complete work. Yet how much greater will be the vast conception embracing all the separate movements of a work, at the same time, uniting them in the way its one general type of feeling and inner logic pervade the whole!

This has been the aim of Sibelius : to achieve complete unity within real diversity, and thereby an extraordinary breadth of vision; in fact, it is largely in this way that he has risen to such greatness and overwhelming mastery of expression in his later works. Before considering how far his approach may have been unconscious and how far deliberate, we will examine the achievement itself, together with the technical symptoms, or the concomitant technical means accompanying its advance.

For the purpose of analysis, these means may be separated into four distinct categories. As a primary essential, Sibelius invariably establishes a sense of proportion between the constituent movements, a balanced relationship between their keys (or tonal centres), and a real consistency of style and mood throughout the work as a whole : secondly, a theme may sometimes find its way unobtrusively from one movement into another, either anticipating or reawakening an idea from another movement : thirdly, Sibelius quite often breaks down the boundaries between two or even more of the movements by welding them together to form one continuous organic whole : and fourthly—and by far the most important of all, both for its intrinsic value and as an example for the future—there is his ever more subtle tendency towards spontaneously evolving his themes throughout an entire work from one or two ' thematic gems '.

In order to understand the full significance of this approach, it may be as well to view it in perspective—as the natural culmination of all progress up to this time. For the attainment of unity within diversity has been a problem which has faced composers, sometimes unconsciously and sometimes rather more deliberately, ever since the sonata became an established form. At least, they paid attention to the tonal connection and to the sense of proportion interrelating and balancing the separate movements, and to the provision of a certain consistency of style and approach within each work as a whole. Yet even as early as in the sonatas of Vitali, Corelli and Tartini, we find the basic principle of cyclic form already in existence. A theme may not only be changed from its position of first subject to that of second subject, or even be transferred from one movement to another, but sometimes each of the movements might be founded on transformations of one main constant theme. In this way, an extraordinary homogeneity of material had been gained even if often at the expense of variety, richness, and breadth of expression. Later, in sonatas and symphonies by C. P. E. Bach, in Haydn's Sonata in A major (No. 26 in the Breitkopf *Gesamtausgabe*) and in Mozart's Symphony in D (K. 181), the individual movements have already begun to be linked together to form one continuous whole, and Haydn and Mozart may at times also relate their minuet thematically to its trio, or their first movement thematically to their finale.

Yet the real problem of establishing a coherence in the complete work was not to arrive with any great insistence until Beethoven began to infuse each of the movements with a strongly marked character of its own, thus inviting a real diversity and sometimes even a deep sense of contrast between their expression. Previously, just as there is not to be found so striking a difference between the various personalities of contemporary classical composers, between their separate works written in the same formal category, or even between different themes written in approximately the same tempo, so too, there cannot be found that same contrast of mood and character between the movements of each complete work. Pattern, or perfection of form, rather than mood or expression, had been the most vital element in music, and variety within pattern naturally implies a far less fundamental type of diversity than does variety of mood and expression. Thus it is not surprising to find that from the time of Beethoven onwards, composers have gradually come to realise, not only a more ambitious contrast between the characters of the individual movements, but also between their tonal centres (as also between the keys *within* each movement); and, at the same time, have been faced with a far more intense and more deliberate struggle to retain an equal correspondence between them.

Beethoven, in his Fifth Symphony and first 'Razumovsky Quartet, extends his scherzo, and in his G major and E flat Piano Concertos, in his Violin Concerto and in several sonatas,[1] extends his slow movements, so that these lead naturally into their subsequent finales; in his Quartet in C sharp minor, he links together all seven movements so as to create one continuous tonal conception. In his sonatas Opp. 13, 31, No. 3, 57, 81, 106, 109 and 110, as also in his Quartet in B flat, Op. 130, we find 'thematic germs' stealing their way imperceptibly into more than one movement; and in his Fifth and Ninth Symphonies, as also in his sonatas Op. 27, No. 1, Op. 101 and in Op. 102, No. 1, themes are brought back in such a way as surely cannot fail to be noticed consciously by the listener.

This manner of interrelating the movements—namely, by the definite interchange or transformation of themes—became the favourite method of later composers. Schumann, Brahms, Chopin, Tchaïkovsky, Dvořák, César Franck, Bruckner and Elgar each contributed towards its advance in many of their most representative works, sometimes allowing themes to recur as an integral part of a later movement (as with Beethoven, or in Schubert's Trio in E flat and in Brahms's Violin Sonata in G major), perhaps in a more organic manner (as in the cyclic form of Franck, Vincent d'Indy and Saint-Saëns, or with the 'representative themes' of Liszt), at times, more for dramatic emphasis (as with the 'motto themes' of Tchaïkovsky and Dvořák) or in a more associative rôle (as with the *idée fixe* of Berlioz or with Richard Strauss). And, contemporaneously, Mendelssohn (in his Scottish Symphony, his Violin Concerto and two piano concertos), Schumann (in his Symphony in D minor), and Liszt (in his Piano Sonata and concertos) were each trying to impart still greater coherence to the whole by grafting together their separate movements, Schumann and Liszt combining this fusion with complete freedom in transferring their themes (as had Schubert previously in his *Wanderer* Fantasia). Although these methods were not always entirely successful in their aims—sometimes interfering with the formal perfection of the individual movements and often being too evidently intentional, rather than latent in the original conceptions—they certainly marked an important stage within the gradual comprehension of entire works as a whole, and undoubtedly were indispensable to recent developments, such as are revealed in the modern tendency towards conceiving, not only tone-

---

[1] Namely the Piano Sonatas, Op. 27, No. 1, the *Appassionata*, the *Waldstein, Les Adieux*, Op. 101 in A, and the 'Cello Sonatas, Op. 69, Op. 102, No. 1, and Op. 102, No. 2.

poems, but sonatas and symphonic works as one single movement,[1] as also to the especially organic achievements of Sibelius.

For Sibelius has furthered and has brought to a higher state of integration all three of these special lines of advance. In his First Symphony, he had brought back and re-emphasised in the opening bars of his finale the long introductory theme to the first movement; yet this single and rather conventional attempt was not sufficient to impart a real sense of unity to four movements otherwise so unrelated. Already in the Second Symphony, though a greater consistency of mood is maintained throughout the movements and despite the contrast between their tonal centres (the trio of the scherzo, for instance, being in E flat minor, the finale in D major), a far greater coherence can be felt within the work as a whole. The technical means by which this has been achieved are apparent, not only in the way the trio section leads uninterruptedly into the finale, but far more by that tendency which, for the purpose of analysis, we have separated into a fourth category—by the manner in which themes throughout all four movements are evolved from one pregnant ' thematic germ '.

It has already been suggested that this latter trend (which undoubtedly can become the most organic of all) had previously been hinted at, even earlier than in the above-mentioned seven sonatas of Beethoven, within certain masses of Palestrina. Michael Haller has shown how in the *Missa Iste Confessor*, at least two-thirds of its total number of bars contain references to seven motives derived from one main melody; whilst in the *Aeterna Christi Munera*, the first hymn is divided into three motives, and these appear in every movement, often being used symbolically in such a significant manner as might even remind us of Wagner's use of leitmotives. This surely shows beyond doubt that Palestrina used the device intentionally. With Sibelius, however, the use of thematic germs seems to be so natural and so much an integral part of his actual conception that at times we cannot but wonder whether he is conscious of their presence. Indeed, it might be added that, after his preliminary attempt in his First Symphony, Sibelius's sense of unity is always achieved (no matter by which technical means) entirely naturally and always quite unobstrusively.

In his Second Symphony,[2] the all-pervading thematic germ consists

---

[1] For instance, the *Kammersymphonie* of Schönberg, the Fourth Symphony of Franz Schmidt, the Third Symphony of Roy Harris, Sibelius's Seventh Symphony, Bartók's Third Quartet.

[2] I must here thank the editor of *Music and Letters* for permission to quote matter contained in my article on ' The Use of Germ Motives by Sibelius ' (January 1942).

of a falling fifth, invariably distinguished by the accented beat falling on the *higher* note. In the first movement, this highly significant germ (which we will refer to as $z$) forms the characteristic phrase of the two main subjects (Ex. 12 and the ' figure of dropping fifths ' mentioned by Mr. Abraham on p. 20), besides appearing in a passage for violins alone (Ex. 11) and being used almost continually in the development section (as well, of course, as returning many times during the recapitulation).

The passage with which the second movement begins, and which is later heard as the accompaniment to its first subject, will be found to refer continually to motive $z$. In the same way, the characteristic phrase of the two other subjects (Exs. 122 and 123) of this section again consists of this same insistent figure. And both these subjects are repeated in many different keys. After two forte statements of motive $z$ in the bass, a new cantabile section is reached, beginning with a beautiful theme which is once again evolved from the thematic germ, as also from a previous subject (Ex. 122).

The scherzo has only one theme which contains our motive; this thematic fragment is played twice by the wood-wind (p. 71 of the miniature score). The theme of the trio which follows is one of infinite sadness and poignant beauty; yet for all its originality we feel we know its story before it has been uttered. This air of profound mystery is surely achieved by the subtle but very significant introduction of the thematic germ, by now firmly rooted in our subconscious minds; it is let fall from the ninth of those repeated B flats. Both the scherzo and trio return once more but, as has already been mentioned, this time the latter is developed so as to lead straight into the finale.

Except for an insignificant mention by the strings (just before letter B, p. 105 of the miniature score), motive $z$ does not appear in this last movement until we reach a passage (un poco con moto, p. 107) which suggests its connection with its own inversion. This inversion, by the way, had already been presented five times within the movement.

The second subject, which is played by the wood-wind, contains a very definite allusion to motive $z$ (p. 109, bar 4). And in mentioning only the occasions in which this all-pervading thematic germ appears in actual *subjects*, we must be careful not to forget how many times it will again be heard in repetitions and developments of these themes.

We have seen, then, to what great extent this vitally pregnant phrase has been used by Sibelius in his Second Symphony. Naturally it would be wrong to expect *every* theme to have been evolved from this single figure, for although such close unity might possibly be confined to one movement (for instance, the first of Beethoven's Fifth Symphony with its characteristic rhythmic germ), it would only become monotonous if extended throughout an entire work. In fact, diversity of thought and mood is quite as important as unity within such large-scale compositions.

Sibelius's next major work—the Violin Concerto in D minor—most certainly cannot be considered to form one *united* conception, nor indeed can it have been originally conceived as such. In fact, as in his First Symphony, not only can little sense of unity be felt between the individual movements (these being only slightly related in style and key), but each movement taken by itself is likewise not distinguished by any complete coherence or, in other words, by such organic form and inevitable continuity as may be found within his finer and more mature achievements. It would seem that, as it is true of the majority of composers, on those occasions in which Sibelius is not inspired by the very highest flights of his genius, each and every aspect of his style bears witness to the fact correspondingly.

In his Third Symphony, Sibelius once again undoubtedly considers the problem of imparting unity to his three movements, though not to the same extent as had been shown in his Second Symphony. In the Third, we do find a close relationship of style and approach between the first and last movements, as also a subtle reference in the finale to the lyric theme of the intermediate movement; yet this middle movement seems to fall rather outside the plan of the whole, and thus the work in its *complete* conception can hardly be said to attain to real greatness and perfection.

But, with the completion of his String Quartet *Voces Intimæ*, and from this time onwards, we shall find that Sibelius has conceived each major work as one coherent whole and has invariably achieved this sense of unity by even more unobtrusive and natural means, and perhaps, on many occasions, largely spontaneously. In his Quartet, this coherence comes about in three distinct ways. Firstly, there is the extensive use throughout the work of purely conjunct motion (pointed out by Cecil Gray); secondly, as Mr. Scott Goddard has already pointed out, various passages will be found to occur practically note for note in more than one movement—and it will be noticed that the second movement follows directly from the first; and thirdly, there is again the use in all five movements of a single thematic germ.

Sibelius has always tended to evolve his themes from mere fragments of scale passages, but in this Quartet, such predominance of conjunct motion goes far in establishing a definite relationship between the individual movements. Of the *second* way in which a sense of unity has been obtained, I will mention only the most outstanding examples. In the first movement, take the second subject (Ex. 91) and the bars immediately preceding it (Ex. 90); in the second movement we meet a passage (figure 2, p. 10 of the miniature score) which is practically identical, except for being in a different key; Mr. Goddard has already drawn attention to the connection between the opening of the second movement (Ex. 92) and Ex. 91. Compare also the passage seven bars after figure 5 in the first movement with bars 11–12 and 15–16 from the end of the second, and the bars before and after figure 1 in the first movement with those before and after figure 3 in the fifth. Naturally, it is very much open to question how far these transformations were intentional and how far they are to be taken simply as symptoms of the underlying unity of his conception; but this matter we shall consider later on.

The 'thematic germ' which Sibelius has used throughout the whole Quartet is again the interval of a falling fifth, invariably characterised by the accented beat falling on the upper note.[1] In the first movement, this figure occurs three times within the second subject alone, the start of which is shown in Ex. 91. In the second movement, it recurs three times within the principal theme (bars 7–9). In the long theme of the slow movement, there are frequent allusions to this germ motive. In the fourth movement, Sibelius does not mention this motive until the last bars of the first subject; but here the reference is particularly noticeable (bars 22–23). Nor is this the only subject to contain the germ motive; it will be seen that two of the subsequent themes continually refer to it.

In the principal subject of the last movement, there are two allusions to the thematic germ, but these, it must be admitted, are not so significant. As a whole, however, this Quartet leaves us with a feeling of unity equalled only in the quartets of Beethoven's last period; nor has the independence of the individual movements been sacrificed or in any way impaired as may be felt in quartets of Dvořák, Smetana, Dohnányi, d'Indy and Franck.

There is no need to prolong this essay with an account of the use of a thematic germ in Sibelius's Fourth Symphony; Cecil Gray has

---

[1] The reader will remember that Mr. Goddard attaches more importance to the falling fourth.—ED.

already shown how the interval of an augmented fourth (or diminished fifth) constitutes the leading figure of all four movements. The use of this striking interval throughout the work, together with its attendant freedom of tonality, and the extraordinary concentration of thought and intensity of mood pervading each movement, succeed in establishing a sense of unity such as has hardly ever been equalled in any other symphonic work.

In the Fifth Symphony, Sibelius's means are particularly original; indeed, are even more so than those he had used on previous occasions. As was true of his Third Symphony, the form of the whole work is tripartite, the first movement consisting of a fusion of two movements (as did the finale of the earlier work) so natural and seemingly inevitable as to result in the creation of one single organism. Furthermore, as again had been the case in his Third Symphony, the first movement is very closely related to the finale in both style and mood, while the sense of progression throughout the work is once more particularly prominent; and, whereas in the finale of the Third Symphony, Sibelius had alluded to the graceful melody of his middle movement, in the intermediate movement of the Fifth Symphony, he anticipates in the bass, two or three times, but even more unobtrusively, the main theme of his finale. But here the parallel ends, for in this later work, the middle movement may also be felt to be completely integrated within the whole; and this relationship has mainly come about by the fact that the characteristic rhythm of its single basic subject had also pervaded the preceding movement. This ' rhythmic germ ' we will consider later when studying the peculiar form of this opening movement.

In his Sixth Symphony, as also in the Seventh and in *Tapiola*, Sibelius reaches the final stage in his quest for, or in his spontaneous attainment of, complete unity. In this work, not only is the entire conception illumined by an all-pervasive lyricism and transcendental maturity of approach, reminding us at times of the modality of the old masters, but all four movements are further inter-related by the recurrence and transformation of one main theme, and once again by the vital presence of a thematic germ. This integral theme, which consists of a minor scale of five notes rising from the tonic, and which finds it way unobtrusively into each movement, is first presented as the main clause of the principal subject (see Ex. 30) as well, of course, as appearing in different forms, sometimes inverted, throughout the first movement. In the allegretto moderato it characterises the concluding part of the main theme, but as before, again pervades practically the entire movement. In the opening subject of the third movement it may be heard, slightly transformed (bars 4 and 5), as also in the answering phrases in the wood-wind; and, naturally, it re-appears in the numerous developments and repetitions of these two themes. But in the finale the germ-theme returns exceedingly frequently, quite often in developed forms, and is finally to be heard in practically its original form during the doppio più lento coda (namely, in bar 7). Yet, once again, it cannot be over-emphasised that the value of this type of thematic transformation by no means rests upon its conscious appreciation by the listener; the fact that this and similar subtleties in Sibelius's music have long passed unnoticed only goes to show how they have performed their true and proper function within the whole—in that they have not in any way intruded consciously on the natural expression and innate logic of the music itself.

The thematic germ, which adds further to the complete unity of the whole, now consists of a rising third, invariably distinguished by the accented beat falling on the lower note; we will refer to this figure as motive *p*. In the first movement, this germ forms the characteristic phrase of the principal subject (Ex. 30), which is shown by the fact that continuations of this theme so often allude to this rising third.

The second theme of the movement is almost entirely evolved from motive *p* (cf. Ex. 31) and the germ motive appears in many different forms throughout the movement, sometimes as developments of the foregoing subjects and sometimes as a figure of accompaniment.

In the second movement, the theme out of which the entire first section is built, refers to motive *p* no fewer than four times, although in rather an allusive way. The second part of the movement consists of tiny thematic fragments presented by the wood-wind against a background of semiquavers played by the strings. The upper part of this long string passage will be seen to consist almost entirely of motive *p* in one or other of two forms (pp. 36 and 38 of the miniature score).

In the third movement, a scherzo which has no contrasting trio section, the thematic germ appears twice in the opening subject and the second theme again alludes to it.

The principal subject of the fourth movement can best be distinguished by its rhythm, since its melodic form changes on each appearance; motive *p* occurs only in two of the many statements of this subject. Although other fragmentary themes are also evolved from the thematic germ, it is not until we reach the coda that it finally assumes real importance. Here, string passages of great originality and harmonic beauty which, however, are intimately connected with the earlier part of the movement, are answered on each occasion by similar bars in the wood-wind. In each of these answering phrases the characteristic interval is once again the interval of a rising third, distinguished by the accented beat falling on the lower note. Ex. 124 is one example. And it is mainly due to the thematic germ recurring seven times in this way, as also, to the final recapitulation of our germ-theme that we feel this last section to be so organically part of the movement. Indeed, although this superb coda might well appear to carry us far away from the music that has gone before, it seems, at the same time, to have grown entirely naturally from the preceding bars and to be an integral part, indeed a culmination, of the entire work as a whole. This surely is symbolical of the extreme subtlety and originality with which Sibelius achieves complete unity and perfection of form without thereby in any way trespassing on the diversity and spontaneity of his thought or mood.

We have seen, then, how Sibelius has at times fused one movement into another; on some occasions has allowed one theme to find its way unobtrusively into each movement; and has used thematic germs throughout his Second and Fourth Symphonies, the String Quartet and the Sixth Symphony. In the Seventh Symphony, Sibelius was to reach a stage in which there was no longer any need even to preserve the four-movement form. In this great single movement he achieves a unity and, at the same time, a diversity of thought and mood, such as even he had never yet attained. Cecil Gray has shown how this coherence is partly achieved by the use of two characteristic melodic progressions throughout the work : firstly by the interval of a semi-tone rising to the tonic, and secondly by the interval of a whole tone descending to the tonic. In the last two bars these two progressions are presented in a way that suggests that Sibelius must have been fully aware of their employment.

Thus the problem is again raised how far the thematic germs throughout all these works were used unconsciously, how far with the composer's full knowledge. No doubt only Sibelius himself could finally answer this question, but, so far, he has given us but one direct clue to its answer. In relating a conversation he had had with Mahler,[1] he tells us : ' When our conversation touched on the essence of the symphony, I said that I admired its severity and style and *the profound logic that created an inner connection between all*

[1] Quoted by Ekman.

*the motives.* This was the experience I had come to in composing. Mahler's opinion was just the reverse : " *Nein, die Symphonie muss sein wie die Welt. Sie muss alles umfassen* ".' (No, symphony must be like the world. It must embrace everything.)

Whether or not these words may be taken to show conclusively that Sibelius was fully aware of his use of thematic germs, we may at least assume that the principle must have been an integral part of his natural conception and never merely the result of independent theorising; as with Beethoven, the immense labour spent on a composition, including all the tentative searchings of the sketch books, must ultimately have been impelled by the sheer intuition of his subconscious mind, never by considerations extraneous to his actual conception. And perhaps this point is not unimportant, for if this great formal idea, or indeed, if any innovation of his, be of example to future composers, it undoubtedly follows that it must be the *vital trend* rather than the outward manner that may serve as ideal. There is an unbridgeable gulf between the deliberate manipulation of themes to connect them to a single motive (such as is found in Schönberg's Quartet in D minor) and the vital organic growth of thematic germs, as exemplified in the music of Sibelius; and it is, without doubt this latter trend that will yield further developments,[1] for not only has the principle been absolutely indispensable to five of the very greatest works of Sibelius, but, at the same time, it must be the most natural advance towards the attainment of ever greater unity than has yet evolved.

Another remarkable feature of Sibelius's style, similar to the one we have just considered, although of less importance, is the manner in which the two highly individual figures which he had used as thematic germs, reappear to characterise important themes throughout his entire output. This phenomenon might be passed over as a mere mannerism, but for the fact that the two motives are so highly significant, are so personal to Sibelius, and yet recur to such an amazing extent in works of every formal category—as much in his earlier style as in the works of his maturity—that it may be nearer the truth to regard them as unconscious 'source motives', as pregnant phrases, so deeply characteristic, or so fundamental to his utterance, as to have remained fertile throughout his development.

The figure consisting of a rising third, invariably distinguished by the beat falling on its lower note, besides pervading the Sixth

[1] Thematic germs have already appeared in Bloch's Piano Quintet, in his Violin Sonata and throughout the whole of his Piano Sonata; they are also to be found throughout Vaughan Williams's Fourth Symphony.

Symphony as thematic germ, reappears in its original and highly characteristic form (thus always resulting in a slight syncopation) twice within the theme of the slow movement of the First Symphony; three times within the great wood-wind subject in the finale of the Fifth Symphony; in the theme of the scherzo-like section of the Seventh Symphony; within a theme in the Violin Concerto (first movement, five bars after figure 3): many times in the theme of the Intermezzo from the *Karelia* suite; twice within the lyrical melody of *Finlandia*. It finally reappears in a theme in *Tapiola* (first present on p. 13 of the miniature score); and naturally it always recurs in the numerous repetitions and developments of these subjects.

But the second figure—consisting of a falling fifth, invariably distinguished by the accented beat falling on its *upper* note—besides pervading the Second Symphony and String Quartet as thematic germ, will again be found to characterise themes in *Rakastava, The Swan of Tuonela*, the first two movements of the First Symphony, the Romance for Strings, two movements of *Pelléas et Mélisande*, the second movement of *Belshazar*, more than one theme of *Pohjola's Daughter*, themes in *Night-ride and Sunrise, In Memoriam*, the first and third movements of the Third Symphony, the last three movements of the Fourth Symphony, themes in *The Bard, The Oceanides*, the middle movement of the Fifth Symphony, the finale of the Sixth, in several excerpts from *The Tempest* and in an equally large proportion of melodies within Sibelius's smaller pieces. Nor is it as if these two figures were of frequent occurrence in music or were in any way insignificant. The motive of a rising third, with the beat falling on the *lower* note, would almost seem to be peculiar to Sibelius's utterance alone; while the figure of a falling fifth, accented only on the *upper* note, although not so exceptional, reveals a most interesting genealogy, which is partly reflected by a study of comparative national folk-music. This figure, that is, in its most characteristic form, seems to be almost quite foreign to music of the Latin races, and hardly less so to English or German expression, but comparatively often to be met in Russian folk-music or in works of the Russian masters (especially in those of Borodin and Mussorgsky), and is a definite characteristic of Finnish folk-music as a whole. Perhaps this is not surprising—that it should be this motive that should be further symptomatic of Sibelius's affinity with the Russian school and should reveal his relationship with the Finnish folk soul in particular; for is it not true that this vital figure happens to be absolutely characteristic of the instinctive directness of expression and of the rhythmic vitality which underlie, not only Sibelius's art, but the expression of both these more elemental races too?

Sibelius's attitude towards the question of form, already discussed by Mr. Abraham and Mr. Wood, constitutes yet a further example of his controlled, yet essentially instinctive approach, as also of the manner in which, basically, his style tends to conform to the ways of Nature. I have already mentioned his almost pantheistic love of the natural world and the force with which its elemental power and beauty have stimulated his mood and inspiration; yet in truth this influence has delved far deeper, right down to the very roots of his expression, affecting as much the growth of a single thematic germ, as the form of an entire movement, indeed (as I have already tried to show when discussing thematic germs) sometimes of his complete work as a whole.

It is true that during the preliminary stages of his development (for instance, in the opening movement of his First Symphony, in the finale of the Second Symphony and in the first movement of his Third Symphony) his ideas and conceptions as yet had not been inspired with sufficient strength and originality to have transcended the boundaries of sonata form, and to have arrived (as from this time onwards, they were to do) at their own natural form and development, together with an attendant freedom as regards tonality, harmony and melodic structure. It is also true, as many writers have observed, that in certain movements Sibelius seems to have evolved a formal principle rather of his own : that in *Lemminkäinen's Home-coming*, in the opening movement of the Second Symphony, in the finale of the Third Symphony, the slow movement of the Fourth Symphony, and to a lesser extent, in the first movements of the Fifth and Sixth Symphonies, he inclines to present us first with melodic fragments, seemingly disconnected ideas, which only gradually grow up to form an integrated whole and then may disintegrate (as in the opening movement of the Second Symphony) or perhaps in this eventual synthesis, form the final culmination of the movement (as in the finale of the Third Symphony). But, as Mr. Wood has insisted, a trend which is far deeper and more essential to his style—and a tendency that underlies even his above-mentioned movements—is his basic insistence on *organic* form, on *natural* growth, on uninterrupted continuity of expression, on the attainment of balance, of unity within diversity, and on the complete freedom of his ideas to achieve their own development and seemingly *inevitable* fulfilment within the whole.

These characteristics, each of which witnesses to the closer harmony of the composer with the ways of Nature, have been becoming more and more prominent ever since sonata form began to emerge from its original rather stereotyped pattern, in which first and second subjects, the exposition, development and recapitulation were each carefully isolated, and methods of development had tended to become systematic rather than inevitable. Mozart, and Haydn in particular, might occasionally evolve members of their second subject from the melodic or rhythmic characteristics of their first subject;[1] Beethoven might achieve this type of growth by still more organic means (as in the first movements of his Fifth, Sixth and Seventh Symphonies, the sonatas *Les Adieux* and *Appassionata*), may even evolve his entire movement from a single rhythmic germ (as in the first movement of his Fifth Symphony), might dispense with the repetition of his exposition, with the formal breaks between the various subjects and sections, and by these means achieve a greater sense of progression and a more real sense of freedom from form imposed from without. Composers of the succeeding era might follow the example of Beethoven—even if not always from the sheer necessity of their own expression—or might aspire to still greater freedom within the domain of the symphonic poem; while Borodin (in the first movement of his First Symphony) and Wagner (in his *Kaisermarsch*) in some ways were to foreshadow the principle of gradual synthesis as later developed by Sibelius. But, as I have already suggested, the Finnish master, within his most representative movements (as also, within certain works as a *whole*) has approached nearest to the complete freedom and organic growth of Nature and to a higher degree of integration than hitherto had ever been achieved. The technical means which have made this possible are revealed in several ways in particular: in his art of transition (rather than by conceiving the work to consist of individual subjects and sections): in the way that a theme may grow by continually shedding and replenishing its component parts, thus always appearing to retain its identity, even if, eventually, it may have completely changed from its initial form : in the manner in which an important theme is invariably foreshadowed (and thus prepared) ever more obtrusively, before its actual arrival : and—most important of all—in the way that each

---

[1] Though in these cases this may have been simply a ' hang-over ' from primitive sonata-form in which the contrast was of key rather than of musical material.

subject may naturally derive from the theme that has gone before, or perhaps an entire movement evolve from a single rhythmic or thematic germ.

Within the limits of this essay, it is possible to suggest only a few of those instances which illustrate this superbly organic form, though actually, these subtleties would seem to be almost illimitable. In his First Symphony, Sibelius was still forced to rely mainly on pre-established structures (not that his ideas were altogether suited to these classical moulds) but already, in the opening bars of his finale proper, we can see how a theme may grow by the constant elimination and replacement of its constituent figures; and this is but the first of many similar instances which appear later. In the first movement of his Third Symphony, Sibelius again has recourse to sonata form, yet even here, his second subject is surely but a lyric reflection of his first theme, although now minor in key and quite contrasted in mood; in this case the affinity between these themes, comes about by the similarity of their melodic curves and by the presence of a semiquaver figure of four notes, which is not only common to both subjects but also pervades almost the entire development section.

The finales of the Fourth and Fifth Symphonies are founded on the balance maintained between two main moods, rather than on the more traditional antithesis of first and second subjects, or on the growth of tiny thematic fragments; yet, in either movement, the thematic contents underlying each main mood are intimately inter-related. For instance, in the Fourth Symphony, the characteristic phrase of the principal theme (which serves to establish the *second* main mood) had been anticipated, ever more obtrusively, both pizzicato in the bass (on three isolated occasions) and once again, as the first figure which constantly recurs during the long spiccato passage for strings; in the finale of his Fifth Symphony, Sibelius had hinted at his principal theme (which again establishes the *second* mood of the movement) not only towards the close of the long winding passage for strings but more fully, twice within the preceding movement.

The opening movement of Sibelius's Second Symphony is distinguished by the presence of both his two most important formal principles: by the tendency towards gradual synthesis, and by the way in which practically every theme evolves from a single melodic germ—in this case, consisting of a descending figure of three consecutive notes. The evolution of this germ might partly be traced if we compare Exs. 9, 11 and 125, the pizzicato passage for strings alone beginning at the end of p. 7 of the miniature score, and the incessant figure of accompaniment, altogether occupying no less than seventy-three bars of the movement, that begins on p. 9. In the final bars the introductory figure of three rising notes which had accompanied the first two themes (and which perhaps may be considered to be an inversion of the thematic germ), at last subsides to conclude the movement, instead, with the all-pervading motive of three *descending* notes.

Both these tendencies (gradual synthesis and the growth of thematic germs) are again in evidence within the finale of Sibelius's Third Symphony, but now, in an even more natural and subtle manner. Nothing is more remarkable than the way in which the motive of a falling third, accented on the upper note (which recurs in countless forms within the many thematic fragments with which the movement is gradually built) grows, ever more insistently, finally to form the characteristic figure of the great culminating theme during its first appearances (p. 53 of the miniature score); later, this triumphant theme, which itself is ever evolving, discards this characteristic progression of a falling third, now to include the motive of a falling fifth (again accented only on the upper note) which had played a similar role as thematic germ within those melodic fragments with which the movement began (for instance, the original form of Ex. 18). This surely is one of Sibelius's very greatest formal achievements, yet is quite independent of any past procedure.

The opening movement of the Fifth Symphony presents us with the first instance of the growth of a purely rhythmic germ—in this case consisting of a distinct syncopation. This motive appears first as the characteristic rhythm of the first subject (Ex. 25) and likewise in each of its many subsequent developments; is then heard still more insistently, and no fewer than six times, within the second theme (Ex. 26a); while it reappears with yet greater emphasis within the remaining third subject (Ex. 26c). Furthermore, the succeeding movement—which, incidentally, reveals the freedom and natural growth of Sibelius's development of variation-form—is based throughout on a rhythmic pattern which again is invariably distinguished by the presence of this rhythmic germ, though now in a less definite manner. Perhaps this latter stage in its evolution may not be appreciated except with repeated hearing; but this point is obviously incidental, for it is not as if any of these subtleties were necessarily intended to be consciously apprehended by the listener; once more, it is often doubtful whether even Sibelius was conscious of their significance.

The themes within the finale of the Sixth Symphony will again be found to have evolved from the distinctive rhythm of the first subject (Ex. 34a), in fact, to such an extent that it may now be nearer the truth to speak, not so much of separate subjects, as of successive stages within the gradual evolution of the first theme. The scherzo of this work is presented as one single whole (as is also that of the Fourth Symphony); indeed, it would now be almost inconceivable for Sibelius to interrupt the continuity and unity of his conception by splitting up his movement into the customary scherzo and trio. And this tendency towards ever more complete unity, natural growth and progression, rises to its very culmination within the succeeding masterpieces, *Tapiola* (in which the entire conception has evolved from the opening subject) and the Seventh Symphony (which is also conceived as one great organic whole). This latter work provides a supreme example, not only of this especially intuitive side to Sibelius's art—in the way that the entire work evolves from two pregnant thematic germs—but also of his more controlled approach to symphonic form—in the balanced symmetry, in the monumental power, in fact, in the timeless architecture of the whole conception. For, besides his deep-rooted insistence on organic form and uninterrupted continuity of expression, the work would seem, at the same time, to have been partly built up of finely balanced, yet definite, structural entities; for there are no fewer than twenty-six groups of bars which are heard more than once (either by being repeated or by reappearing later, often with changed orchestration and texture); and thus, of the total number of two hundred and fifty-three bars, it so happens that less than half that number are heard on one occasion only. Nevertheless, this presence of definite planning or control has been completely submerged beneath the continuous progression, the natural growth, beneath the concentration and the superb unity which pervade the Symphony as a whole.

A sense of balance has here been achieved, not only by the subtle distribution of climaxes and of reversions to the main centre of tonality, but also, by the triple recurrence of the great theme for solo trombone, Ex. 39, a subject which becomes more impressive on each presentation. In his first three symphonies, Sibelius had been content to recapitulate practically his entire exposition; but from this time onwards, in order to bring about a sense of equilibrium and conclusion, he often merely hints towards the end of the movement at his principal theme (as in *The Bard*, the scherzo of the Fourth Symphony and the allegretto of the Sixth Symphony) or instead may mainly concentrate on his principal theme together with its attendant derivations, at the same time re-emphasising the main centre of tonality (as in the opening movements of the remaining four symphonies). In these later works, this sense of tonality usually becomes established by entirely free and natural means, rather than by necessarily conforming to traditional resources of modulation, or to accepted cadences; sometimes this is achieved just by many significant allusions to the triad based on the new tonal centre; sometimes, by stressing this centre as an important and elongated pedal point (which at times is elaborated into an ostinato figure); and occasionally, simply by concentrating solely on the new tonic triad for innumerable bars (a practice that partly contributes towards the vast spaciousness of his style in general). In short, within these widening horizons, Sibelius's approach to tonality is equally free from any set adherence to the classical key system, to its chromatic extensions, to any recent systemisation, or to modality; yet is quite as free to embrace any one of these influences (for instance, bitonality in the Fourth Symphony, or modality in the Sixth) just when the needs of his expression so demand.

Sibelius's harmony, similarly, is quite independent of any fixed approach; its originality lies far more in the free interrelationship of chords than in the very nature of those chords themselves. In the opening movement of his Sixth Symphony, the second theme (Ex. 31) is accompanied by a harmonic progression of three consecutive triads, descending step by step in root position; otherwise Sibelius does not use consecutive fifths, yet, here the effect surely is as beautiful as it is original. In the finale (bars 6–14 after H in the miniature score) the bass part, on which the harmony is founded, descends by ten successive degrees down the whole-tone scale; this, once more, is quite exceptional, but the passage again appears to be an integral part of the movement as a whole. A trend, however, which is far more prevalent, and one that lends further individuality to his harmonic style, is the way in which Sibelius's melodic part is quite often doubled, at octaves, by some other voice within the harmonic scheme. In Ex. 126, to take but one instance, the thematic line (in the first violins) is doubled both by the second violins and violas; and this passage (from *The Swan of Tuonela*) also provides an example of the intense poignancy to which his harmony occasionally aspires;

for very similar passages reappear towards the close of *Tapiola*, the Sixth and Seventh Symphonies; in their great intensity and supreme beauty (as also, in the way that the strings play in their upper registers, subdivided and alone), they provide some of the few instances in which Sibelius's style draws very close to that of Wagner (especially, for example, to the Prelude to *Lohengrin*). But, in general, his harmony may be said to show two main characteristics: firstly, that extensive dissonance (which occurs comparatively rarely, except in the Fourth and Fifth Symphonies and in *Tapiola*) appears to be almost lost within the greater harmony of the whole, and inclines to be formal rather than personal in expression; and secondly, his progressions, as a whole, tend to be conditioned far more by the independent flow of the melodic parts, rather than themselves to condition these individual voices.

Yet perhaps this is hardly surprising, since Sibelius's texture, in general, reveals a gradual advance towards ever more complete integration as his thematic lines, his harmony, his rhythm and orchestration each merge into one single conception, each finally becoming an integral part of the other. Especially in his earlier works, his texture had sometimes been quite elemental, almost primitive, with its occasional accompaniments of plucked strings or arpeggio bowings (across the strings), its long-persistent figures, harmonies or rhythms, its equally protracted pedal points, its almost violent sforzandos for brass, and immense cumulative climaxes. Yet, again, at other times it could be equally refined (as in the Quartet or in *Rakastava*) and throughout its progression, besides becoming ever more integrated, tends to become more subtle and intricate (yet, not necessarily more elaborate) in design. Tempi may quicken within a movement; traditional types of melody or themes (as, for instance, Ex. 8 or Ex. 9) incline to give way to short pregnant motives whose significance lies mainly in their growth and interrelationship, or to other uniquely moulded themes (such as Ex. 37 or Ex. 39); we find bars of complete silence (such as characterised Beethoven's later style), a distinct preference for beginning a theme unobtrusively on a held note starting on an off-beat (as does Ex. 7), a very frequent and characteristic use of consecutive thirds and sixths (esvecially for the wood-wind) and countless appearances of a certain triplet figure which might be regarded as a further 'source motive' (as shown, for instance, in Exs. 46 and 55 and bar 7 of the Violin Concerto). Yet, as a whole, and despite these specific tendencies, Sibelius's texture becomes absolutely as free as every other aspect of his style and technique to conform purely to the needs of his expression alone.[1]

Nor is it as if this freedom implied any laxity or lack of stability; as I hope I have shown, although Sibelius may certainly embrace no fixed style, he is nevertheless an exceedingly fine stylist. And naturally, this truth confronts us, in all its emphasis, within his greatest achievements: in the Seventh Symphony, the Sixth and Fourth Symphonies, in *Tapiola*, (almost equally) in the Fifth Symphony and String Quartet, and (in a less profound manner) in *The Tempest, Oceanides, The Bard, The Swan of Tuonela, Lemminkäinen's Homecoming*, or in *Rakastava*. In fact, on such works as these (and especially on these symphonies of his maturity), Sibelius's real claim to greatness is based. Ultimately, all values in art or elsewhere, may remain purely a matter of individual opinion; and Sibelius may not have achieved so *many* supreme masterpieces as did Beethoven, Bach or Mozart; yet, in certain works, it can be said that he also has risen to supreme heights that transcend all comparisons of greatness. Within his finest symphonies and in *Tapiola*, there will be found united each one of those fundamental attributes which together are associated with true ' greatness ' in art. Within their mastery of form, their breadth of vision, there is complete unity: within their serene beauty, their profundity and their intensity of expression, there is real integrity: and within their comprehension, their freedom and unbounded vitality, Sibelius has achieved the most overwhelming originality; in fact, the closer we examine their style and technique, and the more we become acquainted with such works as these, the more is this complete mastery confirmed.

The combination of such qualities, it must be added, is rarely to be found within any art yet born of the twentieth century. Somehow Sibelius appears to have averted the disillusionment, the restlessness, the excessive sophistication and the escapism so often reflected in the works of his contemporaries. His First Symphony, it is true, may have centered on a personal, a brilliant and almost passionate reaction to the outer world, while his ideas, as yet, had hardly become integrated; his Fourth Symphony may have marked an astounding advance towards greater originality, towards a more elemental and profoundly contemplative mood; but the masterpieces of his maturity, as equally the accounts of his personality at this time, reflect the

---

[1] A striking instance of this is afforded by the long passages in the Fourth Symphony, which consist solely of one thematic line alone.

mind that has finally transcended reaction, that has attained to the deepest serenity by its oneness with Nature and its philosophic approach, that now would rather contemplate realities in their relationship and all discord as essential to one greater whole, that has attained to complete integration, balance and vitality and, above all, to an unbounded love of freedom, of beauty and of life itself.

And it is interesting, indeed significant, that this stage should have been reached subsequently to the conception of the Fourth Symphony and *Luonnotar*; in fact, after Sibelius had approached nearest to the contemporary trends of searching and revolution. For the great tranquillity and all-pervading beauty of this culminating phase—which had contrasted so bewilderingly with the harshness and sophistication of his time—was not really due to Sibelius's vision being rooted in some past approach to life; indeed, such depth and directness of expression could not possibly have so derived. In truth, Sibelius had transcended the contemporary scene, had arrived at a new spirit of classicism[1] and, from the point of view of style alone, had advanced even as far from the symphonic tendencies of later Beethoven, as did Beethoven from Haydn's.

Should this great symphonic style progress—and there is every reason to believe it will—Sibelius's culminating style (and especially his integration of form and the symphony as a whole) must surely remain of special significance for composers who would again assail these heights. While should the comprehensive, the transcendental approach to life prevail, these later works of Sibelius, like those of Beethoven, will inevitably be of great inspiration, not only for us to-day but for generations to come.

---

[1] Sibelius himself had said: ' It is curious, you know, the more I see of life, the more I feel convinced that classicism is the way of the future.'

# Chronology

| | |
|---|---|
| 1865 | Born (December 8th) at Tavastehus, Finland. |
| 1874 | First regular piano lessons. |
| 1875 | First attempt at composition. |
| 1876–8 | At the Suomalainen Normaalilyseo (Finnish Normal School), Tavastehus. |
| 1880 | Begins study of violin. |
| 1881 | Studies Marx's *Lehre von der musikalischen Composition*: first serious attempts at composition (chamber music). |
| 1885 | Becomes law student in University of Helsingfors and special student at Helsingfors Conservatoire of Music. |
| 1886 | Devotes himself entirely to music. |
| 1889 | String Suite and A minor Quartet publicly performed; Sibelius leaves the Conservatoire. |
| 1889–90 | Studies with Albert Becker in Berlin. |
| 1890 | Engagement to Aino Järnefelt. |
| 1890–1 | Studies in Vienna with Robert Fuchs and Karl Goldmark. |
| 1892 | *Kullervo* performed (April 28th); marriage (June 10th); *En Saga.* |
| 1892–1901 | Teacher of theory in Helsingfors Conservatoire. |
| 1893 | *Swan of Tuonela.* |
| 1894 | Visits to Italy and Bayreuth. |
| 1897 | Award of annual grant from Finnish Government. |
| 1899 | First Symphony and *Finlandia.* |
| 1900–1 | Foreign tours as conductor. |
| 1901 | Second Symphony. |
| 1901–5 | Ear trouble. |
| 1903 | Violin Concerto (original version). |
| 1904 | Removal from Helsingfors to Järvenpää. |
| 1905 | First visit to England. |
| 1907 | Third Symphony. |
| 1908 | Throat operation. |
| 1909 | *Voces Intimæ* |
| 1911 | Fourth Symphony. |
| 1914 | Visit to America. |
| 1915 | Fifth Symphony (original form). |
| 1918 | Finnish Civil War; Sibelius's house searched by Red Guards (February 11th and 13th); composer and family take refuge in Lappviken Asylum (March–April). |
| 1919 | Fifth Symphony (definitive form). |
| 1921 | Last visit to London. |
| 1923 | Sixth Symphony. |
| 1924 | Seventh Symphony. |
| 1925 | *Tapiola.* |

# Bibliography

ABRAHAM, GERALD : ' Sibelius's Symphonic Method '[1] (in *Musical Opinion*, London, October 1937–October 1938).

ANON : ' Giovanni Sibelius ' (with ' Bibliografia delle opere musicali di Giovanni Sibelius ') (in *Bollettino bibliografico musicale*, Milan, March 1932).

ANON : ' Mélodies de J. Sibelius ' (in *Le guide musical*, Brussels, 1906).

ARNOLD, ELLIOTT : *Finlandia: the Story of Sibelius* (Henry Holt and Co., New York, 1941).

BENNETT, RODNEY : ' Song-writers of the Day : III—Jean Sibelius ' (in *The Music Teacher*, London, Vol. V, No. 8, August 1926).

BLOM, ERIC : ' Sibelius ' (article in Cobbett's *Cyclopedic Survey of Chamber Music*, Oxford University Press, London, 1929).

CARDUS, NEVILLE : ' Sibelius ' (chapter in *Ten Composers*, Jonathan Cape, London, 1945).

CHERNIAVSKY, DAVID : ' The Use of Germ Motives by Sibelius ' (in *Music and Letters*, London, Vol. XXIII, No. 1, January 1942).

DAVIE, CEDRIC THORPE : ' Sibelius's Piano Sonatinas ' (in *Tempo*, London, March 1945).

EKMAN, KARL : *Jean Sibelius : en Konstnärs Liv och Personlighet* (Helsingfors, 1935); translated as *Jean Sibelius: his Life and Personality* (Alan Wilmer, London, 1936).

ELLIOTT, J. H. : ' Jean Sibelius : a modern enigma ' (in *The Chesterian*, London, Vol. XII, No. 92).

   ' The Sixth Symphony of Sibelius ' (in *Music and Letters*, London, Vol. XVII, No. 3, July 1936).

FLODIN, K. : *Finska Musiker* (Helsingfors, 1900).

   ' J. Sibelius ' (in *Finnische Rundschau*, No. 4, 1901).

FROSTERUS, SIGURD : ' Sibelius Koordinater ' (in *Nya Argus*, Helsingfors, 1932).

FOUGSTEDT, NILS-ERIK : ' Sibelius's Tonsättningar till Rydberg-Texter ' (in *Musik-Världen*, Stockholm, Vol. I, No. 10, December 1945).

FURUHJELM, E : *Jean Sibelius: hans Tondiktning och Drag ur hans Liv* (Borgå, 1916).

GODDARD, SCOTT : ' Sibelius's Second Symphony ' (in *Music and Letters*, Vol. XII, No. 2, April 1931).

GRAY, CECIL : *Sibelius* (Oxford University Press, London, 1931).

   *Sibelius: the Symphonies* (' Musical Pilgrim ' series, Oxford University Press, London, 1935).

KONOW, W. : ' Muistoja Jean Sibeliuksen poikavuosilta ' (in *Aulos*, Helsingfors, 1925).

KOTILAINEN, O : ' Mestarin muokattavana ' (in *Aulos*, Helsingfors, 1925).

---

[1] Partially reprinted, in revised form, in the present volume.

KROHN, ILMARI: *Der Formenbau in den Symphonien von Jean Sibelius* (Helsingfors, 1942).
*Die Stimmungsgehalt der Symphonien von Jean Sibelius* (2 vols.) (Helsingfors, 1946).

LEVAS, S.: *Jean Sibelius och hans hem* (Helsingfors, 1945).

MADETOJA, L.: ' Jean Sibelius opettajana ' (in *Aulos*, Helsingfors, 1925).

MEYER, ALFRED H.: ' Sibelius: Symphonist ' (in *Musical Quarterly*, New York, Vol. XXII, No. 1, January, 1936).

NEWMARCH, ROSA: *Jean Sibelius: a Finnish Composer* (Leipzig, 1906).
*Jean Sibelius: a Short Story of a Long Friendship* (C. C. Birchard Co., Boston, Mass., 1939; Goodwin and Tabb, London, 1944).

NIEMANN, WALTER: *Die Musik Skandinaviens* (Leipzig, 1906).
*Jean Sibelius* (Breitkopf's ' Kleine Musikerbiographien ', Leipzig, 1917).

RINGBOM, NILS-ERIC: 'Litteraturen om Jean Sibelius' (in *Svenska Tidskrift för Musikforskning*, Stockholm, 1942).

ROIHA, EINO: *Die Symphonien von Jean Sibelius* (Jyväskylä, 1941).

ROSENFELD, PAUL: ' Sibelius ' (chapter in *Musical Portraits*, Kegan Paul, London, 1922).

SANDBERG, BÖRJE: *Sibelius* (Helsingfors, 1940).

SOLANTERÄ, LAURI (ed.): *Sibelius* (facsimiles of manuscripts; notes by E. Roiha) (Helsingfors, 1945).

TANZBERGER, E.: *Die symphonischen Dichtungen von Jean Sibelius* (Würzburg, 1943).

TÖRNE, BENGT DE: *Sibelius: a Close-up* (Faber, London, 1937).

TOVEY, DONALD FRANCIS: Analyses of Sibelius's Third and Fifth Symphonies (in *Essays in Musical Analysis,* Vol. II, Oxford University Press, London, 1935).
Analysis of Sibelius's Violin Concerto (in *Essays in Musical Analysis*, Vol. III, Oxford University Press, London, 1936).
Analyses of Sibelius's Seventh Symphony and *Tapiola* (in *Essays in Musical Analysis*, Vol. VI, London, 1939).

WOOD, RALPH W.: ' Sibelius's Use of Percussion ' (in *Music and Letters*, Vol. XXIII, No. 1, January 1942).

# List of Compositions
### (with page references)

---

[1] See also Octet for flute, clarinet and strings under ' Chamber Music '.

[2] Composed as prelude to the unfinished opera, *The Building of the Boat*.

[3] Based on the melodrama of the same name, Op. 15; see also note to Op. 24, under ' Piano Music '.

Opus No.

63   Symphony No. 4 in A minor (1911): 25–8, 33, 35, 44, 53, 56–61, 81–2, 94, 101, 144, 149–50, 162, 165, 167–8, 170, 172–6.

66   Scènes historiques—II (1912): 57, 80–3.

64   The Bard (1913): 56–8, 81, 86, 149, 167, 173, 175.

73   The Oceanides (1914): 54–6, 60, 72, 86, 144, 149, 167, 175.

82   Symphony No. 5 in E flat (1915; revised 1916; largely rewritten 1919): 28–31, 35, 42, 45, 48, 50, 52, 57, 60, 72, 87, 93, 142, 144, 149–50, 163, 167–8, 170–1, 175.

87a   Impromptu (1917).

91   Two Marches (March of the Finnish Light Infantry and Scout March¹ (1918): 45, 50.

96   Three Pieces (Valse lyrique, Autrefois and Valse chevaleresque) (1920): 45. 49.

100   Suite caractéristique (1922): 45, 48, 90.

104   Symphony No. 6 in D minor (1923): 31–4, 40, 45, 50–1, 58, 60, 89–90, 150–1, 155, 163–5, 167–8, 172–5.

105   Symphony No. 7 in C (1924): 25, 31, 34–7, 40, 45–6, 48, 51, 65, 81, 89–90, 150–2, 154–5, 163, 165, 167, 172, 174.

112   Tapiola (1925): 40–6, 48–9, 53–4, 57, 60, 72, 75, 81, 89–90, 115, 144–5, 150, 155, 163, 167, 172, 174–5.

None.   Symphony No. 8 (?): 40, 90.

None.   Tempo di minuetto (date unknown).

None.   Academic March (date unknown).

WORKS FOR SOLO INSTRUMENT WITH ORCHESTRA

47   Concerto in D minor, for violin and orchestra (1903; revised 1905): 58, 67–9, 101, 104, 149, 152, 161, 167, 174.

69   Two Serenades, for violin and orchestra: 57–8
No. 1 in D major (1912); No. 2 in G minor (1913).

77   Two Serious Melodies, for violin (or 'cello) and small orchestra: 52–3
No. 1, Laetare anima mea (1914); No. 2, Ab imo pectore (1915).

87b   Two Humoresques, for violin and orchestra (1917): 45, 50–1
No. 1 in D minor; No. 2 in D major.

89   Four Humoresques, for violin and orchestra (1917): 45, 50–1, 57
No. 1 in G minor; No. 2 in G minor; No. 3 in E flat; No. 4 in G minor.²

WORKS FOR STRING ORCHESTRA

None.   Porträtterna (Portraits) (1901): 69.

42   Romance in C (1903): 68–9, 167.

14   Suite, Rakastava (The Lover)³ (1911): 58–60, 153, 167, 174–5.

¹ The Scout March has ad lib. parts for four-part chorus.
² It appears from the facsimile in the album edited by Lauri Solanterä (see Bibliography, p. 179) that Op. 89, No. 4, was originally numbered Op. 87, No. 1.
³ Based on a male-voice choral setting (1895) of words from the Kanteletar. Nos. 1 and 3 contain a kettle-drum part, No. 2 has a part for triangle.

Opus No.

62a Canzonetta (1911): 58, 60–1.
98a *Suite mignonne*, for two flutes and strings (1921): 45–6, 48–9, 75.
98b *Suite champêtre* (1921): 45–6, 48–9, 75, 89.
None. *Andante festivo* (1924): 40.
None. *Andante lirico* (1924): 40.

WORK FOR BRASS BAND

None. *Tiera* (1894): 72.

CHAMBER MUSIC[1]

None. Trio in A minor (1881–2).
None. Piano Quartet in E minor (1881–2).
None. Sonata for violin and piano (1883).
None. Andantino for 'cello and piano (1884).
None. String Quartet in E flat (1885).
None. Sonata in F, for violin and piano (1886).
None. Piano Trio (1887).
None. Theme and Variations in C sharp minor, for string quartet (1888).
2 Two Pieces (Romance and Epilogue), for violin and piano (1888; revised 1912).
None. Suite in A, for violin, viola and 'cello (1889).
None. String Quartet in A minor (1889).
4 String Quartet in B flat (1889).
None. Piano Quintet in G minor (1889).
None. Piano Quartet in C (1891).
None. Octet for flute, clarinet and strings (material afterwards used in *En Saga*) (1891).
None. Rondo for viola and piano (1895).
20 *Malinconia*, for 'cello and piano (1901): 95.
56 String Quartet in D minor (Voces intimae) (1909): 58, 92–7, 149, 152, 154, 161–2, 165, 167, 174–5.
78 Four Pieces for violin (or 'cello) and piano (1915): 95.
79 Six Pieces for violin and piano (1915): 95.
80 Sonatina in E for violin and piano (1915): 96.
81 Five Pieces for violin and piano (1915): 96.
102 Novellette, for violin and piano (1923).
106 *Danses champêtres*, five pieces for violin and piano (1925).
115 Four Pieces for violin and piano (1929): 39, 96.
116 Three Pieces for violin and piano (1929): 39, 96.

WORK FOR ORGAN

111 Two Pieces, *Intrada* and *Sorgemusik* (Funeral Music), in memory of Gallén-Kallela (1926).

[1] See also under ' Melodramas '.

OPUS No.

## PIANO MUSIC

| 5 | Six Impromptus (1893): 105. |
|---|---|
| 12 | Sonata in F (1893): 98–100. |
| 24 | Ten Pieces (Nos. 1 and 2,[1] 1894; Nos. 3–7, 1985; No. 8, 1900; Nos. 9 and 10, 1903): 97, 106–7. |
| None. | *The Cavalier* (1901). |
| None. | *Finske Folkvisor* (six Finnish folk-songs) (1903): 105. |
| 41 | *Kyllikki* (three lyric pieces) (1904): 98, 100–1. |
| 58 | Ten Pieces (1909): 107. |
| 67 | Three Sonatinas (No. 1, F sharp minor; No. 2, E major; No. 3, B flat minor) (1912): 57, 98, 101–3, 107. |
| 68 | Two Rondinos in G sharp minor and C sharp minor (1912): 57, 98, 103, 107. |
| 40 | *Pensées lyriques* (Nos. 1–7, 1912–14; Nos. 8–10 added later): 106. |
| 74 | Four Lyric Pieces (1914). |
| 75 | Five Pieces (1914): 105. |
| 76 | Thirteen Pieces (1914). |
| 34 | Bagatelles (Nos. 1–8, 1914–16; Nos. 9 and 10 added later): 105–6. |
| 85 | Five Pieces (1916): 105. |
| 94 | Six Pieces (1919). |
| 97 | Six Bagatelles (1920). |
| None. | *Pièce romantique* (1920). |
| None. | *Till trånaden (Longing)* (1920). |
| 99 | Eight Short Pieces (1922). |
| 101 | Five Romantic Pieces (1923). |
| 103 | Five Characteristic Impressions (1924). |
| 114 | *Esquisses* (five pieces) (1929). |
| None. | *Mandolinata* (no date). |

## OPERAS

| None. | *Veneen Luominen (The Building of the Boat)* (sketches only) (Erkko) (1893)[2]: 75, 77, 148. |
|---|---|
| None. | *The Maiden in the Tower*, in one act (Herzberg) (1896): 77. |

## INCIDENTAL MUSIC

| None. | Two Songs with piano trio, for Wennerberg's *Necken (The Watersprite)* (1888): 73. |
|---|---|
| 27 | To Adolf Paul's *King Christian II* (1898): 78–9, 86. |
| 44 | To Järnefelt's *Kuolema (Death)*[3] (1903): 83, 85, 97, 121, 153. |
| 46 | To Maeterlinck's *Pelléas et Mélisande* (1905): 83–5, 138, 149, 167. |
| 51 | To Hjalmar Procopé's *Belshazar* (1906): 83, 85, 149, 154, 167. |

---

[1] Said to be transcriptions from the melodrama *Skogsrået*, Op. 15.
[2] See *Swan of Tuonela*, under ' Orchestral Works '.
[3] Only the *Valse triste* has been published.

Opus No.
54       To August Strindberg's *Swanwhite* (1908): 83, 85–6. 149.
8       To Lybeck's *Odlan* (*The Lizard*) (1909): 83.
None.       To Adolf Paul's *The Language of the Birds* (1911): 58, 86.
71       To Poul Knudsen's pantomime *Scaramouche* (1913): 86–8.
83       To Hugo von Hofmannsthal's *Everyman* (1916): 87, 149.
109       To Shakespeare's *The Tempest* (1926): 40, 87–90, 144, 151, 167.

CANTATAS AND CHORAL MUSIC[1]

7       *Kullervo* (from the *Kalevala*), symphony for soli, chorus and orchestra (1892): 137, 147–8.
18       Six Part Songs for male voices *a cappella*: 1. *Sortunut ääni* (*The Broken Voice*) (from the *Kanteletar*); 2. *Terve kuu* (*Hail Moon*) (from the *Kalevala*); 3. *Venematka* (*The Boat Journey*) (from the *Kalevala*); 4. *Saarella palaa* (*Fire on the Island*) (from the *Kanteletar*); 5. *Metsämiehen laulu* (*Woodman's Song*) (Kivi); 6. *Sydämeni laulu* (*The Song of my Heart*) (Kivi). (No. 3, 1893; Nos. 4, 5, and 6, 1895; No. 2, 1901; No. 1, date unknown.)
None.       *Rakastava* (*The Lover*) (from the *Kanteletar*) for male voices *a cappella* (1895)[2]: 58.
None.       University Cantata (Leino), for chorus and orchestra (1894).
None.       *Min rastas raataa* (*Busy as a Thrush*) (from the *Kanteletar*), for male chorus *a cappella* (1894).
None.       Cantata for the Coronation of Nicholas II (Cajander), for soli, chorus and orchestra (1895): 137.
23       Cantata for the Year 1897 (Forsman), for mixed chorus *a cappella* (1897): 140.
28       *Sandels* (Runeberg), improvisation for male chorus and orchestra (1898).
None.       *Yks' voima* (*One power*) (Cajander), for male chorus *a cappella* (1898).
31a       *Song of the Athenians* (Rydberg), for boys' and men's voices, saxhorn septet, triangle, bass-drum and cymbals (alternative accompaniment for wind-band) (1899): 80.
32       *Tulen synty* (*The Origin of Fire*)[3] (from the *Kalevala*), for baritone solo, male chorus and orchestra (1902): 138, 148.
19       *Thou who Guidest the Stars* (Rydberg), impromptu for four-part women's chorus and orchestra (1902; revised 1910).
None.       *Ej med klagan* (*Not with Lamentation*) (Runeberg), for mixed chorus *a cappella* (1905).
None.       *Carminalia*, three Latin satires for three-part *a cappella* chorus (S.A.B.) or two-part boys' voices (S.A.) with harmonium or piano (1905).
48       *The Captive Queen* (Cajander), ballad for mixed (or male) chorus and orchestra (1906): 58, 139–40.

[1] See also under ' Melodramas '.
[2] Afterwards used in the suite for strings, Op. 14.
[3] Also known as *Ukko the Firemaker*.

# List of Compositions

Opus No.

65    Two Part-songs for mixed chorus *a cappella* (1912). (1) *People of Land and of Sea*; (2) *Bell Melody of Berghäll Church.*[1]

None.    *Drömmarne (Dreams)*, for mixed chorus *a cappella* (1912).

None.    *Uusimaa*, for mixed chorus *a cappella* (1912).

None.    *Juhlamarssi (Festival March)* (Leino), for mixed chorus *a cappella* (1912).

31b    *Har du mod (Hast Thou Courage)* (Wecksell), for male chorus and orchestra (1913).

None.    *Päiv' ei pääse (The Day not ended)* (Erkko), for children's voices *a cappella* (1913).

None.    *Kansakoulunmarssi* (Elementary school march), for children's voices *a cappella* (1913).

None.    *Koulutie (The Way to School)* (Koskenniemi), for children's voices *a cappella* (1913).

None.    Three Songs for American Schools (English words), for children's voices *a cappella* (1913).

84    Five Part-songs for male chorus *a cappella* (1915). 1. *Herr Lager* (Fröding); 2. *På berget (On the Mountain)* (Fröding); 3. *Ett drömackord (A Dream Chord)* (Fröding); 4. *Evige Eros (Eternal Eros)* (Fröding); 5. *Till havs (At Sea)* (Reuter).

92    *Oma maa (Our own Land)* (Kallio), cantata for chorus and orchestra (1918): 137.

93    *Jordens sång (Song of the Earth)* (Jarl Hemmer), cantata for the inauguration of Åbo University, for chorus and orchestra (1919).

95    *Maan virsi (Hymn of the Earth)* (Eino Leino), cantata for chorus and orchestra (1920): 137.

None.    *Jone havsfärd (Jonah's Voyage)* (Fröding), for male chorus *a cappella* (1920).

None.    *Veljeni (Brotherhood)* (Aho), for male chorus *a cappella* (1920).

None.    *Likhet (Resemblance)* (Runeberg), for male chorus *a cappella* (1920).

None.    Two Songs (Schybergson), for male chorus *a cappella* (1920).

107    *Ritual Chorus*, for chorus and organ (1925).

108    Two part-songs (Kyösti), for male chorus *a cappella* (1925) (1) *Humoreski*; (2) *Ne pitkän*.

None.    Two Psalms, for mixed chorus *a cappella* (1925–7):: 39.

110    *The Song of Väinö* (from the *Kalevala*), for chorus and orchestra (1926): 137.

113    *Musique réligieuse*, for solo voice, chorus and organ (1927).

None.    *N. Y. Laulajat*, for male chorus *a cappella* (1929).

None.    *Viborgs Sångarbröder (The Singing Brothers of Viborg)*, for male chorus *a cappella* (1929).

None.    Patriotic March, for male chorus and orchestra.

None.    *Fridolins Dårskap (Fridolin's Folly)* (Karlfeldt), for male chorus *a cappella* (date unknown).

[1] Arranged for piano solo by the composer as Op. 65b.

OPUS No.

21    *Natus in curas*, hymn for male chorus *a cappella* (date
      unknown).

WORKS FOR SOLO VOICE AND ORCHESTRA

3    Arioso (*Flickans Årstider*)(*The Maiden's Seasons*)(Runeberg),
     for voice and string orchestra (1893, revised 1913): 132–3.

33   *Koskenlaskijan Morsiamet*(*The Ferryman's Brides*)(Oksanen),
     for baritone or mezzosoprano and orchestra (1897): 109,
     133–4.

38, No. 1  *Höstkväll* (*Autumn Evening*) (Rydberg), for voice and
           orchestra (1904).[1]

70   *Luonnotar* (from the *Kalevala*), tone-poem for soprano and
     orchestra (1913): 109, 134–5, 149, 176.

SONGS (WITH PIANO)

None.   Serenade (Runeberg) (1888).
13      Seven Songs (Runeberg): 108, 120–2, 131.
        1. *Under Strandens granar* (*Under the Fir-trees*); 2.
        *Kyssens Hopp* (*The Kiss's Hope*); 3. *Hjertat's Morgon* (*The
        Heart's Morning*); 4. *Våren flyktar hastigt* (*Spring is
        Flying*); 5. *Drömmen* (*The Dream*); 6. *Till Frigga* (*To
        Frigga*); 7. *Jägargossen* (*The Young Huntsman*). (Nos. 3,
        4, 5 and 7, 1891; Nos. 1, 2 and 6, 1892).

1       *Julvisor* (Five Christmas Songs)[2] (1895).
17      Seven Songs: 122–4.
        1. *Se'n har jag ej frågat mera* (*And I questioned
        then no further*) (Runeberg); 2. *Sov in!* (*Slumber on!*)
        (Tavaststjerna); 3. *Fågellek* (*Enticement*) (Tavaststjerna);
        4. *Vilse* (*Astray*) (Tavaststjerna); 5. *En Slända* (*A Dragon-
        fly*) (Levertin); 6. *Illalle* (*To the Evening*) (Forsman);
        (7) **Lastu lainehilla** (*Driftwood*) (Calamnius) (Nos. 2, 3 and
        4, 1894; Nos. 6 and 7, 1898; No. 1, 1899).

36      Six Songs (1899): 97, 99, 109–10, 112–4, 117, 119, 132, 135.
        1. *Svarta Rosor* (*Black Roses*) (*Josephson*); 2. *Men min
        fågel märks dock icke* (*But my bird is long in homing*)
        (Runeberg); 3. *Bollspelet vid Trianon* (*Tennis at Trianon*)
        (Fröding); 4. *Säf, säf, susa* (*Sigh, sedges, sigh*) (Fröding);
        5. *Marssnön* (*March snow*) (Wecksell); 6. *Demanten på
        Marssnön* (*The Diamond on March Snow*) (Wecksell).

---

[1] See next section, Op. 38.
[2] It has been impossible to get complete details of Sibelius's Op. 1. No. 1 is
*Nu står jul vid snöig port* (*Now Christmas stands at the snowy gate*) (Topelius) and
No. 2, *Nu så kommer Julen, nu är Julen här* (*Now Christmas has come, now Christmas is here*) (Topelius); the other three consist of *Giv mig ej glans, ej guld, ej prakt
(Give me no splendour, gold or pomp)* (Topelius); *On hangket korkeat (High are the
snowdrifts)* (Joukahainen) and another Topelius setting. Nos. 1 and 2, at any rate,
are written on two staves only (the vocal line being included in the piano part), which
suggests that the composer was thinking of unison chorus rather than a solo voice.

Opus No.
37   Five Songs: 97, 109–11, 115.
     1. *Den första kyssen (The First Kiss)*[1] (Runeberg);
     2. *Lasse liten (Little Lasse)* (Topelius); 3. *Soluppgång
     (Sunrise)* (Hedberg); 4. *Var det en dröm (Was it a Dream?)*
     (Wecksell); 5. *Flickan kom ifrån sin älsklings möte (The
     maiden came from lover's tryst*; generally known as *The
     Tryst)* (Runeberg) (No. 1, 1898, No. 5, 1901; Nos. 2, 3,
     and 4, 1902).
38   Five Songs (1904): 109–10, 114–7, 123–4, 127, 129, 132.
     1. *Höstkväll (Autumn Evening)* (Rydberg)[2]; 2. *På Veran-
     dan vid hafvet (On a balcony by the sea)* (Rydberg); 3. *I
     Natten (In the Night)* (Rydberg); 4. *Harpolekaren och hans
     son (The Harper and his Son)* (Rydberg); 5. *Jag ville jag
     vore (I would that I dwelt)* (Fröding).
50   Six Songs (1906): 109, 118–20, 126.
     1. *Lenzgesang (A Song of Spring)* (Fitger); 2. *Sehnsucht
     (Longing)* (Weiss); 3. *Im Feld ein Mädchen singt (In the
     field a maiden sings)* (Susman); 4. *Aus banger Brust (O
     wert thou here)* (Dehmel); 5. *Die stille Stadt (The silent
     town)* (Dehmel); 6. *Rosenlied (The song of the roses)*
     (Ritter).
35   Tw Songs (1907): 109, 117–8, 123, 135.
     1. *Jubal* (Josephson); 2. *Teodora* (Gripenberg).
57   Eight Songs (Josephson) (1909): 124–6.
     1. *Elfven och Snigeln (The snail)*; 2. *En blomma stod vid
     vägen (The wild flower)*; 3. *Qvarnhjulet (The mill-wheel)*;
     4. *Maj (May)*; 5. *Jag är ett träd (The tree)*; 6. *Hertig Magnus
     (Baron Magnus)*; 7. *Vänskapens blomma (Friendship)*;
     8. *Necken (The Elf-King)*.
60   Two Songs from Shakespeare's *Twelfth Night* (anonymous
     Swedish translation), for voice and piano or guitar (1909):
     126–7, 149.
     1. *Come away, Death*; 2. *When that I was and a little
     tiny boy.*
61   Eight Songs (1910): 108–9, 117, 127–9, 135.
     1. *Långsomt som kvällskyn (Slow as the colours)*
     Tavaststjerna); 2. *Vattenplask (Lapping waters)* (Rydberg);
     3. *När jag drömmer (When I dream)* (Tavaststjerna); 4.
     *Romeo* (Tavaststjerna); 5. *Romans (Romance)* (Tavaventst-
     jerna); 6. *Dolce far niente* (Tavaststjerna); 7. *Fåfäng önskan
     (Idle wishes)* (Runeberg); 8. *Vårtagen (Spell of Springtide)*
     (Gripenberg).
72   Six Songs: 129–30.
     1. *Farväl (Farewell)* (Rydberg); 2. *Orions Gördel (Orions
     Girdle)* (Topelius); 3. *Kyssen (The Kiss)* (Rydberg);

[1] A version for male chorus (T.T.B.B.) appears to have been published as Op. 31,
No. 1.
[2] There is also a version with orchestral accompaniment.

# List of Compositions

4. *Kaiutar (The Echo Nymph)* (Kyösti); 5. *Der Wanderer und der Bach (The Wayfarer and the Stream)* (Greif); 6. *Hundra Våga (A Hundred Ways)* (Runeberg) (Nos. 1 and 2, 1914; Nos. 3–6, 1915).

86   Six Songs (1916): 129–30.
1. *Vår förnimmelser (The Coming of Spring)* (Tavaststjerna); 2. *Längtan heter min arvedel (Longing is my heritage)* (Karlfeldt); 3. *Dold förening (Hidden Union)* (Snoilsky); 4. *Och finns det en tanke (And is there a thought?)* (Tavaststjerna); 5. *Sångarlön (The singer's reward)* (Snoilsky); 6. *I systrar, I bröder (Ye sisters and brothers)* (Lybeck).

88   Song Cycle (1917): 129–30.
1. *Blåsippan (The Anemone)* (Franzén); 2. *De bägge rosorna (The Two Roses)* (Franzén); 3. *Vitsippan (The Star-Flower)* (Franzén); 4. *Sippan (The Primrose)* (Runeberg); 5. *Törnet (The Thornbush)* (Runeberg); 6. *Blommans öde (The Flower)* (Runeberg).

90   Six Songs (Runeberg) (1917): 130–2.
1. *Norden (The North)*; 2. *Hennes Budskap (Her message)*; 3. *Morgonen (The Morning)*; 4. *Fågelfängarn (The Bird-catcher)*; 5. *Sommarnatten (Summer Night)*; 6. *Hvem styrde hit din väg (Who has brought you here?)*.

None.   *Narcissen* (Gripenberg) (1918).
None.   *Segeln (The Sails)* (Öhqvist) (1918).
None.   *Små flickor (Little Girls)* (Procopé) (1918).
None.   *Sammunut (Extinct)* (Busse-Palmo) (1918).
None.   *Sinisorsa (The Blue Duck)* (Koskimies) (date unknown).
None.   *Karjalan osa (Karelia's Fate)* (Nurminen) (date unknown).

## Vocal Duet

None.   *Tanken (The Thought)* (Runeberg), for two sopranos and piano.

## Melodramas

None.   *Svartsjukans nätter (Nights of Jealousy)* (Runeberg), for recitation and piano trio (1888).
15   *Skogsrået (The Dryad)* (Rydberg), for recitation and piano, two horns and string orchestra (1894): 72.[1]
30   *Islossningen i Ule älv (The Breaking of the Ice on Ule River)* (Topelius), for recitation, male chorus and orchestra (1899): 137.
29   *Snöfrid* (Rydberg), for recitation, chorus and orchestra (1900).
None.   *Ett ensamt Skidspar (A Solitary Pair of Skates)* (Gripenberg) (date unknown), for recitation and piano.

---

[1] See also under ' Orchestral Works ' and note to Op. 24 under ' Piano Music '.

# MUSICAL EXAMPLES

191

194

195

**Ex.42**

**Ex.43**

Presto

etc.

**Ex.44**

**Ex.45**

**Ex.46**

Ex. 47

Ex. 48

*) *Sempre una corda ed'un pochettino glissando*

Ex. 49

198

Ex. 53

Sibelius

**Ex. 54**

Vlns.
(div.)

**Ex. 55**

*Andante assai*

Vln. Solo

Orch.

**Ex. 56**

*Andante con moto*

**Ex. 57**

*Allegretto*

Vln. I (div.)
Vln. II (div.)

Vla. (div.)

**Ex. 58**

Vlns. I
II

Vlas.
Celli.
Basses (pizz.)

Ex. 59

Ex. 60

**Ex. 65**

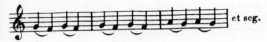
et seg.

**Ex. 66**

etc.

**Ex. 67**

Brass

Strgs.

**Ex. 68**

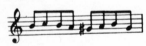

**Ex. 69**

Ex. 71

Ex. 72

Ex. 73ᵃ

Fl. I. Ob. I. Cl. I.
Fl. II. Ob. II. Cl. II
Vln. I. Vln. II. Vla. (pizz.)

Fag. I. II
All Strgs. (pizz.)

Hn. I. II. III. IV

Timp.

Ex. 73<sup>b)</sup>

Ex. 74

205

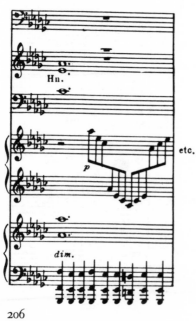

Ex. 76

Ex. 77

Ex. 78

207

Ex. 80

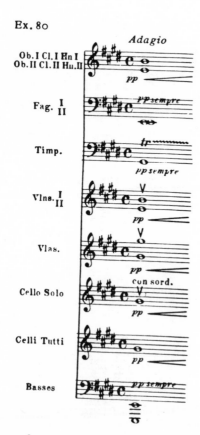

Ex. 82

*Lento assai*

Ex. 84

*dolce espressivo*

Ex. 85

213

**Ex. 103**

**Ex. 104**

**Ex. 105**

**Ex. 106**

**Ex. 107**

**Ex. 108**

**Ex. 109**

**Ex. 110**

etc.

**Ex. 111**

etc.

**Ex. 112**

**Ex. 113**

**Ex. 114**

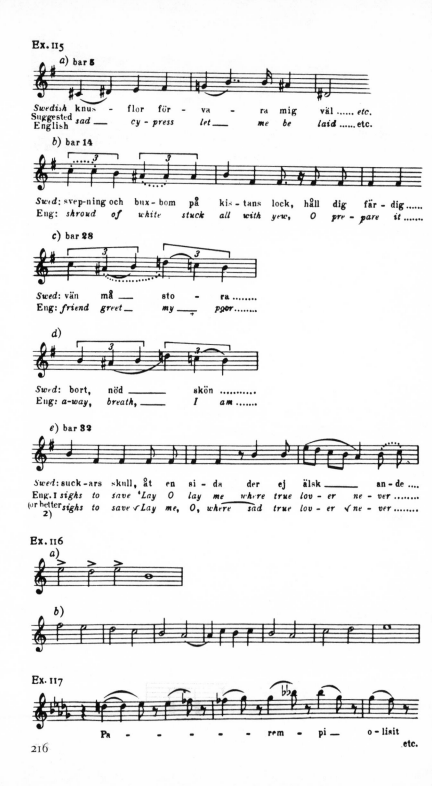

Ex. 115

*a)* bar 5

Swedish knus - flor för - va - ra mig väl ...... *etc.*
Suggested
English *sad — cy - press let — me be laid ......etc.*

*b)* bar 14

Swed: svep-ning och bux - bom på kis - tans lock, håll dig fär - dig......
Eng: *shroud of white stuck all with yew, O pre - pare it ......*

*c)* bar 28

Swed: vän må — sto - ra ........
Eng: *friend greet— my — poor........*

*d)*

Swed: bort, nöd ——— skön ..........
Eng: *a-way, breath, ——— I am ......*

*e)* bar 32

Swed: suck-ars skull, åt en si - da der ej älsk ——— an - de ....
Eng.I *sighs to save 'Lay O lay me where true lov - er ne - ver........*
(or better *sighs to save √Lay me, O, where sad true lov - er √ne - ver......*
2)

Ex. 116

*a)*

*b)*

Ex. 117

Pa - - - - - rem - pi — o - liait
.etc.

216

Ex. 119

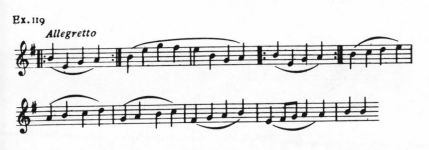

Ex. 120

**Ex. 121**

March time

S.A. / T.B.

*mf* Kun vir - ta vuo - las, nun va-pa-u-den vuo Käy

hal - ki hait - tain, el - kä - pä es - ty vaan.

**Ex. 122**

Poco allegro

*f* Strgs.

**Ex. 123**

Poco allegro
W.W.

*ff*

**Ex. 124**

*p*

*f*

**Ex. 125**

Allegretto
Vlns.

*f*

**Ex. 126**

Andante moderato sostenuto

1st Vln.
2nd Vln.
Vla.

*mf* *f*